SWAMP FOX

SWAMP FOX

THE LIFE AND CAMPAIGNS

OF

General Francis Marion

by

ROBERT D. BASS

SANDLAPPER PUBLISHING CO., INC.
Orangeburg, South Carolina

To
My Mother
Bertha Elizabeth Matthews Bass
whose Matthews ancestors
fought under
Francis Marion

Acknowledgments

THE MOST SIGNIFICANT PERIOD in the career of Francis Marion was that between August 15, 1780, and September 8, 1781. During this time he alone held eastern South Carolina from the British, then helped Henry Lee capture the British posts along the Santee, and finally commanded a corps in the army with which Nathanael Greene drove the British from South Carolina.

Accounts of Marion's activities during much of this period have been vague and historians have glossed over their lack of information with references to the elusive Swamp Fox. I have attempted to clear up these uncertainties by giving Marion's location at least once in every three days. I have also tried to show the causes leading up to each of his actions and the results that followed from his victories.

Although I first began taking notes for this study in 1929, I was unable to finish it until after I had read the unpublished correspondence of Lord Cornwallis. For permission to read these letters I thank Lord Braybrooke, great-great-grandson of Lord Cornwallis. I also wish to thank the Director of the Public Record office in London for permission to use these and other documents.

Many friends, teachers, colleagues, librarians, and others have given me help and inspiration. Among these were the late Joseph M. Woodberry, whose stories about Marion stirred my imagination when I was a schoolboy, and Mr. Ed Woodberry, a brother-in-law, who furnished much information about the country through which Marion campaigned.

I wish to thank the librarians of the following institutions for help and permission to use material: the Library of Congress, especially those in the Division of Manuscripts; Harvard University; Princeton University; University of South Carolina; Enoch Pratt Library; Peabody Library; New York Public Library; Henry E. Huntington Library; and William L. Clements Library. I also thank the directors and staffs of the New York Historical Society and the South Carolina Historical Commission. I am especially grateful to Miss Catherine Jones, of the Greenville Public Library; Dr. Vernon D. Tate, Librarian of the U.S. Naval Academy; Dr. Robert C. Tucker, Librarian of Furman University; and the other librarians of those institutions.

I wish to thank Professor Robert W. Daly, of the U.S. Naval Academy, for his encouragement; Professor Robert M. Langdon, of the U.S. Naval Academy, whose copy of James' *A Sketch of the Life of Brig. Gen. Francis Marion* set me to work anew; and Professor Emeritus Walter B. Norris, of the U.S. Naval Academy, who gave me a copy of an early edition of *The Life of General Francis Marion* by Horry and Weems.

I wish also to express my gratitude to President James L. Plyler and Dean Francis W. Bonner, who have made available to me time for my study as well as the facilities of Furman University.

For help in securing and permission to reproduce pictures, I am indebted to the Culver Service; the Division of Prints of the Library of Congress; the Print Room of the New York Public Library; the Directors and Trustees of the National Gallery and the National Portrait Gallery; and for drawing the maps, to Mr. Green H. Giebner.

Most of all I am indebted to my wife, Virginia Wauchope Bass, for her help in all stages of *Swamp Fox*.

—ROBERT D. BASS

Furman University
Greenville, South Carolina
October 1, 1958

Contents

SWAMP FOX

Prologue

DURING THE CLOSING YEARS of the Revolution, a ragged little guerrilla named Francis Marion moved like a fox through the swamps of eastern Carolina. Hiding in his lair on Snow's Island or Peyre's Plantation by day and emerging stealthily after sunset, he usually struck at midnight, slaughtering and frightening and throwing his enemies into a panic. Before day he vanished again behind the morasses of the Peedee or the Santee River.

Bold and elusive, Colonel Marion was a haunting nemesis to the Tories, terrorizing them from White Marsh to Black Mingo. He was an armed will-o'-the-wisp to the British soldiers, a phantom exacting retribution and justice. With his volunteers in homespun, he cut the supply line between Charleston and Camden. He chased McLeroth out of Williamsburg and whipped Watson's Regiment of Guards. He kept Lord Rawdon in a dither and even brought Lord Cornwallis, convalescent from malaria, back to direct Tarleton's expedition against him.

To the Carolina partisans Francis Marion was a latter-day Robin Hood. They told and retold their tales until his heroic exploits passed into folklore. Romantic legends and family traditions began to cluster around his name. As memory of the war faded, Marion grew more heroic: his skirmishes became battles and his raids became campaigns. The scrawny little Huguenot attained gigantic stature, and William Cullen Bryant sang:

> The British soldier trembles
> When Marion's name is told.

Peter Horry wrote a simple memorial biography of General Marion. Parson Weems rewrote it into a stirring military romance. William James, who as a barefoot lad of fifteen had fought under the General, wrote a prosaic sketch of his hero. William Gilmore Simms then transmuted him into "the Partisan," a Santee counterpart of Chevalier Bayard.

Through song and story, Francis Marion became a hero of the Revolution second only to George Washington. Hundreds of parents named a son Francis Marion. Settlers gave his name to village after village, and now scattered over the United States are some twenty-nine towns and seventeen counties named Marion.

In all of this fantasy Americans forgot the real Francis Marion. He was neither a Robin Hood nor a Chevalier Bayard. He was a moody, introverted, semiliterate genius who rose from private to Brigadier General through an intuitive grasp of strategy and tactics, personal bravery, devotion to duty, and worship of liberty.

By nature Marion was gentle, kind, and humane. Yet his orders, orderly books, battle reports, and personal letters reveal another side to his character. He shot pickets, retaliated from ambush, failed to honor flags of truce, and knowingly violated international law. He could forgive the Tories, and yet he could court-martial his closest friend. Such paradoxical qualities inspired admiration in his officers and love in his men. For two years they followed him through the Carolina swamps without adequate pay, clothing, ammunition, recognition, or hope of reward. In after years they gave him every honor in their power and then cherished his memory as "the Swamp Fox."

CHAPTER I

Apprentice to Mars

FRANCIS MARION was born in midwinter, 1732, at Goat-field Plantation in St. John's Parish, Berkeley County, South Carolina. His parents were Gabriel and Esther Cordes Marion, both first-generation Carolinians. His grandparents were Benjamin and Judith Baluet Marion, and Anthony and Esther Baluet Cordes. Huguenots driven from France by the revocation of the Edict of Nantes, the Marion and Cordes families had come to Carolina in 1685 and settled in St. James' Parish, a low fertile region between Charleston and the Santee River.

These colonists worked to the limit of human endurance. Men and women worked together in clearing fields, and wives paired with husbands in pulling whipsaws. They felled trees and built homes. They planted wheat, rye, and barley. When these crops failed because of the climate, they learned from the Indians how to grow corn. Eventually they learned to grow rice and to cultivate indigo. They then commenced to prosper, and their children began extending their plantations northward along the Santee.

Like their kindred in St. James', Benjamin and Judith Marion were hard-working and temperate, and they clung to their French language and Huguenot customs. Sometime between 1690 and 1695 they had a son whom they gave the Biblical name of Gabriel. They could provide little formal

5

education for him, but as he grew up they taught him to farm the rich earth and to live soberly.

About 1715 Gabriel Marion married Esther Cordes, his first cousin. When her father, Dr. Anthony Cordes, led a new settlement up the Santee to St. John's Parish, Gabriel and Esther went with him. They settled at Goatfield Plantation, built a home, and began rearing their family. In time they had six children: Esther, Isaac, Gabriel, Benjamin, Job, and Francis.

Francis, their last born, was a puny child. "I have it from good authority," said Peter Horry, "that this great soldier, at his birth, was not larger than a New England lobster, and might easily enough have been put into a quart pot." In spite of his scrawny body and poor health, he had a happy childhood.

When Francis was five or six years old, his parents moved from Goatfield to a plantation in Prince George, a parish on Winyah Bay. Apparently they wished to get near the English school in Georgetown, for they dropped their French traditions and provided all of their children with a common school education.

When Francis was about fifteen, he decided to become a sailor. His imagination had been stirred by the ships in the little port of Georgetown. He enjoyed the tales of the seamen, and he loved the exotic smells in the holds of the barks and brigantines. When he asked his parents for permission to go to sea, they willingly consented. They hoped that a voyage through the Caribbean would have tonic effect upon their undergrown son.

Soon afterward Francis signed on as the sixth crewman of a schooner sailing for the West Indies. As they were returning, however, a whale attacked the schooner with such violence as to loosen a plank. The captain and the crew escaped in an open boat, but the ship foundered so quickly that they had no time to save food or water. For five days they suffered under a tropical sun. In desperation they killed a little dog that had swum to their boat when the schooner sank and drank his blood and ate his raw flesh. On the sixth day two crewmen died. Next day the others reached land.

In spite of the peril and hardship, by the time Francis reached home he was in much better health. "His constitution seemed renewed, his frame commenced a second and rapid growth," said Horry, "while his cheeks, quitting their pale, suet-colored cast, assumed a bright and healthy olive."

After his terrible voyage, Francis gave up the sea. Now content with farming, he settled down with his parents. Soon he was their mainstay, for his sister and brothers had begun to marry and move away from home. Esther married John Allston of Prince George, Winyah. Upon his death she married Thomas Mitchell, a well-to-do planter living on Winyah Bay. Benjamin married Martha Alston. Upon her death he married Esther Bonneau, née Simons, and they settled in St. Thomas' Parish. Job married Elizabeth de St. Julien and settled on Walnut Grove Plantation in St. John's. Gabriel married Catherine Taylor, and they, too, settled in St. John's. Isaac married Rebecca Alston, and they settled at Little River on the boundary between North and South Carolina.

Gabriel and Esther Marion continued to live in the old home until his death about 1750. Then, like many other unmarried younger sons, Francis assumed the care of his mother. Quietly, with deep affection for her and for the other members of his family, he followed Job and Gabriel back to St. John's.

Francis Marion began his military career just before his twenty fifth birthday. In the closing stages of the French and Indian War the Cherokees along the border of South Carolina began threatening hostilities, and Governor William Henry Lyttelton expanded his armed forces. When Captain John Postell began recruiting a company of Provincials among the Huguenots, the Marion brothers were stirred by patriotic fervor. On January 31, 1756, Gabriel and Francis joined the militia company of upper St. John's.

They were now the closest of the Marion brothers. They were partners in farming, in hunting and fishing, and in

attending the musters and drills of the militia. When the
Cherokee War finally broke out in 1759, they were veteran
militiamen. Both offered their services to the province. After
receiving a commission as captain, Gabriel recruited a troop
of cavalry in St. John's. Francis enlisted and served under
him. But neither saw active duty. Captain Gabriel Marion's
cavalry was disbanded as soon as Governor Lyttelton had
concluded a treaty with the Indians.

Soon after their demobilization, the brothers separated.
Gabriel, with a growing family to support, moved to Belle
Isle, a fertile plantation in St. Stephen's Parish. Francis
moved up the Santee to live near his brother Job. He had
scarcely settled down, however, before the Cherokees again
rose and spread terror along the frontier.

Colonel Archibald Montgomerie, with his Highlanders
Regiment and the South Carolina militia, immediately
marched to Fort Prince George. From there he started for
Little Tennessee Valley. Near the Cherokee town of Echoe
he fell into a bloody ambush. Rallying his Highlanders,
Montgomerie drove the Indians from their cover with heavy
losses.

Fearing that South Carolina was too weak to protect her-
self against the inflamed Cherokees, William Bull, interim
Governor, appealed to Lord Amherst for help. The Commander in Chief of the British forces in America ordered
Lieutenant Colonel James Grant and twelve hundred regulars to prepare for a campaign against the Indians. In January, 1761, Colonel Grant and his troops arrived in
Charleston. To provide provincial troops for the expedition,
Governor Bull ordered Colonel Thomas Middleton, Lieutenant Colonel Henry Laurens, and Major John Moultrie to
recruit and organize a regiment. Captain William Moultrie
recruited a company of infantry, of which Francis Marion
was First Lieutenant.

About the middle of March, Colonel Grant began the long
march up the Santee and the Congaree. By May 29 he had
reached Fort Prince George, and on June 6 he turned north-

ward along the route followed by Montgomerie. As the loyal
Indian scouts approached the scene of the previous ambush,
they discovered that the Cherokees had again ambuscaded
themselves. Before Grant could advance, he had to dislodge
them. After looking over his young officers, he chose Lieutenant Marion for the hazardous operation and assigned him
a detachment of thirty men.

Francis Marion had never been under fire, but he was as
calm as a veteran. Cautiously, rapidly, he led his men to the
attack. Moving from tree to tree, they advanced into the
pass. When they came within range, the Cherokees gave a war
whoop and began pouring in a deadly fire. Man after man
fell, but Marion kept moving forward. By the time he had
passed the defile, twenty-one of his men lay dead or wounded.
The main column then passed through and advanced uphill. All morning the battle raged, but about noon the Indians broke and fled. Grant rushed forward and burned
Echoe. After that he devastated the Cherokee country, burning fifteen towns and cutting down the growing corn. He
swept the Little Tennessee and the Tuckaseegee Valleys with
fire until Chief Attakullakulla came to him at Keowee and
sued for peace.

Colonel Grant remained in the Cherokee country for
thirty days and then returned to Charleston. As soon as Middleton disbanded his regiment, Lieutenant Marion returned
to his farming. As a veteran who had shown great courage
under fire, he was now accorded a position of respect and
leadership along the Santee. He had also soldiered with and
won the respect of such political and military leaders as
Henry Laurens, William Moultrie, Andrew Williamson,
Isaac Huger, and Andrew Pickens. "He was an active, brave,
and hardy soldier," said William Moultrie, "and an excellent partisan officer."

For several years after Francis Marion returned from the
Cherokee War, he continued leasing fertile farm lands
above the swamps on the western side of the Santee River.

He loved the life of a planter and was contented and sociable. He often visited among his brothers and enjoyed the society of the Cordes, Peyres, DuBoses, Gourdins, Horrys, Mazycks, Porchers, and other Huguenots. He was especially fond of his brother Job, and when Job, a widower, married Elizabeth Gaillard on December 14, 1762, Francis served as his best man. For the next ten years he lived quietly, tilling the soil, hunting and fishing, and exploring every ridge and creek in St. John's and St. Stephen's. In those years he prospered and by 1773 was able to buy a home for himself. Going just above his brother Benjamin's Walnut Grove Plantation, he purchased Pond Bluff, an attractive plantation on the Santee some four miles below Eutaw Springs.

During the years when relations between Great Britain and her colonies were deteriorating, the Marions espoused the cause of liberty. Like other Huguenots, they recalled the hardships their grandparents had suffered for political and religious freedom. And when the Whigs of South Carolina elected their first Provincial Congress, those in St. John's Parish sent Job and Francis Marion to represent them in Charleston.

In a hopeful mood, Francis Marion was in Charleston on January 11, 1775, for the first meeting of the Provincial Congress. Like many of the other delegates, he was disappointed, for the Congress adjourned without taking any constructive action. But on April 19, at Lexington, the Massachusetts militia fired on the red-coated soldiers of the King. Leaders of the Committees of Safety sent couriers speeding through the colonies with news of the battle.

When the news reached Charleston, President Henry Laurens summoned the Provincial Congress to assemble on June 4. This time the delegates came prepared to take all necessary measures. They pledged themselves, under every tie of religion and honor, to stand united in the defense of South Carolina. They adopted the American Bill of Rights urged by the Continental Congress. They also adopted the Act of Association by which the colonies bound themselves not to import goods, wares, and merchandise from Great Britain.

The Provincial Congress then complied with a request from the Continental Congress to raise two regiments of infantry and one of cavalry. On June 12 the members began balloting for the regimental officers. Some consideration was given to family and fortune, but they usually chose young men with military experience. Membership in the militia counted heavily, but they remembered the veterans of the Cherokee War.

In the balloting for captains of companies Charles Cotesworth Pinckney and Barnard Elliott received 140 votes each. William Cattell and Francis Marion received 135 votes each. And Daniel and Peter Horry received 131 each. All captains took their precedence in the regiments according to their standing in the poll.

After designating officers for the First Regiment of South Carolina, the members of the Provincial Congress turned to the Second Regiment. They chose William Moultrie for its Colonel. They also elected Lieutenant Colonel Isaac Motte and Major Alexander McIntosh. They appointed ten captains for the regiment, among whom was Francis Marion.

The Provincial Congress of South Carolina then began rushing its preparations for defense. On June 21 Colonels Christopher Gadsden and William Moultrie organized the First and Second Regiments. Next day Colonel Moultrie, after ordering Captains Eveleigh and Motte to prepare a receiving station in town, sent the other eight captains recruiting. Captain Peter Horry rode down among the Huguenots on the Lower Santee. Captain Francis Marion set off toward St. John's, to recruit among the Huguenots, Scotch-Irish, and English along the Santee, Black, and Peedee Rivers. He soon found sixty men eager to fight, among them Gabriel Marion, his nephew from Belle Isle. Returning to Charleston, he began drilling his men. By September he had them ready to take the field in the first overt act of rebellion in South Carolina.

"You are to detach one hundred and fifty men under such command as you shall judge most proper for the Service; to embark this night at a proper time of the tide to proceed with the utmost secrecy and land at a convenient place on James Island," Henry Laurens, President of the Council of Safety, wrote Colonel Moultrie on September 13. His objective was the capture of Fort Johnson, which commanded Charleston Harbor.

In his General Orders for the Second Regiment, Moultrie wrote: "Ordered, that Captains Charles Cotesworth Pinckney's, Barnard Elliott's, and Francis Marion's companies be immediately completed to fifty men each, from their respective Corps, and hold themselves in readiness to march in three hours."

About eleven o'clock that night Lieutenant Colonel Motte and Captains Pinckney, Elliott, and Marion, with their detachment of 150 men, embarked in a packet at Gadsden's Wharf. After spending an hour crossing a quarter mile of water, the captain anchored his ship a mile from the island. Afraid of the cannon, he refused to sail nearer. Motte began sending his troops ashore, but by dawn only the companies of Elliott and Pinckney had reached James Island. Without waiting for Marion to disembark his men, they rushed against the fort.

To their surprise, instead of fierce resistance, they found the gate open, the guns thrown from their platforms, and a small guard waiting for them. During the night Colonel Alexander Innes, secretary to Lord William Campbell, the Royal Governor, had dismantled the fort and then retreated with the garrison to the *Tamar* and the *Cherokee,* British sloops lying in Rebellion Road.

That evening Lord Campbell sent Innes to demand by what authority Colonel Motte had taken his Majesty's fort. Captain Pinckney replied: "By the authority of the Council of Safety." Pinckney's reply and refusal to admit Innes angered Campbell. Both sides began preparation for action, and Moultrie ordered all South Carolina troops to stand by in readiness. Next morning the *Tamar* and the *Cherokee* closed as if for bombardment, but by then Colonel Motte had three cannon repaired and primed for firing. Seeing men standing on the parapets beside these guns and others deployed to repel any landing party with musket fire, the British captains turned their ships away and again anchored in Rebellion Road.

Because the British sloops remained in the harbor, the Provincial Congress augmented its forces and strengthened the ramparts of Charleston. On November 9 it resolved "by every military operation to oppose the passage of any British armaments." But fearful of some enemy action, as their military stores increased, the Council of Safety ordered the establishment of a depot at Dorchester, a village some thirty miles up the Ashley River.

To this depository the Council sent all public records as well as all accumulations of matériel. Over these it placed a guard of local militia. But as the ammunition piled up, the Council heard rumors from the Back Country that Colonel Scofield and his Tory militia planned to march to the Low Country and seize the gunpowder. To prevent this the Council ordered Colonel Moultrie to send a vigilant officer with troops to Dorchester. For this important command Moultrie chose Captain Francis Marion.

November 19, 1775

To Captain Francis Marion,
   You are to proceed with all expedition, with yours, and Cap. Huger's companies to Dorchester, to reinforce the troops there, and to take special care in guarding and defending the cannon, gunpowder, and public records, at that place. You are to take command of the whole of the troops at that place, till further orders. You are to apply to the committee in Dorchester, for a sufficient number of negroes in the public service, to remove the cannon lying by the water-side to a spot more safe, and convenient, near the fort or barracks, etc.

William Moultrie

Away marched Captain Marion, with Lieutenants Baker, DuBose, and Shubrick and with sixty-four men of his company' and thirty-eight of Huger's. Soon he had the arsenal in a sound state of defense, but he and his troops waited in vain for Scofield. Guard duty was monotonous, and by December 10 Marion had lost forty-five men through sickness and desertion. About Christmas time he requested a change of assignment, and Moultrie recalled him to Charleston to help rebuild Fort Johnson.

The work of repairing the ramparts and of salvaging and mounting the guns of the fort was heavy. Both officers and men remembered the indolent days at Dorchester. In January, one of the lieutenants heard that there was to be a main of famous cocks in the swamp at the head of the Ashley. "O heavens!" he exclaimed, "I would not miss that cockfight for all the world!"

With sorrowful countenance the officer asked Marion if he might visit his father, who lay gravely ill. "To be sure, Lieutenant, go, by all means. Go and wait upon your father," Marion told him, "but return as soon as possible, for you see how much we have to do."

After attending the cockfight, the young officer lingered in Dorchester for two weeks. Returning, he entered the room where Captain Marion sat with other officers, bowed, and started to speak. Having gotten wind of the affair, Marion turned his head away. "I am sorry, Sir, to have overstayed my leave so long," blurted out the discomfited officer, "but I could not help it. But now I am returned to do my duty."

Marion turned his head and remarked drily: "Aye, Lieutenant, is that you? Well, never mind; there is no harm done. I never missed you."

The crestfallen young officer retired, but his comrades never let him forget the rebuke. "I have often heard him say," said Peter Horry, "that nothing ever so completely confounded him as that dry, cutting speech of Marion."

The new year brought information from London that

Major General Charles Cornwallis had begun preparing five regiments for a campaign in the southern colonies. Governor Rutledge decided to fortify the entrance to Charleston Harbor and ordered the Second Regiment to help build a fort on Sullivan's Island. On February 10, 1776, Captain Marion and the detachment he had commanded at Dorchester were encamped at Haddrell's Point. With the increase in fortifications there was need for more soldiers, and so the Provincial Congress authorized the formation of two regiments of riflemen. The members chose Colonel Isaac Huger, Lieutenant Colonel Alexander McIntosh, and Major Benjamin Huger field officers of the First Regiment of Riflemen. They elected Thomas Sumter the Lieutenant Colonel, Commandant, of the Second Regiment of Riflemen. As a result of the promotion and transfer of Major McIntosh, there was a vacancy in the Second Regiment. Because of his seniority, his recognized ability, and his reputation for hard work, on February 22, 1776, the Provincial Congress promoted Francis Marion to the rank of Major.

While Colonel Moultrie was building a fort of palmetto logs and sand on Sullivan's Island, Lord Cornwallis was assembling his expedition at Cork. On February 12 he went aboard the flagship *Bristol,* and Commodore Peter Parker hoisted sail. They had a tempestuous voyage, but by May 1 the transports had begun arriving off Cape Fear, North Carolina. There Sir Henry Clinton took command. He ordered Commodore Parker to turn southward, and on June 4 the British fleet dropped anchor off the bar of Charleston. On the same day Major General Charles Lee, second in command of the American Army, arrived in Charleston.

On the morning of June 28 the British warships began moving into position opposite the fort. At about 11 o'clock Commodore Parker hoisted the signal to attack. The *Thunder* began throwing thirteen-inch shells into the fort. Soon the *Acteon,* the *Bristol,* the *Experiment,* and the *Solebay* joined in the action. At a range of four hundred yards the *Active* began pouring solid shot into the rampart of palmetto logs and sand, but they sank harmlessly into the spongy mass.

The guns in the southwest bastion of the fort replied first. Soon the other cannon joined in the defense. Having only 5,400 pounds of powder, Colonel Moultrie ordered his gun captains to conserve their ammunition. Slowly, deliberately, they aimed and fired, their shot ranging into the ships. Receiving a flattering report of their action from his aide, General Lee crossed over to the island "to encourage the garrison by my presence; but I might have saved myself the trouble; for I found, on my arrival, they had no occasion for any sort of encouragement; I found them determined and cool to the last degree."

Directing their fire principally on the warships *Bristol* and *Experiment,* the Carolinians wrought havoc, wounding Commodore Parker, Lord Cornwallis, Governor Campbell, and Captains Morris and Scott. To silence this cannonading, the *Acteon,* the *Sphynx,* and the *Syren* attempted to round Sullivan's and enfilade the gunners. But the pilots missed the channel and grounded the three frigates.

During the bombardment a ball carried away the Second's regimental standard, a blue flag adorned with a silver crescent and the word Liberty. Upon this Sergeant William Jasper of the Grenadier Company called out to Moultrie: "Colonel, don't let us fight without our flag!"

"What can you do?" asked Moultrie. "The staff is broke."

"Then, sir," said Jasper, "I'll fix it to a halbert and place it on the merlon of the bastion next to the enemy."

Leaping down from the fort, he tore the flag from its staff, and climbed back through a rain of shot and shell. Tying the flag to a sponge staff, he then planted it on the summit of the fort.

There were many other acts of heroism. In the heaviest of the bombardment, Lieutenant Gabriel Marion sprang from the platform, crossed the open space in the fort, and brought up a new supply of powder.

Major Francis Marion commanded the left wing of the fort, in which were emplaced some of the heaviest cannon.

Boldly he directed his batteries throughout the day, and as the battered ships began to slip their cables and withdraw at sunset, he asked Moultrie if he might fire a last shot.

"Yes," yelled Moultrie. "Give them the parting kick."

Aiming one of the largest guns carefully, Marion touched a match to the powder, and watched the ball rip into the flagship.

Sir Henry Clinton failed to renew the battle and on June 30, Colonel Moultrie paraded his victorious troops before General Lee. The General was filled with admiration and praise. In his report to President John Hancock of the Continental Congress, he wrote: "I beg leave, sir, therefore, to recommend, in the strongest terms, to Congress, the commanding officer, Colonel Moultrie, and his whole garrison, as brave soldiers and excellent citizens."

CHAPTER II

Commandant of the Second Regiment

FRANCIS MARION had dreamed of freedom from Great Britain, and now his dream was becoming a reality. On July 4, the day that Governor Rutledge inspected the garrison of Fort Moultrie and gave his sword to heroic Jasper, the Continental Congress passed a Declaration of Independence. As soon as Congress learned of the great victory of the soldiers of one of the United States, it passed a resolution praising them. General Washington felicitated General Lee and added his praise for the gallantry of the defenders of Fort Moultrie.

But while the Whig newspapers of the nation were publishing tributes and resolutions of praise, the heroes of the Second Regiment were employed in a fiasco. Jonathan Bryan, a leading citizen of Savannah, persuaded General Lee to order an expedition against the predatory Tories of East Florida. After preparing the troops of Virginia and North Carolina, Lee marched into Georgia. Rutledge sent reinforcements trailing along under Colonel Moultrie.

When the expedition reached Savannah, General Lee received orders to return to Philadelphia. He turned the command over to Colonel Moultrie, but by that time the army was in a terrible state. Marching in the subtropical heat of August had decimated the corps and nearly every officer lay dangerously ill. In the advanced camp at Sunbury, heat and malaria were killing soldiers at the rate of fifteen a day, and so Moultrie ordered his troops to return to Charleston.

While Colonel Moultrie and the Second Regiment were in Georgia, the Congress of the United States established a national Army. At its invitation, on September 20 the General Assembly placed the South Carolina troops upon the Continental establishment. Colonels Christopher Gadsden and William Moultrie were promoted to the rank of Brigadier General. There were consequent changes and promotions, and on November 23 Isaac Motte became the Colonel, Francis Marion the Lieutenant Colonel, and Peter Horry the Major of the Second Regiment of South Carolina.

These Continentals had scarcely returned to Charleston before General Robert Howe, who had succeeded Lee, ordered some of them to return to Georgia. On February 23, 1777, an express rode in with information that Captain Richard Winn and fifty men of the South Carolina Rangers at Fort McIntosh on the Satilla River were being attacked by Indians and Tories. Under Howe's orders Lieutenant Colonel Marion hurried off with a detachment of 107 men. Before Marion could reach Fort McIntosh, however, Captain Winn had surrendered to British regulars under the command of Major General Augustine Prévost, and so on March 18 Marion loaded his weary troops aboard transports and brought them back to Charleston.

For the next year Lieutenant Colonel Francis Marion served in and around Charleston. After General Prévost had driven the American troops from Georgia and settled British regulars in Savannah, the war in the South became a stalemate, and Howe's Continentals were confined largely to the city and spent their time in dreary garrison duty. In the long months of gun polishing and waiting, duty became dry routine. The monotony of standing guard disgusted the more intelligent and vigorous soldiers, and they left the army upon the expiration of their enlistments. Those remaining were often lazy and shiftless and devoted much of their time to playing cards and gambling. There were also heavy drinking and fighting, and one row ended in a fatal duel.

The officers of the various regiments tried to maintain discipline. Courts-martial heard case after case. A private in the Second Regiment was charged with stealing silk stockings. Another was tried for stealing a linen shirt from an officer. One hungry offender was punished for taking fruit from an officer's servant. An entire squad was found guilty of tearing the frames from the doors and windows of a private home and using them for firewood. The quality of personnel deteriorated so badly that in 1778 the Legislature ordered all vagrants, harborers of deserters, and persons convicted of killing deer after shining lights in their eyes, to be sentenced to serve in the Continental regiments. Howe ordered Lieutenant Raphael court-martialed for "having behaved in a manner unbecoming an officer and a gentleman in having threatened to take the life of a person who gave evidence against him at a court-martial." General Moultrie ordered Colonel Owen Roberts, Commandant of the Regiment of Artillery, put under arrest for "quitting his post and being too frequently in town without leave of the Commander-in-Chief." Jealousy and strife reached even the highest ranks. After receiving orders from Major General Howe for six months, Brigadier General Christopher Gadsden decided that he was senior and demanded to know by what right Howe commanded in South Carolina. Howe stated his position and authority. The quarrel dragged along until Gadsden's friends brought the matter before the General Assembly. When Gadsden lost, he resigned from the army, charging Howe with insincerity and duplicity. Howe challenged him to a duel. They met on July 30, 1778. Gadsden fired into the air, and at eight paces Howe missed!

During these months of inactivity, Francis Marion observed perfect decorum. There was never a rumor of criticism of his conduct. As the executive officer of the Second Regiment, he devoted himself to maintaining its *esprit de corps.* He was proud of his officers and men.

On the second anniversary of the battle of Fort Moultrie, June 28, 1778, some of the leading women in Charleston gave a splendid dinner to the defenders. The officers of the Second Regiment presented their troops with a hogshead of claret and three barrels of beer. "Colonel Marion hopes the men will behave with sobriety and decency to those ladies who have been so kind as to give them so genteel a treat," said his Regimental Order.

A man of deep religious instincts, Marion nurtured the same spirit among his men. "On Saturday, 10 o'clock in the morning, divine service will be performed by the Chaplain in St. Michael's Church," he said in his Regimental Order of June 23, 1777. "All officers and men are desired to parade with their side-arms at the new barracks at nine o'clock in the morning, from which the regiment will be marched to church."

To prevent his troops from appearing with the long hair and beards that men frequently develop while idling in barracks, Marion ordered regulation haircuts. "As long hair gathers much filth, and takes a great deal of time and trouble to comb and keep clean and in good order, the Lieut.-Colonel recommends to every soldier to have their hair cut short, to reach no further down than the top of the shirt-collar, and thinned upwards to the crown of the head, the fore-top short, without toupee, and short at the side," he said in his Regimental Orders. . . . "Any soldier who comes on parade with beards, or hair uncombed, shall be dry-shaved immediately, and have his hair dressed on the parade."

Francis Marion showed an instinctive feeling for discipline. Without being a martinet, he was rigid with his officers. He knew that they alone could maintain the regiment in fighting spirit, and he sometimes censured as well as praised them. "As the regiment, by being in town too long, have lost a great part of their discipline, and it is necessary to reform all abuses and neglect of discipline, the Lieut.-Colonel calls upon every gentleman in the regiment to true and exact discipline, that they may regain their former credit, and be an honor to themselves and their country," he said in his Regimental Orders of January 8, 1778.

The common-sense measures were effective and popular. Marion's officers admired him. "The truth is," said Horry, "Marion wished his officers to be gentlemen. And whenever he saw one of them acting below that character, he would generously attempt his reformation. And few men, perhaps, ever knew better how to manage truants from duty."

Marion's men loved him. "Indeed," said Peter Horry, "I am not afraid to say that Marion was the *architect* of the Second Regiment and laid the foundation of that excellent discipline and confidence in themselves, which gained them such reputation whenever they were brought to face their enemies."

Francis Marion's integrity, diligence, and attention to duty were recognized throughout the Southern Army. When Colonel Isaac Motte resigned on September 23, 1778, Marion assumed command of the Second Regiment. But he was not promoted. British regiments were commanded by lieutenant colonels; and, as that made a disparity in prisoner exchange, Congress stopped promotions to the rank of colonel. His title was changed, however. He was now Lieutenant Colonel Francis Marion, Commandant of the Second Regiment.

In the spring of 1778 General Howe led a campaign against the Indians and Tories in Georgia, but Lieutenant Colonel Marion and his crack Second Regiment were left at Fort Moultrie to guard Charleston. Howe sent a detachment of Continentals under Colonel C. C. Pinckney and of militia under Colonel Andrew Williamson as far as the Altamaha River. The expedition collapsed from sickness and July heat.

Howe retreated across the river to Purrysburgh, where he was soon afterward relieved of his command by General Benjamin Lincoln. On January 16, 1779, Colonel Richard Richardson, who commanded the militia east of the Santee, joined Lincoln. But his undisciplined militiamen refused to obey their officers. On being chided by his captain for being absent from a sentry post, a private answered roughly. After having been arrested, he tried to shoot the captain. When Lincoln attempted to convene a court-martial to try the offender, many of the militia officers refused to serve on the grounds that militiamen could be tried only under the militia laws of South Carolina.

In disgust Lincoln declared the militia no longer under his command. Turning them over to Moultrie, he marched off toward Augusta with his Continentals. After watching Lincoln for three months, General Prévost decided to invade South Carolina. Crossing the Savannah River, he began advancing along the Charleston road, his troops threatening to outflank and get behind those of Moultrie.

Leaving a rear guard westward of the Coosawhatchie River, on May 1 Moultrie retreated to the east of the Tulifinny River. He had planned to hold the passes over the rivers, but a long drouth had so lowered the water that he changed his strategy. He began retreating toward Charleston.

Crossing the Ashley near Dorchester, Moultrie entered the capital on May 9 and immediately strung all available troops, militia and Continental, across Charleston Neck. To form his anchors, he sent Colonel McIntosh and the Fifth Regiment into the redoubt on the right flank. Into the redoubt on the left flank he sent Colonel Marion and 140 men from the Second Regiment.

Prévost crossed the Ashley River on June 10 and next morning moved into position in front of the line. All day the light troops skirmished. About three o'clock next morning, Governor Rutledge came to Moultrie and asked if he should open a parley with the enemy. After earnest debate, Moultrie sent an inquiry to Prévost. "General Moultrie, perceiving from the motions of your army that your intentions are to besiege the town, would be glad to know on what terms you would be disposed to grant a capitulation should he be inclined to capitulate."

About eleven o'clock Prévost sent his brother, Colonel J. M. Prevost, with an answer. Rutledge summoned his Council to the Governor's House. While they were reading the terms of surrender, Captain Thomas Dunbar dashed in with a message from Colonel Marion. The British had observed work on the defenses continuing during the parley, and Prévost had sent an ultimatum warning that if it were not stopped he would immediately attack.

Rutledge and his Council studied Prevost's terms during the night. By morning they had reached a decision: "To propose a neutrality during the war between Great Britain and America, and the question, whether the state shall belong to Great Britain, or remain one of the United States be determined by the treaty of peace between those two powers." Although asserting his willingness to carry the proposal to General Prévost, Colonel Prévost reminded the emissaries that the British had not come in a legislative but in a military capacity, that his business was with General Moultrie, and that as the garrison was in arms they must surrender as prisoners of war.

"I am determined not to deliver you up as prisoners of war!" Moultrie exclaimed to the Governor and his Council. "We will fight!"

Moultrie began strengthening his lines and preparing his troops against the coming assault. But on the following morning he discovered that the enemy had decamped. Learning that General Lincoln, rushing up from Georgia with his Continentals, was almost in position to seal his escape route, General Prévost had recrossed the Ashley during the night. Slowly Prévost moved on down the coast, and by early summer he had his troops again billeted in Savannah.

After the retreat of Prévost, Governor Rutledge, General Lincoln, and Monsieur Plombard, who was the French Consul in Charleston, settled upon a campaign to drive the British from Georgia. To Count D'Estaing, the French Admiral cruising in the waters of the West Indies, they proposed a combined French and American attack upon Savannah. The Count agreed. In early September his squadron of forty-one vessels dropped anchor off Tybee Island, Georgia. In loose cooperation Lincoln mustered the American Army. He ordered Colonel Marion and the Second Regiment from Fort Moultrie, called in his other Continentals and the Charleston militia, and set off for the rendezvous.

But D'Estaing was impetuous and rash. Before Lincoln arrived, the Count disembarked his troops, moved upon Savannah, and summoned the British to surrender. General Prévost asked for twenty-four hours in which to consider the ultimatum, and D'Estaing granted the delay. "My God!" cried Marion when Lincoln reported D'Estaing's action, "who ever heard of anything like this before? First allow an enemy to entrench, and then fight him!"

Never before had Peter Horry seen Marion in such towering passion. "I was actually afraid he would have broken out on General Lincoln."

Marion was right. Upon the approach of D'Estaing, General Prévost had called in Lieutenant Colonel John Harris Cruger from Sunbury and Lieutenant Colonel John Maitland from Beaufort. Collecting several hundred slaves from surrounding plantations, he set everyone digging trenches and erecting fortifications. By the end of the truce, his position was too formidable for D'Estaing to risk an attack. Thereupon the French and American troops began a combined operation. On October 4 they opened a bombardment. They continued it for four days, but with little effect. Then the Admiral decided to storm the fortifications.

D'Estaing set the assault for the early morning of October 9. The plans were for all troops to move in a single column under the skirt of a wood and, as they came into the open to break into different columns, each with its objective. But before all of his troops were in position, the Count led the first units against Spring Hill redoubt, the anchor of the British line.

The American column, led by Colonel John Laurens with

the Light Infantry and supported by Colonel Marion with the Second Regiment and Captain Shepperd with the Charleston militia, followed Count Pulaski and his legion up Spring Hill. In a rain of musket shot they reached the fosse. Francis Marion, sword in hand and shouting encouragement to his men, plunged into the ditch. There he stood urging his men forward while the enemy riflemen sprayed death around him. Up to the parapet Lieutenant John Bush carried the blue flag of the Second Regiment.

But Lieutenant Colonel Thomas Brown, whom the Whigs had once tarred and feathered, was holding the redoubt with his regiment of South Carolina Loyalists. His Tories fought with valor, and their marksmen wreaked havoc among the troops of the Second Regiment. One of Brown's marksmen wounded Lieutenant Bush, who passed his flag to Sergeant Jasper. As the hero of Fort Moultrie carried the flag uphill, a sharpshooter struck him down. Before dying he handed the flag back to Lieutenant Bush. Into the ditch beside Marion charged Bush and, when a musketeer toppled him, he died with the blue ensign crumpled beneath him. Before the sharpshooters marked him for death, Lieutenant James Gray planted the red flag of the Second Regiment on Spring Hill redoubt.

Gray's heroic act was the high point of the attack. The momentum of the advance was spent, and the parapet was too high to be scaled under fire. Seeing his men were not gaining any ground, D'Estaing ordered a retreat. Sergeant McDonald snatched Gray's red ensign from the redoubt and followed Marion down Spring Hill. Behind them the ground was covered with the dead and wounded. Of the six hundred Carolinians who had charged uphill, more than two hundred and fifty did not come down again.

"I went with a heavy heart on parade, to take a review of the sad remains of the battle," said Peter Horry. "The call of the roll completed the depression of my spirits. To every fourth or fifth name there was no answer—the gloomy silence which ensued told us where they were."

About twelve o'clock D'Estaing sent an officer under a flag to ask Prévost's permission to collect his men who had been killed. "We then proceeded to bury our dead," said Horry, "which was done by digging large pits, sufficient to retain about a hundred corpses. Then taking off their clothes, with heavy hearts, we threw them into the pits, with very little regard to order, and covered them with earth."

After his defeat, Count D'Estaing hurried his men aboard ship and sailed back to the West Indies. Soon afterward General Lincoln crossed the Savannah at Zubley's Ferry, paused at Ebenezer Heights, and finally encamped on the Bull Plantation at Sheldon. From there he hurried on to Charleston, leaving the survivors of his three regiments under the command of Colonel Marion.

Francis Marion now commanded the only field army in South Carolina. Although only a lieutenant colonel, he had been entrusted with the responsibilities of a brigadier general. For the three months he remained at Sheldon he performed his duties in an exemplary manner.

While Marion was at Sheldon, Governor Rutledge received orders from the Continental Congress to reduce the number of South Carolina regiments on the Continental establishment. "Congress have resolved that the regiments of this state should be incorporated and formed on the plan ordered by them for the Army of the United States. . . ." General Lincoln wrote Marion on December 30: "I have the Governor's permission to inform you that he wishes this business may be conducted in a manner most agreeable to the line of officers." Marion immediately polled his officers and reported their preference to General Lincoln.

By January 20, 1780, Rutledge and Lincoln had decided that Lieutenant Colonels Francis Marion, William Scott, and William Henderson would command the three regiments after the reduction. They had also selected Majors Isaac Harleston, Edmund Hyrne, and Thomas Pinckney. Rutledge and Lincoln instructed these officers to appoint twenty-seven captains on the basis of seniority. When the new regiments, were formed, Lieutenant Colonel Francis Marion was the senior field officer in South Carolina. He had risen from the postion of an unknown captain to that of the most respected commanding officer in South Carolina.

In the late summer of 1779 Lord Cornwallis, who had been in England with his dying wife, returned to New York. With him he brought instructions from the War Office for the conquest of the Southern Provinces. During the autumn Sir Henry Clinton organized a vast expeditionary force. As soon as it was aboard transport, Sir Henry joined Vice Admiral Mariott Arbuthnot on the *Romulus,* and on December 26 Captain John Plumer Ardesoife hoisted signal on the flagship. The armada broke through the thin ice in New York Harbor and turned southward toward Tybee.

As soon as General Lincoln learned of Sir Henry's move, he began concentrating his forces. "The state of affairs is such as to make it necessary that we draw our force to a point as much and as soon as possible," he wrote Marion on January 31, 1780. "No troops will be kept in the field except two hundred light infantry and the horse. You will, therefore, please to select from the three regiments with you, two hundred of your best men, and those who are best clothed, and organize them into corps with proper officers. . . . After that I wish to see you as soon as possible in Charleston."

During the excitement over the coming invasion the General Assembly of South Carolina had hastily conferred dictatorial powers upon Governor John Rutledge, adopted a resolution to defend Charleston to the last extremity, and adjourned. Rutledge immediately called out the South Carolina militia. He ordered General Moultrie to establish a receiving station for militiamen at Bacon's Bridge near Dorchester. To this post Lincoln sent Marion in early February. He assigned him the task of properly drilling these citizensoldiers. "No officer in the Union was better calculated to command them, and to have done more than he did," said Peter Horry.

By then the British had begun arriving. After a stormy voyage, on February 1 Admiral Arbuthnot anchored his fleet off Tybee. With favorable wind he then moved his transports up to within thirty miles of Charleston, and on February 11 Sir Henry Clinton began disembarking his troops on John's Island. Sir Henry passed unmolested to James Island. There he waited for Lieutenant Colonel Banastre Tarleton, then remounting his green dragoons with horses rustled from the planters around Beaufort, and for Brigadier General Patterson who was bringing his army up from Savannah.

With Sir Henry closing in, Lincoln called in his best commanders. On February 19 he sent Lieutenant Colonel William Henderson to Bacon's Bridge, and recalled Francis Marion to the Second Regiment. For the next month Marion worked heroically in helping prepare the defenses of Charleston. On March 19 the Colonel was with his regiment. But about that time Captain Alexander McQueen, Adjutant General to General Moultrie, gave a dinner party at his home on the corner of Orange and Tradd Streets.

After dinner the host locked the door, and these ardent Whigs began toasting liberty and victory in bumpers of sparkling wine. While Marion drank lightly, having drawn his six and a half measures of rum on March 1, he would not get drunk. He began looking for a way to escape. Finding no better, he jumped from the second story window. In landing he broke his ankle. "When the story got about in Charleston, most people said he was a great fool for his pains," said Peter Horry, "but the event soon proved that Marion was in the right, and that there is no policy like sticking to a man's duty."

The British were moving toward Charleston. On March 18 Tarleton marched from Beaufort. Three days later he took the van of Patterson's army. On March 25 they joined Sir Henry Clinton at Stono River, and four days later Sir Henry crossed the Ashley and strung his troops across Charleston Neck. On April 1 he sent Tarleton to seize Bacon's Bridge. Clinton then began a vigorous siege. Fearful of ultimate surrender, on April 12 General Lincoln sent Governor Rutledge and part of his Council from the beleaguered city. To disencumber his army of all but fighting men, Lincoln also issued an order "that all supernumerary officers, and all officers who are unfit for duty, must quit the garrison and retire into the country."

Francis Marion, his ankle swollen and useless, left Charleston in a litter, crossed the Cooper River, and disappeared among his friends and kindred along the Santee. But his hiding was precarious. The British were combing the country. On April 14 Tarleton defeated the troops under Lieutenant Colonel William Washington at Moncks Corner. The arrival of reinforcements on April 18 enabled Sir Henry to dispatch Lord Cornwallis and Tarleton across the Cooper to St. Thomas' Parish. Tarleton began sweeping the country. On May 6 he struck Colonel Anthony White's dragoons at Lenud's Ferry and drove them into the Santee.

General Lincoln surrendered on May 12, 1780. General Moultrie and the officers and men of the South Carolina regiments became prisoners of war. Major Isaac Harleston marched the Second Regiment to Haddrell's Point, where they encamped to await exchange or release.

As soon as Sir Henry Clinton had firm control of the capital, he set the British Army in motion to conquer South Carolina. He sent one column up the Savannah to Augusta. He sent Lieutenant Colonel Nisbet Balfour and the Light Infantry to Ninety-Six. And he sent Lord Cornwallis and the main army toward Camden. On May 18 Cornwallis marched to Lenud's Ferry. Sending Tarleton across the Santee, he ordered him to sweep the country around Georgetown.

Conditions were now too hot for the Continentals furloughed from Charleston. Colonel Peter Horry forgot his rheumatism and prepared to flee. Dressed in his uniform, he rode into Georgetown. "I saw a distant group of people, to whom I rode up, and with *great civility,* as I thought, asked the *news*," said Horry. "To which a young fellow very scornfully replied, that 'Colonel Tarleton is coming, and the country, thank God, will soon be cleared of Continental colonels.' "

In spite of his swollen ankle, Francis Marion also put on the uniform of the Second Regiment, called Oscar, his faithful Negro servant, and slipped across the Santee ahead of Tarleton. Through the Whig settlements in All Saints Parish on Waccamaw Neck he rode, pausing at the home of his brother Isaac at Little River. Then, burning with hope to serve his country again, he rode boldly northward to meet the American Army marching toward the Carolinas.

CHAPTER III

Release of the Prisoners

WHILE FRANCIS MARION, Peter Horry, and the other Continentals who escaped from Charleston were riding northward to meet the American Army, Lord Cornwallis was overrunning South Carolina. After crossing the Santee at Lenud's Ferry, he marched the British Army slowly along the road leading to Camden. As he was breaking camp near Nelson's Ferry early in the morning of May 27, he dispatched Colonel Tarleton and his British Legion in chase of Colonel Abraham Buford and the Third Regiment of Virginia Continentals who were retreating toward Salisbury. Tarleton rushed away, most of his horses carrying a dragoon and an infantryman. On the night of May 28 he bivouacked at Camden. News of his arrival spread quickly.

Henry Rugeley, an English settler who owned mills and a plantation named Clermont twelve miles above Camden, had that night as guests Governor Rutledge and the two members of his Council whom Lincoln had sent out of Charleston. Feeling strongly the demands of hospitality, Rugeley waked the Governor, warned him of the approach of Tarleton, and helped him escape into North Carolina.

Foiled in capturing Governor Rutledge as he had bagged General Charles Lee at Baskingridge in 1776, Tarleton continued after Buford. At three o'clock on the afternoon of May 29 he overtook the Virginians at the Waxhaws. When

Buford rejected his terms, Tarleton formed the British Legion and charged. A rifleman killed his horse and, before he could find another and remount, his green-coated dragoons were out of control and massacring the defeated Americans. "I am extremely fatigued with overtaking the Enemy & beating them," he wrote Lord Cornwallis from the battlefield.

Cornwallis, who reached Camden on June 1, rushed the report and a letter of encomium to Sir Henry Clinton. Thinking that Tarleton's victory had ended all resistance in South Carolina, on June 3 General Clinton issued a proclamation that all paroles would "be null and void" after June 20. He ordered all holders of paroles to resume the character of British subjects and to take part in forwarding the military operations of Lord Cornwallis.

Admiral Arbuthnot detached Captain John Plumer Ardesoife, placed him in command of HMS *Loyalist,* and left him to assist Cornwallis. Ardesoife immediately began sailing along the coast and frightening the sea islanders. In late June he sailed into Winyah Bay and dropped anchor off Georgetown. Going ashore, he published the proclamation of Clinton, and ordered the inhabitants to come in and swear allegiance to King George. His decree angered and aroused the Scotch-Irish of Williamsburg. They chose Major John James, the hero of Tulifinny, to go to Georgetown and seek a clarification from Ardesoife. Did the proclamation mean that those returning to allegiance would have to take up arms against their fellow countrymen? The Major, in the plain garb of a planter, rode off on his horse Thunder. He found Captain Ardesoife at his headquarters and asked the question propounded by the assembly.

"The submission must be unconditional," replied the Captain haughtily.

"Will the inhabitants be allowed to stay at home upon their plantations in peace and quiet?" enquired James.

"Although you have rebelled against his Majesty, he offers

you a free pardon, of which you are undeserving, for you ought all to be hanged," stiffly retorted the naval officer. "But as he offers you a free pardon, you must take up arms in support of his cause."

"But the people I came to represent will not submit on such terms."

"You damned rebel," shouted Ardesoife, "if you speak in such language, I will immediately order you to be hanged up to the yardarm!"

Ardesoife wore his uniform and was armed with his sword. At his cursing, Major James sprang up, seized the chair on which he had been seated, and brandished it in his face. He then backed through the door, jumped astride Thunder, and galloped off toward Kingstree.

"You must take up arms in support of his cause" rang from All Saints Parish on the Atlantic to St. John's across the Santee. The inhabitants became thoroughly aroused. All refused to shed the blood of their countrymen. Covenanter spirit flamed and the men of Williamsburg decided to fight. Since Major James had represented them in the General Assembly, they selected him to command them in the field. For captains they chose William McCottry, Henry Mouzon, John James (a second cousin of the Major's who lived on Lynches Lake), and John McCauley. While they were organizing, their neighbors joined in the movement for freedom. Lieutenant Colonel Hugh Giles raised a regiment of militia in the neck between Lynches River and the Peedee. Across the Peedee Colonel John Ervin called out the Britton's Neck Regiment.

Lord Cornwallis had posted his regiments at strategic points. He sent Lord Rawdon and his Volunteers of Ireland to the Waxhaws. To overawe the Whigs along the eastern frontier, he sent Major Archibald McArthur and his battallion of the 71st Regiment of Highlanders to Cheraw. But many of his Highlanders were prostrated by malaria. Faced with the task of getting the ill to Charleston, McArthur called out the Loyalist militia commanded by Lieutenant Colonel Robert Mills. Loading Lord Nairne and 106 ill and invalid troops aboard sequestered flatboats, he sent Mills and his Tories to escort them to Georgetown. But Colonel John Ervin learned of their movement and waylaid the flotilla near Mars Bluff. Mills and some of his officers swam ashore, but Ervin's men captured the others, with their arms and equipment. They also seized the invalids under Lord Nairne.

Confronted with insurrection and violence, Lord Cornwallis put into effect an idea used successfully in the North: set Americans fighting Americans. "I agreed to a proposal made by Mr. Harrison, to raise a provincial corps of five hundred Men, with the rank of Major, to be Natives of the Country between the Pedee and Wateree, and in which it is at present extremely probable he will Succeed," he wrote Sir Henry Clinton on June 30.

As violence mounted, Lord Cornwallis, who with Tarleton had returned to Charleston and established headquarters at Drayton Hall, sent Major James Wemyss and his battalion of the 63rd Regiment to Georgetown. In keeping with his policy, he told Wemyss to help Lieutenant Colonel James Cassels in forming a regiment of Loyal militia. But with the Williamsburg militia assembled and ready to strike, the Tories in Georgetown refused to join Cassels. And so on July 30 Cornwallis ordered Major Wemyss to march to the High Hills. "Nor can you in the present situation of things do any good toward forming a militia at Georgetown," he wrote. "I cannot permit therefore of your making any longer stay there."

In Williamsburg, meanwhile, the revolting militia remained under arms. Learning that Gates and the American Army were rapidly approaching South Carolina, Major James sent an emissary to ask him to appoint for them a commander from the Continentals. Then he posted Captain McCottry and his riflemen near Indiantown. With the infantry he encamped at Witherspoon's Ferry, where the main highway crossed Lynches River.

While Lord Cornwallis was in Charleston directing his troops in the field, trying to set up a provisional government and preparing for his fall campaign, Baron de Kalb was marching an army of Continentals through North Carolina. General Washington recommended that this army be put under command of Major General Nathanael Greene. Congress, however, appointed Major General Horatio Gates, the hero who had captured the army under Burgoyne at Saratoga. Gates immediately set out to join the army. In early July he issued a proclamation for all Continental officers still at liberty in the South to join him at Hillsboro, North Carolina. In obedience, Colonels Francis Marion and Peter Horry, with about twenty officers, men, and servants, came out of hiding and rode on to meet the army. They found De Kalb encamped at Wilcox's Mill on Deep River and were with the friendly old Baron on July 25 when Gates reached camp and took command.

Gates immediately marched on his campaign. "Instead of moving on as old de Kalb had done, with a prudent regard to the health and refreshment of his troops," said Peter Horry, "he, Jehu like, drove them on without regard to either." He crossed the Peedee at Mask's Ferry on August 3 and began advancing relentlessly toward Camden. By August 7 he had reached Little Black Creek, only forty miles from the British at Logtown. From there an officer of the Continental Line wrote the South Carolina delegates in Congress: "I take the opportunity of the present express to inform you, that two days ago, Major General Gates entered South Carolina at the head of the Maryland division, with a park of artillery, Colonel Armand's Corps, and a regiment of Virginia State Troops, and a party of South Carolina refugees, under Colonel Marion."

Alarmed at the rapid march of Gates, Lord Rawdon began preparing the British Army for battle. He recalled the advanced detachments under McArthur, Turnbull, and Balfour from the frontier, and he began urging Lord Cornwallis to return to Camden. Rawdon was also alarmed by the insurrection around Kingstree. As he watched the long train of wagons bringing provisions and ammunition from Charleston, he began fearing some bold stroke. On August 1 he complained to Cornwallis: "I am still afraid of some party getting over the Santee and disturbing our convoys."

Cornwallis tarried at Drayton Hall, but he ordered Tarleton to gather the convalescent troops of the British Legion and the 17th Dragoons and return to Camden. "I directed him to pass at Lenew's Ferry and proceed up the Santee," he wrote Major Wemyss in Georgetown. "He is informed fully of the State of Things in those parts and will take any steps in his power to contribute to the security of your movement and to intimidate the Enemy."

Guided by Tories, late in the afternoon of August 6 Tarleton's dragoons crossed Lower Bridge and dashed into Kingstree. As the red-coated dragoons and the green-coated legionnaires went into bivouac, the people watched grimly. The time had now come to fight for home and hearth. Messengers galloped away to summon Major James and the militia. But there were also Loyalists in Kingstree. After dark the wife of Captain John Hamilton, a notorious Tory who had formerly been a merchant in the village, slipped into the British camp to warn Tarleton of the approach of James. Fearless partisan that he was, Tarleton knew when to fight and when to run. Unheedful of the orders of Cornwallis to arrest the most violent of the Whigs, he aroused his troops. Silently they crossed Kingstree Bridge and disappeared up the western bank of the Black River.

The messengers found Captain McCottry and his riflemen at Indiantown. Without waiting for Major James and his mounted infantry, McCottry dashed off toward Kingstree. Arriving a little before midnight, he found that the British had decamped. Without waiting for orders, he dashed across the bridge and set off in pursuit of "Bloody" Tarleton. But as William James drily remarked, "perhaps fortunately without overtaking him."

On August 4 Major Wemyss wrote Cornwallis that he would march in four or five days. On August 8 he wrote: "I shall march tomorrow morning." Then, to relieve the General's anxiety, the Major added: "The militia although collected in some numbers are I think tolerably quiet. I expect little or no annoyance from them on my march." Late that evening, after placing his sick in wagons and mounting his convalescents on horses, Wemyss set off for Camden. Unaware that Tarleton's raid had aroused the Scotch-Irish, he crawled along with his caravan until they were in the neighborhood of Lenud's Ferry. Here the Tory guards told him that Major James and five hundred militiamen lay under arms at Kingstree. Realizing that the road passed within thirteen miles of this formidable encampment, Wemyss began forcing his march. All day and into the night he drove his troops. Next morning from Nelson's Ferry he reported to Cornwallis: "I got here last night with the detachment of the 63rd Reg't."

At the house of Colonel Thomas Sumter at the Great Savannah, six miles above Nelson's Ferry, Wemyss rested his troops for several days. On August 11 he reported to Cornwallis: "The militia from St. James and St. Johns who were with Col. Tarleton returned yesterday and found everything quiet on the road to Camden."

Like McArthur, Tarleton, and Wemyss, the other British commanders were marching their troops toward Camden. Turnbull abandoned Rocky Mount and brought in his New York Volunteers. Captain Rousselet and the infantry of the British Legion evacuated Hanging Rock. From Ninety-Six Balfour sent four companies of the Light Infantry. As these detachments swelled the British Army, Lord Rawdon marched out to Little Lynches Creek to dispute the passage of the American Army.

During this concentration, Rawdon sent messenger trailing messenger to Charleston. On the evening of August 10 Lord

Cornwallis left Charleston with an escort of light dragoons. On August 12 he crossed at Nelson's and paused to confer with Major Wemyss. During the night of August 13 he galloped into Camden and took command of the British Army. "I was greatly alarmed for a small detachment which I had sent under Major Wemyss to reduce the people of Georgetown to some order," he wrote Sir Henry Clinton. After discussing the commotion along the Peedee, he concluded: "Major Wemyss performed his march from Georgetown without loss, and is now in the neighborhood of this place."

While the British were strengthening their concentration, General Gates was marching steadily toward Camden. On August 10 he reached Little Lynches Creek. Finding his passage blocked by Lord Rawdon's troops, he paused to gather strength. Next morning he moved four miles upstream, threw the army across Lynches at a secret ford, outflanked the British, and struck for Rugeley's Mills. Here he established Camp Clermont.

In the meantime, Colonel Sumter, plunging after the retreating British, had retaken Rocky Mount and Hanging Rock. He was still following them, seizing fords and burning ferryboats. On August 12 he wrote Gates, urging that a powerful detachment be thrown across the Wateree to sweep down behind Camden. General Gates liked Sumter's strategy. Confident of finding Cornwallis just another Burgoyne, he conceived a movement to close all escape routes behind him. On August 14 he dispatched Colonel Thomas Woolford with one hundred Continentals and three hundred North Carolina militiamen to swing north of Camden, cross the river, and join Sumter in his foray down the Wateree.

Francis Marion, still a supernumerary officer with the American Army, approved of Gates' plan for Sumter. He had talked with an emissary from Major James and knew that the Scotch-Irish were already in arms and waiting for a leader. Eager to get back into the struggle, he asked Gates' permission to swing far south of Camden, take command of

the Williamsburg militia, and start a boat-burning foray up
the Santee.

"Col. Marion, a gentleman of South Carolina, had been
with the army a few days, attended by a very few followers,
distinguished by small leather caps, and the wretchedness
of their attire," Colonel Otho Williams, Adjutant General
of the Army, wrote in his *A Narrative of the Campaign.*
"Their number did not exceed twenty men and boys, some
white, some black, and all mounted, but most of them miser-
ably equipped; their appearance was in fact so burlesque,
that it was with much difficulty the diversion of the regular
soldiery was restrained by the officers, and the General himself was glad of an opportunity of detaching Col. Marion,
at his own instance, towards the interior of South Carolina,
with orders to watch the motions of the enemy and furnish
intelligence."

Among the refugees with Marion were Lieutenant Colonel
Peter Horry, Major John Vanderhorst, and Captains James
Theus, Lewis Ogier, and John Milton. "It was on the morn-
ing of August 15, 1780, that we left the army in a good posi-
tion near Rugeley's Mills," Colonel Peter Horry wrote in
his life of Marion. In his *Journal* Horry was more explicit:
"Col. Francis Marion & Myself was ordered to go Down the
Country to Destroy all boats & Craft of any kind, we found
on Santee River in Order to prevent Cornwallis & his Troops
Escaping him."

Riding off on the road from Rugeley's to Salem, Marion
and his followers covered less than a dozen miles before
dark. "Night took place & we could Go no further on Road
we were unacquainted with," said Horry, in relating that
they stopped at the home of a Tory, "so we Lay down in the
hall & Piazza on our blankets and Coats first Posting a
Centinal or two to Prevent our being suprized." About two
o'clock next morning Marion was awakened by the sound of
distant firing. Realizing that Gates had opened his attack,
he and his followers hastily mounted and headed toward
Williamsburg. Late in the afternoon of August 17 they

reached the camp of the Williamsburg militia at Witherspoon's Ferry.

Shouts, huzzas, and other exclamations of joy rang across
the muster field, for many of the militiamen recognized
Marion, having served under him in the earlier days of the
war or having seen him when their militia units served with
the Continentals. Major James dashed up to welcome the
Continentals. He introduced Marion to his officers and men.
Then the Major called up his fifteen-year-old son William.

William Dobein James never forgot his first sight of
Francis Marion. "He was below the middle stature of men,"
he wrote long afterward. "His body was well set, but his
knees and ankles were badly formed; and he still limped
upon one leg. He had a countenance remarkably steady; his
nose was acquiline, his chin projecting; his forehead was
large and high, and his eyes black and piercing."

The lad watched the Colonel with fascination. "He was
now forty-eight years of age; but still even at this age, his
frame was capable of enduring fatigue and every privation,
necessary to a partisan. His wisdom and patriotism will become henceforth conspicuous. Of a character so much venerated, even trifles became important. He was dressed in a
close round-bodied crimson jacket, of a coarse texture, and
wore a leather cap, part of the uniform of the second regiment, with a silver crescent in front, inscribed with the words,
'Liberty or death.' "

Francis Marion was still Commandant of the captured
Second Regiment of South Carolina. As an officer of the Continental Line, on special assignment but without rank in the
militia, he had no legal authority over James' troops. Nevertheless, he immediately took command. As soon as he had
become acquainted with his new corps, inspired by the fearless temper of the men, he began carrying out his orders
from General Gates.

As his first action Marion ordered Colonel Horry to ride
on and take command of the militia on Lower Santee.

Lynch's Creek, Aug. 17, 1780
Sir,

You will take the command of such men as will be collected
from Capts. Bonneau's, Mitchell's and Benson's companies,
and immediately proceed to Santee, from the lower Ferry to
Lenud's, and destroy all the boats and canoes on the river, and
post guards at each crossing place, to prevent persons from
crossing to or from Charleston, on either side of the river——
you will give all necessary intelligence, and the number of
men you may have collected as early as possible. You will
procure about twenty-five weight of gun-powder, and a pro-
portionable quantity of ball or swanshot, also flints, and send
them up to me immediately, to the Kingstree, by an express.
I am with esteem

Your obedient servant,
Francis Marion

N. B. You will also take the command of Capt. Lenud's
company, and furnish your men with arms, wherever you can
find them, giving receipts.

After the departure of Horry, Marion waited while Major
James and his captains gathered provisions and called out
reinforcements. He then marched his new command to Kingstree and next day moved on to the Santee. Striking the river
near Lenud's, he began a slow ascent, his troops zealously
destroying canoes and burning flatboats. They were determined that no redcoat should escape destruction at Camden.

But as Marion was moving up the Santee, some Whigs
came to him. In secret they told him an almost unbelievable
story. On the morning of August 16 Gates and Cornwallis
had fought one of the bloodiest battles of the Revolution.
They had marched against each other during the night, and
about two o'clock their advance guards had clashed about
halfway between Rugeley's and Camden. At daybreak they
had formed their lines, and then Cornwallis had opened the
battle. At the approach of Colonel Webster's red-coated infantry, the Virginia troops had thrown down their guns and
run. Wheeling his troops, Webster had then rolled up the

American left wing. Baron de Kalb and the Marylanders on the right had fought off Lord Rawdon's advance until Tarleton had cut in behind them with his Green Horse. Then the Marylanders, too, had fled, leaving the Baron mortally wounded. All day Tarleton had chased the fugitives, never halting his dragoons until they had reached Hanging Rock. Gates had fled into North Carolina.

The emissaries also reported that the upper jaw of Gates' pincers had been destroyed. On August 15 Sumter had captured Fort Carey which guarded the ferry behind Camden. But instead of moving on down the Wateree to meet Marion, next morning, with his command glutted with prisoners and captured supplies, he had begun a slow retreat. But at Fishing Creek, forty miles above Camden, Tarleton and his dragoons had overtaken him. In a fierce charge that had caught Sumter's midday bivouac by surprise, Tarleton's green horsemen had cut the few defenders to pieces, bagged the survivors, and rescued the prisoners. During the melee, Sumter had sprung astride a horse without a saddle and disappeared in the direction of Charlotte.

What should Marion do? South Carolina lay prostrate. The British held the capital, and there was no civil government in the state. Cornwallis had shattered any hope of military rescue. As soon as Tarleton had rested his bloody dragoons, he would ride into Williamsburg to chastise her people for perfidy and revolt.

But Francis Marion was at his best when the odds were most desperate. He never hesitated. He had orders to burn boats, and so concealing the debacle at Camden from his troops——not even warning Peter Horry——he continued to march and burn. During the night of August 23, he sent a small detachment in canoes across the Santee at Murry's Ferry with orders to burn every flatboat. Next day he marched on to Nelson's Ferry.

In the meantime Colonel Horry had ridden on to Lower Santee and called out the militia. "Not content with destroying the common scows and flats at the ferries," he wrote, "we went on to sweep the river of every skiff and canoe we could lay hands on." But, as he admitted, "it was a serious thing to the planters, and their wrath waxed exceedingly hot against us."

On toward Lenud's Ferry moved Horry's militia, enthusiastically destroying boats to cut off British stragglers. "Among the fleet of boats and flats that perished by our firebrands or hatchets, there were two that belonged to my excellent old uncle, Colonel E(lias) Horry," wrote the Colonel. "The old Gentleman could hardly believe his Negroes, when they told him that we were destroying his boats." The old Huguenot saddled his horse, got his fowling piece, and rode down to the Santee. With mingled French and English curses he halted his nephew's destruction. Peter remonstrated that he had orders from Colonel Marion who had orders from General Gates! The grizzled planter snorted that Cornwallis had chased Gates into North Carolina. Peter Horry was dumfounded. As further destruction would be useless, he decided to release the militia and await orders from Marion.

In spite of his great victory, Lord Cornwallis was also in trouble. He feared that malaria and smallpox would break out among the American prisoners. He wrote Sir Henry Clinton:

> I therefore sent them off as early as possible, by Divisions of 150 each, under the Escort of 38 Men, about two thirds of which were composed of the 63rd, and Prince of Wales Regiments, the rest Militia. In order to cover their March, altho' I did not apprehend much danger, I posted Major Wemyss with a Part of the 63d at the High Hills of Santee, and I sent Lieut. Colonel Tarleton with a detachment of the Legion & Lieut. Colonel Hamilton's Corps & some Militia to Ratcliffes Bridge on Linches Creek, which I thought would effectually awe the lower Country.

Unaware of the march of the prisoners, on the evening of August 24 Colonel Marion and his men lay in bivouac at Nelson's. During the evening his scouts brought in an ensign of the Loyalist militia. From this deserter Marion learned that a British escort under Captain Jonathan Roberts and a batch of a hundred and fifty American prisoners had camped for the night at Sumter's house at the Great Savannah.

Long before daylight Marion roused his men. After riding as quickly as possible to the Great Savannah, he sent Major Hugh Horry and sixteen men to seize the pass over Horse Creek. Then with the main body, he began circling around Sumter's house. As the mansion sat on an elevation above the Santee Swamp, he approached it unobserved behind a screen of live oaks and cedars. But in the darkness Horry's patrol stumbled upon a British sentinel. He fired. At the alarm Horry dashed down the lane toward the house. Marion's party closed in from the rear. They found the enemy's muskets stacked carelessly outside the front door. In a brief scuffle they killed or captured twenty-two of the escorting troops and two Tory guides.

Marion released a hundred and fifty Continentals of the Maryland Line, but to his chagrin eighty-five of them refused to obey his commands or to follow him. They insisted that as prisoners of war they be allowed to go on to Charleston. After all persuasion had failed, he gathered his prisoners and the remaining Continentals, turned back along the Santee Road, and retreated rapidly toward Kingstree. Late on Saturday afternoon, August 26, he crossed Lynches River at Witherspoon's Ferry.

"I am sorry to acquaint you that Gen. Gates is defeated with great loss; he was obliged to retreat to Charlotte, which obliges me also to retreat," Marion wrote Colonel Peter Horry the next day. "You will without delay retreat with what men you can get, to Briton's neck, where I have encamped."

Lieutenant Colonel Hamilton at Ratcliffe's Bridge first learned of Marion's retreat into Britton's Neck. On Monday evening he rushed a letter to Lord Cornwallis. "I have this moment received certain intelligence from Kingstree," he said, "that the Rebell party who retook the Rebell prisoners consisting of 150 men under the Command of Col. Marion, passed over Lynches Creek last Saturday towards Pedee."

On the return from Sumter's house, all except three of the Continentals deserted their liberator. On October 6 Colonel Otho Williams disgustedly reported to Governor Lee of Maryland: "Of the 150 men retaken by Marion only about 60 rejoined their corps——some were sick but most of them just departed."

Cornwallis ordered Major Wemyss to investigate this affair. "One thing is certain, that Captain Robert's party, the night they were surprised, lay not only without their accoutrements, but without their coats," Wemyss reported from the High Hills on September 3. "They were so completely surprised, that about 100 infamous Militia seized most of their arms without Opposition." And he concluded sardonically: "I am afraid negligence will mark the whole of it."

When Marion reached Lynches River, most of the Williamsburg militia turned back home. Undaunted by this wholesale desertion, he crossed the Peedee with Major James and his steadfast comrades. At Port's Ferry he waited for Colonel Peter Horry. He was among staunch Whigs. As soon as they learned that Colonel Francis Marion was in Britton's Neck, many visited his camp. Several joined his band. Among these were Francis Goddard and his half brothers Samuel and Britton Jenkins. They were sons of Widow Elizabeth Jenkins who lived about ten miles below the ferry. They were veterans of the Second Regiment and had served in the disastrous campaign against Savannah.

Constant to Continental traditions, as soon as Marion was safe from pursuit, he wrote his official report. On the morning of August 29, he handed it to Lieutenant Keating Simons and instructed him to deliver it to the commanding general wherever he could be found. Simons overtook the remnants of the American Army at Hillsboro, North Carolina. "Colonel Marien, of South Carolina, has surprised a party of the enemy near Santee-River, escorting 150 prisoners of the Maryland division," General Gates reported to Congress on

September 9. "He took the party and released the prisoners, who are now on their march to Cross Creek, where I have sent Lieutenant Col. Ford, and proper officers to conduct them hither."

News of Marion's brilliant exploit cheered a drooping Congress. He had saved a morsel from the destruction of the Southern Army. Charles Thompson, Secretary to Congress, forwarded the extract from Gates' letter to leading Whig newspapers throughout the country. *The Boston Gazette, The Country Journal, The Connecticut Courant,* and *The Pennsylvania Journal* featured the report. For the first time patriots from Maine to Georgia read the name of Francis Marion. But from that perversity which ever dogs military dispatches, it was spelled Marien.

CHAPTER IV

Retreat to White Marsh

AFTER CROSSING the Peedee River, Francis Marion was safe, for he lay under the protection of zealous Whigs. Like the valiant Scotch-Irish whose cabins dotted the banks of the Black River and were concentrated around the King's Tree, the English settlers on the lonely sand ridges of Britton's Neck were rebellious. They were Associators, adherents of the Liberty Boys, and partisans of the Liberty Tree. Under Colonel John Ervin they were mustered and pledged to defend their lands and homes and families against the soldiers of the King.

Their kinsmen on Catfish Creek, along the Little Peedee, and up the branches of Drowning Creek, however, were still loyal to their King. Their communities were peaceful, and they continued planting their fields and raising stock on the ranges. Only a few of them had enlisted in the Continentals and taken part in the struggle. Instead, they had formed a regiment of Loyalist militia under the command of Major Micajah Ganey. The Major, who lived on a large plantation between Catfish Creek and the Little Peedee, was a handsome, soldierly man, intelligent, but somewhat overbearing and truculent and, when aroused, hot-tempered and violent.

Captain Jesse Barefield was second in command of the Loyalist regiment. "Cap'n Barfield," as the English people in the district called him, lived in the Barefield settlement between Drowning Creek and the Little Peedee. A man of good family, common school education, and considerable property, he had patriotically enlisted in the Second Regiment in 1776 and served faithfully as a Continental under Marion. But fancying himself slighted by an officer, he appealed to his superiors for vindication. Receiving no satisfaction from them, and appalled at the Low Country indifference to backwoodsmen, he returned home at the end of his enlistment and again swore allegiance to his King. With his younger brother Miles, he soon thereafter raised a troop of eighty Tory horsemen.

The news that Marion had camped at Port's Ferry quickly spread among the Tories. Ganey called out his militia. Soon the mustering field on the Little Peedee was stirring with 250 men, confident and eager for adventure. Before day on September 4 the Major set out to surprise the rebels. After ordering Barefield to follow with the infantry, he cantered off with an advance guard of forty-five horsemen.

But Francis Marion was never caught napping. He kept his scouts and patrols moving, searching, listening, always on the *qui vive*. Thus he had learned of the Tory muster and in his taciturn way had begun evaluating his position. What could he do with only fifty-two men? He could run—and forfeit forever the trust of the patriots. He could await Ganey's attack and then fight him behind every gut or slough in Britton's Neck. Or he could attack first. Deliberately, without emotion, he made his decision. He would stake his life and the lives of his men at odds of one to five. Incommunicative, knowing that no gossip could whisper a secret until after he had heard it, he told no one his plans.

Long before daylight on September 4 Marion was up, limping about his camp, rousing, cheering, and instructing his followers. He took every precaution for their safety. So that his militiamen might distinguish each other from the Tories, since all wore homespun, he ordered them to mount white cockades in their caps. Then he rode quietly away from

Port's Ferry and headed across the sand hills. Alert and cautious, he sent a picked squadron under Major James to serve as advance guard. He then took command of the main body. For two hours he and his men rode leisurely. The morning was warm, and the road wound across sand ridges covered with scrub oaks and partridge peas and through swamps flaming with leaves of black gum trees. Briskly they turned into the Tory settlement along the Little Peedee. Suddenly a scout wheeled back in alarm. A troop of armed horsemen blocked the road.

Without waiting for Marion's orders, Major James clapped spurs to Thunder and charged, shouting and huzzaing for his comrades to follow. Recognizing Ganey, he dashed straight toward him, his sword bristling and flashing. But the Tory Major had been caught off guard. In a moment of panic, with his surprised troops squandering in every direction, he turned and fled. For half a mile the Majors raced, their horses snorting and blowing. At that point Ganey paused with several Tories who had rallied behind a thicket. James, realizing that he had outrun his men, spurred Thunder into the group. "Come on, boys!" he shouted to imaginary companions. "Come on! Here they are! Here they are!"

Again the Tories fled. They never looked back nor reined their horses until they were safe in the bogs of Little Peedee Swamp. Their rout was comic. Thoroughly terrified, they thought only of escaping. No stalwart dreamed of warning Barefield's infantry of Marion's approach.

From the prisoners Marion learned that the Tory foot soldiers were only three miles away. With a shout he headed toward them. Ten minutes later he met the enemy in full march. But Jesse Barefield had learned tactics from Marion himself. Quickly he formed his line and stood his ground. Two hundred men with muskets at the draw were too formidable for a frontal assault, and Marion signaled retreat. At the Blue Savannah, an open sandy swale surrounded by a dense growth of scrub pines and an undergrowth of gallberry and yellow jessamine, he checked his flight. Leaving the road, he began cautiously circling back. Then, after halting and concealing his men behind a screen of pine saplings, he waited.

Captain Barefield was courageous; no Loyalist ever boasted more valor. But he was not cautious and he led his excited regiment straight into the ambush. As the straggling line came opposite his concentration, Marion charged, his fifty horsemen at his back, all shouting, their pistols smoking and their swords flashing. Barefield steadied his troops and they delivered one volley, the buckshot toppling three men and killing two horses. Too hard-pressed to load their muskets again, the Loyalists faltered, broke ranks, and then darted for the covering woods. They, too, never stopped until they were safe in Little Peedee Swamp.

Marion's horsemen pursued the Tory infantry to the edge of the morass. But they dared not penetrate the black ooze beneath the cypress and tupelo trees. Like Comanches they prowled along the rim, screaming, cursing, firing at the trembling fugitives. Marion soon called them off. After caring for the wounded and prisoners, he turned slowly back toward Port's Ferry. As he rode, the excitement of battle faded and he calmly reflected on his victory. He was satisfied. He had dispersed the Tories without serious bloodshed. It was better so. The wounds of civil strife would heal more quickly if there were no dead kinsmen to remember.

Next morning Marion sent a patrol back to the Blue Savannah. After riding over the battlegrounds, they returned with a report that during the night the Loyalists had crawled out of the swamp and slunk off to their cabins. In two skirmishes, at a cost of having four men wounded and two horses killed, he had broken the power of the Tories east of the Peedee.

During the day sixty volunteers rode into camp. With his command doubled, Marion began fortifying his retreat. To protect the ferry and blockade the post road which ran from Savannah to Boston, he threw up a small redoubt of logs and

clay on the eastern bank of the Peedee. Behind the rampart
he mounted two small cannon brought to him by the militia.
Charged with grapeshot and primed, their brazen muzzles
pointing along the road and across the river, they stood
guard on a desperate venture.

Marion's victories at Sumter's house and the Blue Savannah first surprised, and then angered the British. To protect
Georgetown, the anchor of their right flank, Colonel Balfour
rushed Major James Moncrief and a battalion of the 7th or
Royal Fusilier Regiment. He instructed Moncrief to build
a redoubt and make the seaport impregnable. Balfour also
called out the Loyalists west of the Santee and dispatched
Colonels John Coming Ball and Joseph Wigfall with the
regiments from St. James' and St. Stephen's parishes to
Georgetown.

Lord Cornwallis also acted swiftly. He knew that a victorious band of guerrillas astride the long supply line between
Camden and Charleston would be fatal. As soon as he had
learned of Marion's strike at Sumter's house, he ordered
Major Wemyss to march the 63rd Regiment from the High
Hills to Kingstree. "I should advise your sweeping the country entirely from Kingstree Bridge to Pedee, and returning
by the Cheraws," he wrote on August 28. "I would have you
disarm in the most rigid manner, all Persons who cannot be
depended on and punish the concealment of Arms and ammunition with a total demolition of the plantation."

Without exact knowledge of Marion's strength, but knowing that the 63rd Regiment was still weak from malaria,
Cornwallis ordered all available Loyalist forces to cooperate
in the movement. From Camden he sent Major John Harrison's Provincials and Colonel Samuel Bryan's North Carolinians. He also requested Colonel John Hamilton to send
one hundred of his troops from Ratcliffe's Bridge. On August
28 Hamilton replied: "The detachment from my regiment
shall be in readiness to join Major Wemys."

James Wemyss was tough and wily. Faced with a march of

one hundred and fifty miles, with even the possibility of trudging all the way back to New York, he decided to mount his regiment. Calling together all the Whig planters in the High Hills and along the Santee, he harangued them for an hour on the theme "that the British are come to rescue you from tyranny and oppression." But his oratory was nothing more than a blind for perfidy. While he was attracting the attention of the countrymen, his troops were scouring the neighborhood, rounding up their horses. The discovery of the rustling brought dismay, wrath, and violent language. But in vain. The horses were in British corrals, guarded by veterans with fixed bayonets. "The enraged countrymen walked home," said David Ramsay, "but soon after many of them repaired to General Marion."

After having turned his regiment into mounted infantry, on September 5 Wemyss set off down the familiar Santee Road. "Don't stay any longer in that country than is necessary to do your business," Cornwallis cautioned him. "Balfour will order the militia under Ball and Wigfall to proceed directly to Georgetown. I would not however have them remain on the east of Santee after your return."

Fearing that the departure of Wemyss would tempt small parties of marauders to seize the line between Nelson's Ferry and Camden, Cornwallis sent Captain Frederick DePeyster and a detachment of Turnbull's New York Volunteers to the High Hills. For reinforcement he told the Captain to call out and to try to "model the militia of Major Tynes." But his lordship knew the caliber of the Tories and he warned DePeyster: "Major Tynes is a weak, well intentioned man."

With intuitive grasp of guerrilla warfare, Marion expected a concentration against him. On September 7 he sent Major James and a picked squad back to Kingstree to reconnoiter. Then, after leaving fifty men to guard his camp, he led a hundred of his followers across the Peedee and camped at Indiantown. In the meantime Major James and his companions were carrying out their mission. Late that evening they

hid in a deep thicket beside the high road into Kingstree.
Soon they saw Wemyss' tired horsemen filing past in the
brilliant moonlight. As their rear guard rode by, the Major
and his men sprang up and, before the surprised Briton
could even fire an alarm, they had trussed him up and were
dragging him through the broom sedge toward Black River
Swamp. Half an hour before daybreak they reached their
rendezvous with Marion in a pine forest near the James
Plantation.

Marion questioned the prisoner. He learned that some two
hundred troops had already reached Kingstree and that
Major Wemyss was expected to bring two hundred more during the night. From a captured orderly book he also learned
Moncrief had reached Georgetown. With this depressing
news he and his staff retired for a council while the men sat
their horses. The conference was long and heated. The har-
dier advocated fighting. The realistic advised dispersal. Although as courageous as any of them, Marion knew the
mettle of his men, the number of the enemy, and the odds
against him. He knew that it would be folly to lead one hundred militiamen against a concentration of eight hundred
British regulars and Loyalist militia. He also knew that a defeat would shatter the morale of the Whig militia. So he
dismissed the men and all but the most ardent of his officers.

Leaving Captain John James, the son of the Major, and
ten chosen men to gather intelligence and aid the distressed,
Marion and his heavy-hearted followers recrossed the Peedee.
They spent the day resting near their redoubt. All afternoon
scouts rode in with distressing news. Wemyss had crossed
the Peedee River at Yauhannah; he was trying to get behind
Marion's fort. Moncrief had dispatched Ball and Wigfall
north of the Black River. He had ordered them to cross the
Peedee at Britton's Ferry and march up through Britton's
Neck. And Ganey had again begun mobilizing his militia.

Marion had now a simple strategic choice: fight or run.
With him were only sixty men, and arrayed against him were
some thousand to fifteen hundred men from nine militia,

provincial, and regular British regiments. Calmly, without visible discouragement, he chose flight. Wheeling out the two field pieces, he dismantled his fort and at sunset began retreating toward North Carolina. That night and all next day he led his companions, never flagging, never stopping. Across the sand hills, with the gray sand crying beneath the hoofs of their horses, through the dark swamps and over the puncheoned causeways they rode, while the field pieces lumbered and rumbled behind.

As soon as Marion had crossed the Little Peedee and was safe from attack by Ganey, he ordered the cannon spiked, dragged off the road, and left to rust in the swamp. Then on he went. After covering forty miles he halted and pitched camp in the friendly Whig settlement around Amis' Mill on Drowning Creek. He kept his counsel, but he had begun to worry. He had saved the fighting men from the vengeance of Wemyss, but to what flagellation had the enraged Scotsman subjected the unarmed and the innocent? At daylight he asked Major James and a few volunteers to go back and find out how the redcoats had treated their wives and children. Marion then resumed his retreat. He knew that Brigadier General William Harrington's corps of North Carolinians lay at Cross Creek. With a growing feeling of security he headed in the direction of Cape Fear. Finally he called his men, turned off the road, and followed his guides into the eastern fringe of the Great White Marsh, a wilderness enfolding the southern branch of the Waccamaw River.

In Williamsburg, meanwhile, Major Wemyss was on a rampage. At Kingstree he had been joined by Captain Amos Gaskens, a hated, conniving Tory, and guided by him had attempted to cut off the patriots. Learning that Marion had decamped, he turned back to carry out the orders of Cornwallis to disarm in the most rigid manner all those who had joined in the uprising. "This is a sedition shop," he snorted, as he burned the Presbyterian Church at Indiantown.

Surrounded by his minions, he then galloped to the home of Major James. The sound of tramping horses and the sight of armed men in her front yard might well have frightened Jean James. But she was a Calvinist, fearing neither man nor devil, and so she calmly opened the door. Wemyss was resplendent in his great red coat, leather boots, and side arms. He was polite and conciliatory. "If Major James will come in and lay down his arms," he said courteously, "he shall have free pardon."

"I have no influence over my husband," replied the wife through whose heart flowed the Covenanter blood of the Dobeins. "In times like these his conscience compels him to take a part, and he has taken the part of his country."

The Major and the housewife argued, but she baffled him. In exasperation he ordered his men to lock her and her children in one room of their home. For two days he lay waiting, hoping that Major James would come to his family. The lure failed, and somehow Wemyss, demon though he was, seemed blind when Captain David Campbell of Edisto pushed food and water to the prisoners through a back window.

Captain John James, whom Marion had left in Williamsburg, had been captured in the fall of Charleston. He was on parole, but in this new revolt, even though he knew that the punishment might be hanging, he had again taken up arms in defense of freedom. So outraged was he at the treatment of his mother and family that he fired upon a small party of Tories raiding McGill's Plantation. Wemyss sent a patrol to the Captain's home to take him into custody. "If he is found to have broken his parole," the Major swore, "he will be hanged in the morning to yonder tree!"

Next morning Wemyss held a drumhead court-martial. He could extract nothing from members of the James families, and so he called in their slaves and forced them to testify. The loyal Negroes, however, kept silent or pleaded ignorance. So the court, with great reluctance, acquitted the Captain. Wemyss then released the James family, but like a barbarian burned their home before their eyes. "I felt an early inclination to record these events; but Major Wemyss burnt all my stock of paper, and my little classical library, in my father's house," wrote William James, "and, for two years and a half afterwards, I had not the common implements of writing or of reading."

Under the guidance of Harrison's Tories, Wemyss and his Myrmidons burned a swath fifteen miles wide along the seventy-mile route from Kingstree to Cheraw. Believing that the way to suppress rebellion was to hang the leaders and destroy the resources of the rebels, he ordered his men to break up the looms, fire the grist mills, and destroy the blacksmith shops. To deprive the Whigs of even the means of existence, his troops shot their milk cows and wantonly bayoneted their sheep.

Wemyss even found a scapegoat upon whom to vent his wrath. Adam Cusac, who had also been paroled at Charleston, had refused to ferry some British officers across the Black River. They had argued and cursed, but still he had refused. In dudgeon he afterward shot across the river to frighten a slave of Captain John Brockington, a noted Tory of Kingstree. He missed, but Wemyss ordered his arrest. Then, as a deterrent example, he dragged him along to Cheraw. There he tried the frightened civilian by court-martial. Whether or nor the court was legally constituted or had jurisdiction, it found Cusac guilty of breaking his parole by resorting to firearms, and the president of the court sentenced him to die by hanging.

Wemyss ordered a scaffold erected beside the road at Long Bluff and personally superintended the execution. As his Jack Ketch adjusted the noose, Mrs. Cusac and her children prostrated themselves before the Major, screaming and begging him to spare their loved one. Angered by their outcries, Wemyss spurred his horse to ride down the suppliants. But a junior officer seized the Major's bridle rein and stopped his horse short of the foul deed. Just before the soldiers tripped the platform under the prisoner, Dr. James Wilson,

a physician of Long Bluff, interceded. As punishment
Wemyss later destroyed much of the doctor's property,
burned his home, and drove his wife into North Carolina.
Aroused and undaunted, Wilson joined Marion's band.

"On my arrival at Kingstree Bridge, I was joined by the
Detachment of Colonel Hamilton's Corps, Harrison's of 50,
and about 50 militia," Wemyss reported to Lord Cornwallis
from Cheraw on September 20. "I have done everything in
my Power to get at Mr. Marion, who with Giles commanded
about 150 Men on my arrival in this part of the Country.
Although I never could come up with them, yet I pushed
them so hard as in a great measure to break them up; the
few that still continued together have retreated over Little
Pedee."

The Major closed his letter with a survey of the rebellion
in the district between the Santee and the Peedee. Almost
every family was involved: the women sullen, the slaves hiding out, and the men run off with Marion. In a postscript he
added: "I forgot to tell your Lordship that I have burnt and
laid waste about 50 houses and Plantations, mostly belonging
to People who have either broke their Paroles or Oaths of
Allegiance, and are now in Arms against us."

Lord Cornwallis replied with a characteristic appraisal:
"It gives me great pleasure to hear that your detachment is
healthy; in other respects your account is not so agreeable."
But to Colonel Turnbull he confided testily: "I am much
disappointed in that business."

In Georgetown the Loyalists were elated. On September
15 a correspondent there wrote *The South Carolina and
American General Gazette:* "Major Wemyss has been scouring the country to the northward of this. Several of the inhabitants who, after giving their paroles, joined Marion and
Horry in their late incursion, have gone off with them. Some
of their houses have been destroyed *in terrorem.*"

CHAPTER V

Victory at Black Mingo

Francis Marion established a simple camp in the Great White Marsh. His troops, all experienced woodsmen who had lain outdoors many nights while hunting and fishing, merely turned from the road into the wood, hitched their horses to saplings, and bedded down. The provident had brought a quilt or blanket. The others raked up beds of leaves and pine needles. Marion had only one blanket. Unluckily, fire broke out, scorching it badly and charring his leather cap with the silver crescent. Thereupon he kicked up a pile of straw, pillowed his head against the root of a tree, and slept as soundly as his orderly.

The men cooked their own rations, two or three banding together in small messes. Coarse food was plentiful: corn meal, beef, pork, hominy grits, cow peas, and sweet potatoes. But salt, that staple of health and taste, was a luxury. After Major James had ridden on his dangerous mission, Marion paid friendly attention to young William James, and one day invited the lad to dine with the officers. "The dinner was set before the company by the General's servant Oscar, partly on a pine log and partly on the ground; it was lean beef, without salt, and sweet potatoes," James later wrote in his sketch of the life of Marion. "The author had left a small pot of boiled hominy in his camp and requested leave of his host to send for it; and the proposal was acquiesced in, gladly. The hominy had salt in it, and proved, although eaten out of the pot, a most acceptable repast. The general said but little, and that was chiefly what a son would be most likely to be gratified by, in the praise of his father."

During the first three or four days of the encampment, Marion was busy establishing communications. From Brigadier General Harrington at Cross Creek he learned that General Gates had collected the scattered remnants of his defeated army at Hillsboro. Marion felt that as a Continental officer he should report to his commanding General. Writing was hard, for he was scarcely literate, but he had risen to the command of a regiment because of his attention to exacting details. And so, laying his paper on the fallen pine that served as his dining table, he began struggling with spelling and grammar. Slowly he wrote. Soberly, without complaining or bragging, he traced the spectacular events of the first week in September.

White Marsh, Bladen County
15 Sept. 1780

Sir

I wrought you by Mr. Simons the 29th Augt (per Express) who is not yet returned——I have not been able to Learn anything of your Situation which has very much dispirited the friends of America.

I have sent the Prisoners I took the 25th Augt. with the Continentals to Wilmington, Many of the later has left me, & my Situation growing more Critical I could not possibly keep them any longer.

On the 3rd Instant I had Advice, that upwards of two hundred Torys Intended to attack me the next day. I immediately marched with 52 men, which is all I could get, on the 4th in the morning I surprised a party of 45 men which Escaped. I then marched immediately to attack the main body, which I met about 3 miles in full march towards me. I directly attacked them to flight (though they had 200 men) & got into an impassable swamp to all but Torys.

I had one man wounded in the first action & 3 in the second & two horses killed; finding it impossible to come at them I returned to Camp——the next day I was informed they all disperst——On the 5th I was joined by about 60 men; I then throughed up a small redoubt, to secure my camp from being surprised by the Torys Should they again collect.

On the 7th I crossed PD & Lynches Creek with one hundred men, & left 50 to secure my camp & the river; to attack a party of regulars and militia sd to be 150, which was in Williamsburg township, a burning all the houses of those men who had joined me, when I had got to Indian Town Capt. James who I had sent to reconoitre the Enemy met me, he had taken a prisoner belonging to Col. Ferguson's rifle regt. by whom I learnt that they was 200 British & a number of Torys, & that Majr. Whimes with 200 more was to join them that night; they was seen after dark on their march, & by an orderly book taken with an officer's baggage with the above prisoner, I found their Intentions was to remove me & to proceed to the Cheraws; I also had Intelligence that 200 men just regulars had arrived in Georgetown from Santee, which oblige me to return to my camp which I did that Day. On the 8th I had Intelligence that they Maj. Whimes had crossed Black river & Uhaney to fall on my rear, the Torys which I had lately Disperst was collecting on my right, which would Compleatly surround me & cut off my retreat, which Oblige me to retreat to this place with 60 men, the rest left me to see after their family which had their houses burnt; they have burnt a number of houses on Black river, Lynches Creek & Waccamaw.

I shall remain here untill I hear from you, or I have an Opportunity of Doing something.

I have the honour to be with respect yr most obt. sert.

Francis Marion

Marion then turned to purely military duties. He began a constant routine of vedettes and patrols, employing small squadrons in scouting, foraging, and convoying. Soon, however, his men began to complain and sicken. The summer had been exceedingly rainy, and the creeks and marshes had often been in freshet. Mosquitoes were now teeming in the woods. They swarmed in the camp, singing and biting, while the patriots tossed and scratched and swore. Quietly, without any warning buzz, the insidious females of the anopheles filled their victims with malaria. Young William James came down first, trembling, sweating, vomiting. Captain George Logan was next, his teeth chattering and his forehead burning. Finally Colonel Peter Horry was prostrated by the ague.

After an absence of about ten days, Major James found Marion's hiding place in the Great White Marsh. He brought maddening news. The British had devastated Williamsburg. Wemyss and Harrison had plundered and burned and slaughtered. Like Mohawks they had spread destruction, desolation, and death from Georgetown to Cheraw. " 'Tis a harsh medicine," said Marion, "but it is necessary."

At Georgetown, in the meantime, Major Moncrief had finished the redoubt and had placed a garrison of Fusiliers in it. He then began posting the Loyalist militia. From James Cassels he had learned of the strategic value of Britton's Neck, the twenty-mile stretch of sand hills, woods, swamps, and creeks that lay between the Peedee and the Little Peedee. "Colonel Cassel's Reg't is going to Britain's Neck, which is a very good post," Moncrief informed Cornwallis, in revealing his moves to prevent Marion's return. "But if he should hear of any superior force he is to fall back to Black River; if he finds in the course of Ten days that there is no force in his front, he will move up the Corps left at Black River, Potatoe, and Raggs Ferry to cover the Pedee."

Engineer Moncrief then turned strategist. He recommended that Cornwallis keep a hundred troops at Georgetown, fifty at Wragg's Ferry, fifty at Potato Ferry, fifteen at Black River Ferry, and three hundred at Kingstree Bridge. As part of this deployment, he recalled Cassels and posted him in Georgetown. And then, in spite of Lord Cornwallis' warning not to leave Ball and Wigfall east of the Santee, Moncrief sent them north of the Black River to overawe the most rebellious section of Williamsburg.

Colonel Wigfall commanded only fifty men, but he boldly took a position near Black River Church. Even more daring, Colonel Ball, with only forty-six men, moved up to Shepherd's Ferry on Black Mingo Creek. He pitched camp around the Red House, a respectable tavern run by Patrick Dollard, and stationed his troops athwart the great post road. From this pivot he could smite the Whigs around Indiantown or in Kingstree.

The boldness of the Loyal militia disturbed the British commanders. From Charlotte, into which the British army had marched on September 24, after waiting at the Waxhaws for two weeks for Colonel Tarleton to recover from yellow fever, Lord Cornwallis wrote Turnbull at Camden: "Moncrief has established a Militia at Georgetown under Colonel Cassels." Then, in some agitation, he continued: "By letter which I received this day from Major Wemyss, I am very uneasy about all the Lower Country and am much afraid that the two Regiments of Militia of Ball and Wigfall and that lately embodied by Col. Cassels will meet with some serious disaster."

Well might Cornwallis tremble for the safety of Ball and Wigfall. Retribution was imminent. At the camp in the Great White Marsh on the afternoon of September 24 there was stirring and bustling, packing and mounting. Finally Colonel Marion limped to his horse, swung into the saddle, and gave a shrill whistle. Quickly the horsemen followed him into the highway. Eagerly, like soldiers going home on furlough, they rode through the fading twilight and cool night. Late the next evening they reached Kingston and bivouacked under the spreading live oaks along the Waccamaw.

Before dawn Marion and his troopers were up, cooking, eating, and tending their horses. Quietly they mounted and cantered off on the sandy road leading to the Little Peedee. For five miles they rode along the infrequented way, passing Cypress Creek and Hunter Swamp. Then the Jenkins boys left the highway and guided the troops into Little Peedee Swamp. There the woods were cool and shadowy, immense live oaks spreading their mottled foliage against the morning sun and giant cypress trees rearing their fronds into the sky, their knees protruding from the soggy black loam and their limbs draped with streaming Spanish moss. From all around came the sour, pleasant smell of decaying vegetation and mucky soil. After three miles of shadows and marshy odors, the riders burst into the sunlight. Before them flowed the dark rippling waters of the Little Peedee.

Francis Marion could not swim and there was no ferry. Although he feared water, he did not fear death. As their leader, he beckoned his men and then plunged his horse into the river. Clinging to the pommel of his saddle, he floated across beside the swimming animal. Safely he scrambled up the boat landing on the Woodberry Plantation. Anxiously he watched his men cross. Then, wet and bedraggled, he climbed into his saddle and followed the Jenkinses along the quiet road toward Hickory Hill, past the home of Widow Jenkins, their mother, and on toward the Old Neck Church. As they jogged along, they saw a lone horseman galloping behind them. He was Captain Logan. Early that morning he had arisen from his sick bed at White Marsh, taken leave of William James and, with the pallor of death upon his face, had trailed his comrades for sixty miles.

On rode the valiant band, crossing the sand ridges on which the scrub oaks, sweet-scented loblolly, and majestic long leaf pines stood shrouded in deep autumnal haze. Late in the afternoon of September 28, they reached Port's Ferry. Without pausing at their old redoubt, they crossed the Peedee in flatboats and then jogged on to Witherspoon's Ferry. In the twilight they crossed Lynches River. There Captain John James and his squad of ten men waited. With him also were Captain Henry Mouzon, Lieutenant John Scott, and a few volunteers from their company of militia. They had exciting information. Colonel Ball still lay at Shepherd's Ferry, his troops encamped around Dollard's in great insecurity.

As Marion listened, his eyes glowed. He looked at his men. They were nearly exhausted. Since daybreak they had ridden thirty miles and crossed three rivers. But without asking he knew their wish—to drive the intruders from their doors. He swung back into the saddle and reined his horse in the direction of Black Mingo.

Colonel Ball's camp lay west of Black Mingo Creek, that chasm of black water once haunted by Mingo Indians. But Marion's men were now among their own farms and plantations, and every road or path, every branch or creek, every ford or bridge was familiar to them. In the starlight they rode the twelve miles, moving slowly in hope of finding the enemy in deep slumber. Just before midnight Major James turned Thunder's head toward Willtown Bridge, an old structure about a mile above Shepherd's. The approach to the bridge was over a puncheoned causeway, broken and boggy. The bridge was rickety, its flooring loose and rattling. As the hoofs of the horses struck the ramp, the planks began to rumble. The noise echoed up and down the Mingo, and in the Tory camp a sentinel fired an alarm gun.

At the sound Marion hunched forward, tightened his reins, and spurred his horse. With his men crowding around him, he galloped toward Dollard's. Striking the post road some three hundred yards west of Shepherd's, he dismounted his men—except for a squadron to serve as cavalry. Thinking that the Tory Colonel had turned the Red House into a bastion, he sent Captain Thomas Waties and the supernumerary officers to make a frontal assault upon it. To support them he sent Major Hugh Horry and the infantry to the right flank. His cavalry he sent to the left of Dollard's. With his small reserve he followed the attack.

John Coming Ball was crafty. At the sound of the alarm gun he sprang up, roused his men, and rushed them out into the old field west of the tavern. There he calmed them as they listened nervously to the clatter of Marion's galloping horsemen. He walked among his troops, cheering and steadying them, as they listened to Marion deploying his men in the darkness. When Hugh Horry's infantry came charging through the broom sedge and dog fennels, Ball waited: fifty yards, forty yards, thirty yards——"Fire!"

Muskets flashed and thundered, shattering the night like lightning. Buckshot whistled, then splattered on weeds and leaves and buildings. Captain Logan sagged, coughed, and

died. Captain Mouzon and Lieutenant Scott fell, badly
wounded. Terrified by the flashing and roaring, Major
Horry's men faltered and began falling back in disorder. But
Captain James, a veteran hardened to the sound of gunfire
and the evil smell of burning powder, steadied his own men,
rallied those of Mouzon, and checked the retreat. Cautiously,
he led the patriots, as they began creeping forward, firing,
loading, and firing again at every moving shadow. By that
time Waties and the supernumeraries had skirted the Red
House and begun advancing against the enemy's right flank.
Caught between the troops of James and Waties, Ball's men
delivered a scattered, ineffective volley. As they saw the flaming guns of the advancing foe and heard the screams and
groans of wounded and dying friends, they, too, wavered.
Then, dropping their empty guns and forgetting King, country, and honor, they fled into the swamp of Black Mingo.

"On their retreat, they would not halt a moment at
Georgetown, though twenty miles from the field of battle,"
said Peter Horry, "but continued their flight, not thinking
themselves safe until they had got Santee river between him
and them."

The Battle of Black Mingo lasted only fifteen minutes, but
for the scant hundred men involved it was bloody. Of his
forty-six men, Ball left three dead and thirteen wounded or
prisoners. Several others died of their wounds before reaching home. Marion left two dead: Captain Logan and a private. Besides Scott and Mouzon, so badly riddled by buckshot that they never again saw action, he had six wounded.
These he left at Dollard's inn.

Marion's troops captured the enemy's guns, ammunition,
and baggage. Their triumph, however, was the capture of the
blooded horses of the Tories, strong-boned Chickasaws raised
in the limestone pastures around the Springs of Eutaw.
Among these was a spirited sorrel gelding that had been Colonel Ball's charger. Marion claimed the horse, bridle, and
saddle of his defeated rival. With puckish humor he renamed

the steed Ball, and as a terrifying symbol rode him ever after in his campaigns through eastern Carolina.

Colonel Wigfall still slumbered at Black River Church. Tireless, Marion called on his men to surprise him. But the militiamen began to murmur. They wanted to go home to their wives and children. They wished to see for themselves the destruction wrought by Wemyss and the thieves under Harrison. Marion understood their anxiety. Praising their endurance, courage, and valor, he bade them: "Go to your families."

Even though flushed with victory, when Marion turned to the Loyalists his heart filled with compassion. He knew each of them: the dead, the wounded, and the prisoners; he also knew their fathers and brothers. He began talking to the captives. So earnest, magnanimous, and convincing was he that five of them renounced the King, swore allegiance to the United States, and joined his band.

Having crushed the enemy, succored the wounded and prisoners, and furloughed his militia, Marion mounted his horse Ball. With Colonel Giles, Major Hugh Horry, Major King, Captains Waties and Milton, and about a dozen others of his most loyal officers and men, he took the narrow, sandy road to Britton's Ferry. The gallant little band rode another twenty-six miles without stopping. Late the next morning Ferryman Britton rowed them across the Peedee. Safe from pursuit, they halted and rested. Next morning they jogged over the familiar roads of Britton's Neck, galloped across the old battleground at the Blue Savannah, and by evening were encamped near Amis' Mill on Drowning Creek.

"Marion, Giles, and a Col. Ford from Cape Fear with several other leading men are assembled at Drowning Creek with about 400 men and these are increasing daily," Major Wemyss immediately wrote Cornwallis. "They are burning houses and distressing the well affected in a most severe manner."

Part of Wemyss' accusation was false. Francis Marion had

not burned any houses nor had he distressed any women and
children. He was too humane, too tender-hearted; besides,
during the last three weeks, he and Giles had been in hiding
or riding and fighting. Others in the concentration on
Drowning Creek, however, were guilty, the most notorious
miscreant being Captain Maurice Murphy.

Powerful, raw-boned, and reckless, Murphy was a fearless
partisan. With horsemen recruited around his home at Sandy
Bluff, Little Peedee, he had scourged the Tories from Wahee
Neck to Socastee Swamp. After Ganey's defeat at the Blue
Savannah, he had tried to run down the survivors. Among
these were several Blackmans, sons of a noted Tory who lived
on Catfish Creek. Riding to Blackman's home, the Captain
tried to learn the hiding place of these sons. When the old
man refused to tell him, Murphy's guerrillas tied him to a
gate post.

"Who are you for?" Murphy asked.

"King George," replied Blackman.

At Murphy's nod his men gave Blackman fifty lashes with
a bull whip.

"Now who are you for?" demanded Murphy.

"King George," snarled Blackman.

The guerrillas laid another fifty lashes on the old man's
lacerated back.

"Now, by God, who are you for?" shouted Murphy.

"King George!" roared Blackman.

They gave him another fifty stripes.

"Who are you for?"

"King George!"

Blackman was prepared to die. In the crude settlements in
the backwoods of South Carolina no man had greater love
for his King. Even Murphy recognized valor. He cut the
bonds and called off his fiends.

On his way home, Murphy stopped for breakfast at the
home of Gideon Gibson, an uncle. Gibson upbraided the
Captain for his cruelty. Words followed; oaths flew. Murphy
sprang from the table and stalked out of the house. Gibson,

spawned from the same violent clan, followed, shouting and cursing. Outside the door the Captain turned, drew his pistol, and deliberately shot his uncle dead. Three of Gibson's sons were members of Murphy's troop. All witnessed the brutal deed, but so terrified were they of their cousin's desperate courage that none raised a hand. Nor did they ever avenge the murder.

Francis Marion despised Murphy. He detested any man who was cruel, overbearing, or bigoted. His own motives were pure, his actions inspired by love of country, and to him the shooting of a defenseless man, the flogging of a septuagenarian, or the burning of a home just emptied of women and children, was abominable. He condemned the Captain in his report to General Gates.

Drowning Creek S.C. 4th Oct. 1780

Sir

I set out from the White Marsh on Sunday evening 24th Sept. & took a tour to Kingston, from whence I turned & crossed Little Pedee at Woodberrys & made a force march across big PD to Black Mingo, where was a guard of forty Seven men of the Militia of St. James Santee & St. Stephens, commanded by Capt. Cummin Ball, which I immediately attackt about 12 o'c. pM the 28th Sept; they had intelligence of our coming & Drew up near a Swamp & received our fire within thirty yards which they returned twice & then took into the Swamp——we killed three Dead on the Spot, & wounded one, took thirteen prisoners, my loss was Capt Logan of the Continentals & one private killed one Capt. & one Lt & Six privates wounded——I have since heard that several of their men has been found Dead, & b'd in the Swamp & adjoining Woods—— all their horses & Baggage fell in our hands——it was my intention to brake up another Guard at Black river Church of fifty men, but so many of my followers was so desirous to see their wifes & family which have been burnt out, that I found it necessary to retreat the next morning across Big PD at Britton's ferry to this Place, & have Delivered Col. Brown nine of the prisoners taken at B. Mingo & three of the 63rd Rgt. taken at the Great Savannah some time ago, which I Parole to a house on Account of their being Sick & incapable of marching.

The prisoners taken are men of family and fortune which I hope may be a check to the Malitia taking arms against us. I must beg that these men who have a Cross before their names in the Inclosed list may be showed as much favour as possible, as they had showed themselves, before this last Action to be Good Men——I would not give them Paroles as I thought it would be Acknowledging them to be British subjects and woud give my followers Great Discontent, for the British imprison all those who are our friends & have hanged one Cusag for breaking his Parole. I am sorry to Acquaint you that Capt. Murphy's Party have burnt a Great Number of houses on Little Peedee, & intend to go on in that abominable work—— which I am Apprehensive May be Laid to me; but I assure you, there is not one house Burnt by my Orders or by any of my People, it is what I detest to Destroy poor women & children——

The British marched from Georgetown for Camden the 29 Sept; it is sd 220 men, part of them Marines——Major Whimes is at the Cheraw with about 90 men of the 63rd Regt. Burning & plundering Negroes & everything in their way; the Torys are so affrighted with my Little Excursion that Many's moving off to Georgia with their Effects, Others are rund into Swamps. If I coud raise one hundred men, I shou'd certainly pay a visit to Georgetown, my whole party has not been none more than sixty men of all ranks. I expect Genl Harrington will be by this near Cheraw, where I mean to join him with Col. Brown (abt. 100) who is within eight miles of me, & remove Majr Whimes from his Post——I have great fatigues but I surmount every Difficulty & am happy with the assistance of Major King & Capt. Milton who are Excellent Officers. Major Vanderhorst I have rec'd also great assistance from, the little time he has been with me—I have sent him with a flag to Santee to get cloathes & necessarys for the prisoners, by whom I hope to gain some Intelligence.

Please Present my Compliments to Gen. Huger & Majr Richmond. I am with respect yr Honours most ob. servt.

Francis Marion

CHAPTER VI

Escape of the Fox

FOR TWO WEEKS Marion remained with Ford and Giles at Amis' Mill. Their forces, powerful and mobile, and roughly centered in a triangle based on Georgetown, Cheraw, and Cross Creek, were highly strategic. They protected and encouraged the Whigs while Gates was reorganizing his army. They overawed the Loyalists, intimidating Ganey and holding in check Colonels Hector McNeil and David Fanning, leaders of the Tories in eastern North Carolina. And they put pressure against the rear of the advancing British.

From Charlotte Lord Cornwallis began deploying his regiments to meet this threat. He ordered Major Wemyss to return to Camden with the 63rd Regiment and Hamilton's North Carolinians, and to leave Harrison at Cheraw "to keep some kind of hold on the country." He then dispatched Major Thomas Fraser with eighty mounted infantrymen to combine with Harrison's Provincials in "hope he will be able with the Help of the Militia of the Lower Districts to secure the Country tolerably well."

Wemyss knew that Harrison and Fraser could not hold the Peedee country. His house-burning foray had engendered too much hatred. Marion's daring reprisal at Black Mingo had terrorized the Loyalists. Colonel Robert Mills had resigned the command of the Loyal regiment in Cheraw; in his place Balfour had appointed Robert Gray. Ball and Wigfall now refused to take the field. And so, as he prepared to evacuate Cheraw, on September 30 Wemyss wrote Cornwallis: ". . . presuming in regard to Harrison's Corps to disobey your directions, being convinced that were they left here, that they would disperse in two or three days. They are if possible worse than militia, their sole desire being to plunder and steal, and when they have got as much as their horses will carry, to run home."

Scarcely had the Major reached Camden and settled in the old camp at Logtown, when an express from Lord Cornwallis ordered him to rouse Harrison and march into Williamsburg. "I have ordered Wemyss to mount his whole Regiment and guard the Country east of Santee," Cornwallis hastily wrote Balfour on October 7. But Wemyss and Harrison never reached Kingstree. Disaster was moving too swiftly. Even while Cornwallis was writing, at King's Mountain only twenty-eight miles away, American militiamen were ruining his campaign. The Back Water Whigs from the foothills of the Blue Ridge Mountains were destroying forever any hope of a substantial Loyalist militia.

Major Patrick Ferguson, with a well-drilled corps of one hundred Provincials and one thousand militia, the latter recruited among the Loyalists around Ninety-Six, had been marching to join the British Army at Charlotte. Aware that the Back Water men commanded by Colonel Isaac Shelby were trailing him along the Cherokee Road, on October 6 he wrote Cornwallis: "Something must be done soon." His call for help reached the British headquarters at one of the decisive moments in the history of nations. Lord Cornwallis was languorous from chills and fever. He begged Tarleton to take his feared Green Horse to Ferguson's rescue. But having just recovered from an almost fatal attack of yellow fever, Tarleton was too weak to sit his horse.

During this day of indecision in Charlotte, the Back Water men were pressing Ferguson. About noon on October 7 Colonels Isaac Shelby, John Sevier, William Campbell, and Benjamin Cleveland, with nine hundred horsemen, caught up with him at King's Mountain. They dismounted, formed for battle, and stormed up the hill. They found Major Ferguson and his men drawn up and waiting on the crest of the mountain. On the Whigs charged, exultant, unappalled, their long rifles crackling and their muskets roaring. The Tories fought bravely. But after a bullet had dropped gallant Major Ferguson, Captain Abraham DePeyster raised a white flag. Only those Loyalists away on a foraging party escaped death or capture. Not a survivor reached Charlotte. Lord Cornwallis was not certain of Ferguson's defeat until the night of October 9. Next morning he sent Tarleton to succor the wounded and protect the stragglers. He also sent an express, galloping with orders recalling Wemyss to Camden.

The British had now lost the initiative. Although Turnbull and Wemyss held the depot at Camden, with Shelby and the Back Water men on his left and Marion, Giles, and Ford on his right, Lord Cornwallis was in a precarious situation. Thomas Sumter, appointed Brigadier General of Militia by Governor Rutledge on October 6, had taken the field. When the Gamecock began calling out Whig regiments and forming his brigade in the New Acquisition below Charlotte, the British position became untenable. So Lord Cornwallis decided to shorten his line, concentrate his forces, settle among friends with food and fodder, and wait for reinforcements which he had ordered Major General Alexander Leslie to bring down from the Chesapeake.

Cornwallis abandoned Charlotte on October 14 and set out toward central South Carolina. By the time he had reached the Waxhaws, he was desperately ill of malaria. Lord Rawdon took command of the army and paused for two weeks while the doctors treated Cornwallis. During the delay, however, he sent Tarleton and his dragoons on ahead to locate a site for a winter camp. The Green Dragoon selected Winnsboro, situated in the midst of fertile Whig plantations and containing a perfect site on the rolling hills around Mount Zion Academy. Here the army could winter in close proximity to its supply base at Camden, to its out-

post among the Loyalists of Ninety-Six, and to the rich farming district in the Dutch Fork.

News of the victory at King's Mountain spread rapidly
across the Carolinas. At Hillsboro, where he was rebuilding
the American Army, General Gates alerted his forces for a
second blow at the staggering British. On October 11 he ordered General Harrington to attack Gray and Fraser at
Cheraw. "I desire you will acquaint Colonels Marion and
Giles with your intentions," he told Harrington, "and recommend it to them to make diversions against the enemy's
posts below."

On the same day General Gates, pleased with Marion's
successes, wrote him a warm letter of encouragement.

Hillsborough 11 October 1780
Dear Colonel
    I received your Letter yesterday by Capt. Conyers, I am ex-
treamly pleased with your managem't & success & request you
earnestly to continue your Hostilities against our Tyrannic &
cruel Enemies——I have by this express wrote to Gen. Harrington at Cross Creek who has the Command of a Brigade des-
tined to take post immediately upon Pee Dee, opposite the
Cheraws, which I am well assured the Enemy have abandoned
——I desire you to Correspond with the General & as far as
for the Benefit of the Common Cause, cooperate with him——
The Enemy may be much destracted and divided by your
different attacks & the Country well covered by your Joint
endeavors to protect the persons and estates of our Friends
the Whiggs——I shall desire Governor Rutledge who is here
to write you by this Express and give you his Instructions in
regard to your prisoners, as with those you have taken & those
you may hereafter get into your possession——With much
Esteam I am Dr. Col.

Yrs. Sir
Col. Marion   H. G.

As soon as Marion received Gates' instructions, he
marched back into Britton's Neck and settled in his old camp

at Port's Ferry. From there he issued a call for the militia to assemble. He expected prompt obedience from the veterans of Black Mingo. But war had passed Williamsburg. The scarred country was again peaceful. Instead of rushing to arms in an attempt to throttle the slender supply line of the retreating British, they lingered around their desolate plantations.

Accustomed to commanding disciplined troops of the Continental line, Marion became annoyed at their tardiness. Slowly he became discouraged. What could he accomplish with undisciplined, independent horsemen who fought like Tartars when aroused, but who remained at home when they wished? After a week he called in his officers for a council of war. Sadly he told them that he had decided to abandon the Low Country and rejoin General Gates. Major Hugh Horry, his closest friend in the council, begged him to remain in South Carolina. Horry realized that militiamen could scarcely measure up to the standard of Continentals. But he knew that they were honorable men. He believed that they would obey the summons. "The services of Col. Hugh Horry in the field, were certainly highly meritorious; but he never rendered his country more effectual aid than by this act of friendly persuasion," said William James. "The militia at length came in."

As his troops began straggling into camp, Marion again became confident. He began actively campaigning. In every direction he dispatched patrols, five or ten horsemen who rode at sunset and returned at daylight. Over the silent highways, along country lanes, and through trackless woods they rode, gaining intelligence, encouraging the Whigs, and frightening the Tories. On the morning of October 24 a patrol galloped down the Black River Road from upper Williamsburg with stirring news.

To bolster the sagging British line, left unshored by the hasty withdrawal of Wemyss, Colonel Balfour had ordered the embodiment of the Loyalist militia in the High Hills. In response Colonel Samuel Tynes had called out the Tories from Nelson's Ferry to Salem. Into camp had ridden lads from the High Hills, from the headwaters of Pocotaligo River, and from the swamps of Lynches River. From the depot in Camden they had drawn brand-new English muskets, with plenty of powder and shot, as well as new blankets and bridles and saddles. Proud, careless, and completely unmilitary, they were now camping at the old muster field bordering Tearcoat Swamp.

The news of Tynes' encampment set Marion's blood racing. Here was an opportunity for "a diversion against the enemy's posts below." He called for a muster. When one hundred and fifty men responded, he crossed the Peedee at Port's. From Witherspoon's he marched to Kingstree. Cautious, secretive, afraid that Tynes would get wind of his coming, he kept his plans to himself, but all the while he spread rumors that he was on his way to McCallum's Ferry to chastise Harrison's Tories.

At Kingstree on the morning of October 25 Marion turned up the road toward Salem. Swiftly he led his troops, his scouts on the alert, dashing in and out of the main body, vigilant against surprise or ambush. Scarcely stopping, he rode during the afternoon, and in the evening he turned abruptly off the highway and forded the Black River. As he approached "the Tarcoat," as the English settlers called the little stream, he sent two nimble-footed lads to spy out the Tory camp. From them he learned that Tynes had turned aside from the road and camped in an overgrown field, his rear against Tearcoat Swamp and his defense in great insecurity. Some of the Tories had already tossed their blankets over the crab grass and were asleep on the ground. Others, like farm boys on a fishing trip, were merry, their voices ringing with song and laughter. Around campfires still others were talking and playing cards. Captain Amos Gaskens was winning. "Hurrah! At him again, damme! Aye, that's a dandy! My trick, by God."

Marion waited until midnight. Then he attacked. Using tactics proved at Black Mingo, he divided his troops into three parties. Sending a detachment to swing around and approach the field from the right and a second detachment to foreshorten its steps and move to the left, he headed toward the center of the camp with his main force. At the flash of his pistol the three divisions charged, shouting and screaming and firing as they galloped.

Completely surprised, the Tories sprang up, frightened and bewildered. Sleepy lads bounced from their pallets and bolted for the dark woods along the Tearcoat. Surprised gamblers tumbled into the morass. Colonel Tynes vanished.

The rout was gory. Marion's men killed three, wounded fourteen, and captured twenty-three men and boys. Among the dead was Amos Gaskens. Clutched in his hand were the ace, deuce, and jack of clubs. The Captain held high, low, and jack, and was reaching for game. But Death played the joker.

Marion's men captured eighty spirited horses, with bridles, blankets, and saddles, and eighty muskets. They also seized the baggage, food, and ammunition of the enemy. Never did the fury of their striking power more impress the Tories. "The most of Tynes' men soon after joined General Marion and fought bravely," said William James.

But Marion was disappointed. John Coming Ball had fled from him at Black Mingo. Now Samuel Tynes had escaped him at Tearcoat Swamp. He chafed at his misfortune, for he wished to capture the officers, destroy the leadership, and leave the Loyalist rank and file to wither away. So he tried another tack. Calling in Captain William Clay Snipes, one of his boldest riders, he sent him to the High Hills to bring in the Tory Colonel. Then, after tending the wounded, securing the prisoners, and refreshing his troops, he started his march back to Kingstree.

Brigadier General Harrington had chased out Fraser and Gray and established his headquarters in Cheraw. Thus he became the senior militia officer in South Carolina. To him Marion sent Colonel Tynes and the Tory militiamen to be confined in a prisoner camp in North Carolina. He respected

Harrington. And yet, as a Continental, he had no desire to be commanded by the North Carolina Brigadier. So he decided to clear up that point with General Gates.

Slowly, painfully, Marion wrote his report of the Battle of Tearcoat, his style still laconic and his language ungrammatical. He was optimistic. His victories at Black Mingo and Tearcoat Swamp had put spirit and resolution into the militia. They were trooping in. For the first time since coming to Williamsburg, he could envision a regiment of four hundred horsemen. He wrote:

> I hope I shall be Able to keep the North side of Santee clear of the Enemy, & prevent them from driving off Much. The Militia is now turning out better than they have done for some time past, my Strength the 25th Oct. was 150 of all ranks, & at present Upwards of 200, & I expect in three or four days it will be double.
>
> There is in Georgetown 60 British Invalids and as many militia from the South of Santee, which I hope to remove in a few days——Col. Giles is with me & has been very Active and Serviceable, but I believe Genl Harrington will Order him from me greatly against his Inclinations, and much to the Dissatisfaction of all his Officers. Genl Harrington has wrought to Majr Horry Orders as if he Commanded Col. McDonald Regt., which you had Given to me, & I cannot think it is your Intention I should be under his command.

Marion wrote a similar letter to Governor Rutledge. The Governor forwarded it to the South Carolina delegates in Congress. As the little victory at the Tearcoat was the only encouragement that Congress could offer the American people at the moment, it published an excerpt from Marion's letter in many of the Whig newspapers:

> Having intelligence of a party of militia embodying in the forks of Black River, I crossed Pedee the 24th of October, and on the 25th at night surprised Colonel Tyne, with a body of 200 men, killed 6, wounded 14, and took 23 prisoners, 80 horses and saddles, and as many muskets, &c. This surprise was

so compleat, that I had not one man killed; our loss was only two horses killed——my party consisted of only 150. A few days after the above afair, I detached Capt. Snipes with a party of men to the high hills of Santee, to seize all the militia and civil officers, which he found means to do, and took Colonel Tyne and a few other officers of militia, two justices of peace, in the British service, all of whom have sent to General Harrington, at Charraw Hill.

The news of Marion's smashing victory over Tynes brought Lord Cornwallis, still convalescent from malaria, back to the command of the British Army. "Bad as the state of our affairs was on the Northern Frontier, the Eastern was much worse," he wrote Clinton, pessimistically. "Col. Tynes, who Commanded the Militia of the High Hills of Santee, and who was posted on Black River, was Surprised and taken, and his Men lost all their Arms."

Colonel Balfour rushed fifty soldiers from Charleston to Moncks Corner to prevent Marion from crossing the Santee River. "But," he complained to Lord Cornwallis, "the numbers & spirits of the rebell partys so far outballances that of our militia, that a post at the High Hills of Santee, or Kingstree Bridge, is now absolutely necessary, otherwise communication is at an end betwixt the Army and this town."

Francis Marion, whom Lord Cornwallis less than three months before could identify only vaguely as "a Colonel Marion," had now become the scourge of the British. He seemed ubiquitous, lurking everywhere: hiding in an unknown rendezvous, creeping stealthily along on a raid, or leading a midnight attack. To add to the enemy's alarm, he kept his patrols constantly moving up and down the Santee Road. British wagoners were afraid to cross at Nelson's, but took the longer, more tortuous route to Camden by way of Friday's Ferry on the Congaree River.

From Camden on November 1 Colonel Turnbull wrote Tarleton, begging him to bring his green dragoons and chase the rebel horsemen from the supply line. The Green Dra-

goon had encamped at Brierley's Ferry on the Broad River,
his British Legion poised to strike at Shelby or Sumter or to
protect Winnsboro or Ninety-Six. Tarleton forwarded Turnbull's letter to Lord Cornwallis. "I can make nothing of
Turnbull's letter to you, as he only seems to describe Parties
of ten or twelve Rebels, which of course it is not intended to
employ the Legion to hunt," Cornwallis replied on November 2. But he gave Tarleton permission to go, saying: "You
will of course not be long absent and let me hear from you
constantly."

Ban Tarleton, fully recovered from yellow fever, and eager
to inflict another Waxhaw upon the King's enemies, ordered
his Green Horse to prepare for a campaign. True to his
motto of "Swift, Vigilant, and Bold," he led his dragoons
across the Wateree at Camden on the afternoon of November
3. "Col. Turnbull has informed me of People assembling at
Singleton's on Wateree," he reported to Lord Cornwallis.

"I received yours of yesterday," replied Cornwallis, "and
sincerely hope you will get at Mr. Marion."

Turnbull then reported: "Two men have arrived this
morning from Black Creek who assure us that Marion and
Snipes have their quarters at Singleton's Mills. We have
sent a spy who we expect to be back by Morning, and Tarleton will regulate his Route accordingly." As soon as he had
heard the report of the spy, with Harrison's Provincials as
guides, Tarleton and his troops cantered away from Logtown. He found the Santee Road open. There were no rebels
at Singleton's.

Nevertheless, astride Ball and with four hundred horsemen
at his back, Francis Marion was moving fearlessly up the
Santee Road. He planned to stop all traffic between Nelson's
and Camden, and to disrupt and delay as much as possible
the flow of supplies to Winnsboro. On the evening of November 5, knowing that he was among friends, he went into
bivouac on Jack's Creek, about ten miles above Nelson's
Ferry.

"A Negro has just told me of a Party at Jack's Creek,"

Tarleton reported to Cornwallis that night. "I shall proceed to General Richardson's and if I get no satisfactory intelligence before I arrive there, I shall take post and destroy the Country between there and Kingstree." He realized that the party at Jack's Creek was Marion and his men. Eagerly he set out to cross swords with the man who had crushed Ball and Tynes. He spread rumors that he was returning to Camden. As he moved toward the plantation of the late Brigadier General Richard Richardson, he sent out small patrols, hoping to lure Marion into ambush. On the evening of November 7 he reached Widow Richardson's, emplaced his two cannon, and lay with his Legion and Harrison's Provincials in full armor.

Marion, attracted by the lights reflected above the camp-fires, began creeping forward. He had heard of several small patrols and hoped to surprise them. But Widow Richardson sent her son Richard, a Continental officer who had been captured at Charleston and who had been paroled after he had caught smallpox in a prisoner camp at Haddrell's Point, to warn the Americans of ambush.

Brave, a man without fear, one who had stood in the hottest fire at Fort Moultrie and Savannah without flinching, Francis Marion was not afraid of Banastre Tarleton. And yet he was not foolhardy. Without any bravado or qualms about running from an enemy, he wheeled his corps around and called to his men to follow him In profound darkness he skirted the bogs of Woodyard Swamp. He never checked Ball until he had ridden across Richbourg's Mill Dam on Jack's Creek. He then exclaimed: "Now we are safe!"

During the confusion of their flight, Marion's men let a Tory prisoner escape. He ran to alarm the British and was brought before Tarleton just before dawn on November 8. There was an immediate call to arms. At the break of day, with Harrison leading the way, the Green Horse galloped off toward Richbourg's Mill Dam.

But Francis Marion was as quick-witted as Ban Tarleton. Before daylight he was also in the saddle. Calling in the men most familiar with the great pine barrens between the Santee and Black Rivers, he placed them in the van of his horsemen. To Major James he entrusted his rear guard. Then, easing out of his bivouac into open country, he tossed the rein to Ball.

From Richbourg's Marion raced toward the head of Jack's Creek and then circled down the Pocotaligo River. He let Ball set the pace, and his excited troopers urged their foaming steeds in his wake. All morning he fled along country roads, across harvested fields, through trackless pine woods, and over boggy swamps. Down the Pocotaligo River he sped, ready to take to water the instant he should see Tarleton's van. After he had reached familiar roads along the Black River, he slowed his gallop, and at Benbow's Ferry he turned Ball into the chill waters.

For seven hours Tarleton trailed Marion. "The Corps under my command were ordered under arms immediately and made a rapid march of 26 miles through Swamps, Woods, & Fastnesses toward Black River without a Halt," he reported to Lord Cornwallis. "The enemy by being all mounted, obtaining so much time previous to the pursuing & owing to the Difficulties of the Country could not be brought to action."

At Ox Swamp, a branch that flows into the Pocotaligo River about twenty-three miles above Kingstree, Tarleton halted. Ahead lay a roadless bog. His dragoons were tired and hungry; their horses were winded and heaving. Slowly he reined his horse around. In his imagination he was contrasting fleeing Marion with fighting Sumter. "Come, my boys! Let us go back, and we will find the Gamecock," he cried in the thick accents of Lancashire. "But as for this damned old fox, the devil himself could not catch him!"

Tarleton's weary dragoons chortled gleefully at his calling Marion a "damned old fox." Harrison's Tories also chuckled, and from Ox Swamp to Camden they spread the story. The Whigs along the Santee, too, were grimly amused. They seized upon Tarleton's epithet, turned it euphemistically into Swamp Fox, and fastened that nickname forever upon their hero.

All afternoon and evening the "damned old fox" waited at Benbow's. Craftily he set his defenses in readiness for a proper reception. He had his men fell trees in the single defile that led down through the bluff to the ferry slip. For advance skirmishers he dotted the western shore with McCottry's riflemen. As a precaution, he told his men that, if Tarleton should force his way across the river, they should scatter. After escaping they should come together again and lie in wait for the Green Horse successively at the narrow passes through Pudding Swamp, Claps Swamp, and Flat Swamp on the road to Kingstree.

But Tarleton never came closer than Ox Swamp. Next morning he trotted back to the Santee and began punishing sedition with the torch. Between Jack's Creek and the High Hills he burned thirty houses. His punishment of Widow Richardson for warning Marion was ghoulish. He ordered his troops to dig up General Richardson, who had lain in the plantation graveyard for six weeks, in order that he might "look upon the face of such a brave man." As the Richardsons wept anew, his green dragoons plundered their home. Like a conqueror, he called for dinner. After he had dined, with a spirit of vengeance hitherto unrevealed in his bloody rampages, he ordered his troops to drive all of the cattle, hogs, and poultry into the barn. Then, as Governor Rutledge wrote the South Carolina delegates in Congress, "he consumed them, together with the barn and the corn in it, in one general blaze."

Satiated and weary, on November 10 Tarleton wrote a vainglorious report to Lord Cornwallis: "I returned on my steps & laid the Houses & Plantations of violent rebels waste about Richardson's and Jack's Creek. The Country seems now convinced of the error of Insurrection. People join me from the Swamps. The Torch is stopped & I have issued the enclosed Proclamation. Thus my Lord I have used my best Abilities to settle the Affairs of this part of the Province, but

if there had been one individual of the Country attached
to our Cause & Exempt from Fear the total Destruction of
Mr. Marion had been accomplished."

There is, however, sometimes in the fortunes of men something called poetic justice. On the day that Tarleton burned
Sumter's mills on Jack's Creek, the Gamecock ended the
career of house-burning James Wemyss.

As soon as Tarleton had set off after Marion, Lord Cornwallis ordered Major Wemyss to bring the 63rd from Camden to Winnsboro. In the absence of the Green Horse, he
could use the mounted infantry for scouting, foraging, and
seeking intelligence. Everything was quiet between the Broad
and the Wateree. But on November 7 a patrol rode in with
information that General Sumter, with ten militia colonels
and their troops, was at Moore's Plantation only thirty miles
above Winnsboro. The next afternoon Cornwallis sent Major
Wemyss, with the 63rd and forty dragoons from the British
Legion, in quest of Sumter. Unknown to the British, Sumter
had moved, and about one o'clock on the morning of November 9 Wemyss unexpectedly stumbled into the Gamecock's
new camp at Fishdam Ford on the Broad River. Surprised,
the Major changed his original plan of attacking at daylight,
and gave battle. But the silhouettes of his horsemen made
splendid targets. Of the first five shots, one broke Wemyss'
arm and another splintered his knee. After a few minutes of
confused fighting, both sides withdrew. Lieutenant Stark left
Wemyss and the other wounded under a flag of truce. About
noon Sumter returned and paroled them. In Wemyss' pocket
he found a list of the houses the Major had burned along the
Peedee. With impulsive magnanimity, Sumter threw it into
the fire. He knew that should his men find the list it would
serve as the Major's death warrant.

The capture of Wemyss shocked the British. On November
8 Lord Cornwallis had written a sleepy letter of advice to
Tarleton: "The enemy is, I believe, in no great force, and
Marion is cautious and vigilant," he said. "If a blow could

be struck at any body of the rebels it might be attended with good consequences; but I do not see any advantage we can derive from a partial destruction of the country." Next morning the strategic situation had entirely changed. The presence of one thousand victorious American horsemen within twenty-five miles of Winnsboro alarmed Cornwallis. He wrote an order recalling Tarleton and the British Legion and sent it to Turnbull with a note: "Pray forward the enclosed immediately by an Officer to Tarleton whose Presence in these Parts is absolutely necessary."

Tarleton returned swiftly from Singleton's. At Camden he found Lord Rawdon who, on November 13, had relieved Lieutenant Colonel Turnbull. Suffering from malaria, Turnbull had received permission to go home, and Lord Cornwallis had given Colonel Welbore Ellis Doyle command of the New York Volunteers. The Green Dragoon was chagrined at Marion's escape, but he was warm in his praise of his guides. Rawdon reported to Cornwallis: "I hear much of the prowess of Harrison's Rangers, upon the Expedition with Tarleton: a valiant friend of Government is a Prodigy of which the World talks." But the young Irish Lord double-crossed the valiant Rangers. He knew their reputation. In his secret cipher he informed Cornwallis: "They want to plunder and not do regular duty."

In the early light of November 14 Lieutenant Colonel Banastre Tarleton and his Green Horse, their saddles creaking and their bridles jingling, cantered through the sleeping village of Camden and headed for Winnsboro. The bloody dragoon was passing from the Santee Road forever.

"Col. Tarleton has burnt all the houses, and destroyed all the corn, from Camden down to Nelson's Ferry," Marion reported to Gates from Benbow's Ferry on November 9, ". . . has behaved to the poor women with great barbarity; beat Mrs. Richardson, the relict of Gen. Richardson, to make her tell where I was, and has not left her a change of raiment. He not only destroyed all the corn, but burnt a number of cattle in the houses he fired. It is distressing to see women and children sitting in the open air around a fire, without a blanket, or any clothing but what they had on, and women of family, that had ample fortunes, for he spares neither Whig nor Tory."

CHAPTER VII

Murder of Gabriel

THE SWAMP FOX sat gazing across the turbid water at Benbow's Ferry. He was ragged and unkempt, he still limped when he walked, but he was in high spirits. All afternoon he had awaited the coming of Tarleton's Green Horse. Now he knew that the enemy had abandoned the chase. He and his men were safe. As he gazed, his thoughts turned to the future. What next? He began thinking about Georgetown with its garrison of sixty invalids. He knew that guns, ammunition, clothing, and salt——especially salt——lay in the British depot. With the morale of his citizen-soldiers running high, he wondered if he could take the town by storm. After carefully considering the possibilities of surprise, with the strategic effect of victory and the consequences of defeat, he decided to make the attempt.

Marion confided his plans to no one. To divert attention from his real objective, he followed Tarleton back to Nelson's. From there he sent patrols scouting past Singleton's Mills. As soon as he was convinced that the dragoons had been recalled to Winnsboro, he opened his campaign. Setting out in secrecy on the evening of November 14, he led his horsemen swiftly through Williamsburg. Avoiding Kingstree, he crossed the Black River at secluded Potato Ferry and moved through Gapway Swamp.

In war it is axiomatic that your enemy can do everything

you can and probably do it better. Unknown to Marion, the British had sent reinforcements to Georgetown. As soon as the Swamp Fox had decamped at Drowning Creek, Captain Barefield had called out the Tory militia on the Little Peedee. Upon orders from Balfour, he began rounding up horses to mount Colonel Doyle's New York Volunteers. But Colonel Thomas Brown, commanding the American militia on the upper Peedee, stopped the marauding. "I have killed Miles Barfield, and wounded two others of the Barfields; and it is said, Jesse Barfield is shot through the hand, but the certainty I cannot tell," Brown reported to General Harrington on November 4. "I have got four more of the Barfields well ironed and under guard, whom I am very choice of."

As soon as Balfour learned of the drubbing of Tynes, he reasoned that Marion would next attack Georgetown. Unable to spare any more regulars, he ordered Captain Barefield to reinforce the garrison there with his horsemen. With address worthy of a better cause, Barefield crossed the Little Peedee, slipped down Waccamaw Neck, and entered Georgetown while Marion was outrunning Tarleton. His arrival was reported to Balfour. "We are authorized to inform the public that about 200 of the inhabitants near Pedee River, over whom Mr. Marion and his associates for some time past have exercised the most despotic and cruel tyranny, lately collected together in arms, and fell in with a gang of banditti, whom they routed and entirely dispersed. The leader of the rebels, a Col. Murphy, was amongst the killed," *The South Carolina Gazette and American Journal* reported on November 15. "A few days since, the victorious Loyalists joined the King's forces in Georgetown."

Without suspecting this reinforcement, Marion and his troops passed through Gapway Swamp before daybreak on November 15. The Swamp Fox knew the vicinage. As a boy he had rambled over every road and byway along Winyah Bay. He had explored every creek and swamp near Georgetown. So he led his men into White's Bay and concealed them in a rendezvous afterwards known as The Camp.

At daylight Colonel Marion sent Peter Horry and his horse-men across White's Bridge and along the road toward the Black River. The neighborhood was quiet until Horry reached White's Plantation. Here he found a party of Tories from Captain James Lewis' company killing beeves. At the approach of Horry's partisans, they fled, firing as they ran. Hearing the sound of shooting, their comrades dashed out from the village. "Then you might have seen the woods all covered with armed men," said Horry, "some flying, others pursuing; and with muskets, and pistols, and swords, shoot-ing and cutting down as fast as they could."

In a few moments Colonel Horry was alone except for a fourteen-year-old lad named Gwinn. Eight or ten men gal-loped up. Horry shouted: "Are you friends?"

"Friends!" answered Lewis as he lifted his musket. "Friends of King George!"

Young Gwinn pulled the trigger of his musket. Captain Lewis pitched from his saddle, blood spurting from buckshot wounds. With the courage of a dying animal, he raised him-self in his final spasm and fired. Horry's horse crumpled under him. The sound of the shots brought the partisans whooping and halloing back. "The Tory party then fired at us and fled," said Horry, "leaving four of Marion's men, whom they had just taken and beaten very barbarously with the butts of their muskets."

Learning of another Tory party camping at the Pens, the plantation of Colonel Alston, Marion sent Captain Melton and his horsemen to surprise them. With them as a super-numerary rode Lieutenant Gabriel Marion. Unfortunately, as they were passing through a dense swamp, Melton's van-guard stumbled into Captain Barefield and his troop. Both sides fired. The Tories killed the horses of Francis Goddard and young Marion. The Americans fired a load of buckshot into the face and shoulders of the Tory leader. In the melee young Goddard outran the Tories, sprang on another horse, and fled to the camp. But the Tories seized Gabriel. As they began clubbing him, he recognized a man whom he had met at the home of his Uncle Francis. He called to him for mercy. But at the name of Marion, they shouted: "He is one of the breed of that damned old rebel!"

The Tories were maddened by the sight of blood streaming down the face of Jesse Barefield. They remembered Miles dead and the younger Barefields in irons. As they began howling for Gabriel's blood, he grabbed and clung to his acquaintance. They shouted to the soldier that if he did not shove young Marion from him, they would blow him to pieces also. Then, tearing Gabriel away, they thrust a musket against his chest and fired a load of buckshot through his heart. "The instrument of death," said James, "was planted so near that it burnt the linen at his breast."

Francis Marion had seen many heroes die in the cause of freedom. But Gabriel was the first kinsman who had died following him, and he grieved for his nephew as for an only son. Like some Biblical character, lamenting the dead, he turned from his companions. They did not see his tears, but they knew his sorrow. Next morning, however, he called them in. "As to my nephew, I believe he was cruelly murdered," he told them calmly. "But living virtuously, as he did, and then dying fighting for the rights of man, he is no doubt happy. And this is my comfort."

During the day Marion's troops captured a Tory mulatto named Sweat. They suspected that he had killed Gabriel, and feeling against him was overpowering. That night, as they were crossing the swamps of the Black River on their return to Williamsburg, a militia officer rode up to Sweat, who was marching in a line of prisoners under guard. Clapping his pistol to the head of the wretch, he shot him dead.

The wanton murder of Sweat infuriated Marion. Seldom did he show temper, but now with flaming cheeks and flashing black eyes he sent for the captain of the guards. With vivid phrase and violent tongue he upbraided the unhappy man. Why had he not protected Sweat, even killing the perpetrator to prevent so savage a deed? "Of all men who ever drew a sword, Marion was one of the most humane," said Horry. "He not only prevented cruelty in his own presence, but strictly forbade it in his absence."

When his tired troops reached Shepherd's Ferry on Black Mingo, Marion sent them into bivouac. Next morning he ordered them to form a circle. As they stood puzzled by the strange formation, a sergeant led the horse of Captain Lewis into the ring. He was a noble steed, accoutered with English bridle and saddle, and with portmanteau, sword, and pistols lying across the saddle. As the horsemen gazed with envy, Marion called young Gwinn from the ranks. Placing his hand on the lad's tousled head, he exclaimed: "A brave little man." Gwinn turned crimson. The Colonel pointed to the horse and arms of Lewis and said: "There is the reward for your gallantry."

Confused and hesitant, Gwinn looked around at his comrades. "Dear me, now," he finally blurted out as he reached for the reins, "what will Mammy think——and the children ——when they see me riding up on this famous horse, with all these fine things? I know well enough how Mammy will have a hearty cry——that's what she will——for she will think I stole him." Marion smiled at the simple youth. He warmly commended his bravery. And then, he sent his compliments to Gwinn's mother for bringing up such a brave, honest son. "I've always hated the Tories," Gwinn told his comrades after the pageantry. "They will not fight for their country."

After the little parade, Colonel Marion turned to his problems. The rebuff at Georgetown had not lowered the ardor of his troops. They were holding eastern Carolina in readiness for the advancing American Army. But where was that Army? Where were the troops, ammunitions, clothes, and medicine expected from Gates? Hoping for an answer to those questions, Marion wrote General Harrington:

Sir   Black Mingo, 17 Novr, 1780
    Since my last to you, Colonel Tarleton retreated to Camden, after destroying all the houses and provisions in his way. By

information, I was made to believe there was but fifty British in Georgetown, and no militia, which induced me to attempt taking that place. But unluckily the day before I got there they received a reinforcement of two hundred Tories under captains Barfield and Lewis from Pedee. The next day the Tories came out and we scrimmaged with them.

Captain Barfield was wounded in his head and body, but got off. Captain James Lewis, commonly called "Otterskin" Lewis, was killed. I stayed two days within three miles of the town, in which time most of the Tories left their friends and went home.

Finding the regulars in the town to be eighty men, besides militia, strongly entrenched in a redoubt, with swivels and cohorns on their parapet, I withdrew my men, as I had not six rounds per man, and shall not be able to proceed on any operations without a supply of ammunition, which I shall be obliged to you to furnish me with by Captain Potts, who commands a detachment to guard the prisoners taken. I have not heard anything from General Gates since the letter you sent me.

A man from the high hills of Santee, within eight miles of Camden, says that Washington's Horse is at Rugely's Mill, one mile from there. I beg to know where our army is, and what news from them.

I am, with esteem,

Your most obedient Servant
Francis Marion

Hon. Brig. General Harrington
Pedee

While Francis Marion was at Black Mingo, Banastre Tarleton reached Winnsboro. He told Lord Cornwallis a glowing tale of having chased the Swamp Fox from the High Hills to the impassable swamps of the Black River. Now he was eager to pick a fight with the Gamecock. Cornwallis was delighted with the report of the dashing cavalryman and told Major McArthur: "I hope we shall soon put a stop to Mr. Sumter's bragging."

About nine o'clock next morning the Green Dragoon

reached Brierly's Ferry. His tired troops rushed down to the edge of the Broad River to wash up and clean their horses. While they were busy, a party of some one hundred and fifty of Sumter's men dashed up to the opposite bank and delivered a volley. A horse crumpled and a private of the 63rd Regiment screamed. Tarleton opened with his cannon and sent the raiders scampering. Then, concealing the green uniforms of his dragoons, so that Sumter would not learn that he had returned from the Santee, he crossed the Broad River. At daylight on November 19 he set out and marched his troops all day. He bivouacked near the Enoree River, but during the night a malcontent of the 63rd deserted, stole a horse, and fled to Sumter.

At dawn Colonel Tarleton resumed his pursuit. Reaching a ford over the Enoree River in early afternoon, he learned that Sumter had crossed only two hours earlier and was forcing his retreat toward the Tyger River. Leaving his infantry and artillery to march at a slower pace, Tarleton hastened forward with eighty mounted infantry of the 63rd and one hundred and ninety dragoons of his Legion. About five o'clock he clashed with Sumter's rear guard under Colonel Thomas Taylor. The Gamecock had posted his troops on the hills around the house of a man named Blackstock, with their rear against the Tyger River.

Not wishing to attack one thousand well-posted militia before the arrival of his infantry and cannon, Tarleton dismounted the 63rd under Major John Money and placed them at the lower end of Blackstock's field. Then, taking station with his dragoons near a wood, he waited. True to his fighting instincts, Sumter opened the battle. He sent four hundred infantrymen against Major Money, but the 63rd drove them back with the bayonet. Hand-to-hand, bloodily, furiously, at odds of five to one, they fought, the officers leading, shouting, waving their swords; and the men advancing, sweating, thrusting with their blood-reddened bayonets. Major Money dropped, mortally wounded. Finally they drove the Americans into the woods beyond Blackstock's house.

During the fighting, General Sumter rode to order Colonel Edward Lacey to attack Tarleton's idle dragoons. But as he turned back toward his command post, a British sharpshooter wounded him. The rifle ball pierced his right shoulder, ripped through his shoulder blade, and chipped a splinter from his backbone.

"General, you are wounded!" exclaimed Captain Robert McKelvey when he heard blood sprinkling on the dry leaves.

"I am wounded," Sumter replied courageously. "Say nothing of it."

When they reached the command post, Colonel Henry Hampton helped Sumter from his horse, put his sword into his scabbard, and told an orderly to lead his horse away. "Say nothing about it," Sumter cautioned him. "Request Colonel Twiggs to take the command."

By then the American militia had begun driving back the 63rd. To prevent his infantry from breaking, Tarleton charged at the head of his Green Horse. Uphill they thundered, bursting through the cordon across the highway. But Hampton's men, firing from fence jams and the log houses, toppled horses and riders so fast that the dying choked the road. Seeing Major Money lying on the field, Tarleton sprang from his horse and, in defiance of Hampton's sharpshooters, lifted his wounded comrade into his own saddle. By then the 63rd had rallied and was retreating in order, and so the dragoons left the field.

With the coming of twilight Tarleton withdrew and sent his troops into bivouac on a hill two miles from Blackstock's. Colonel John Twiggs concentrated his militia around the house and barns. Both expected to renew the battle at daylight. But by dark General Sumter was unable to stand or to speak. After stretching an uncured bull hide between two horses, Twiggs placed the Gamecock in it and sent him to the camp of Colonel Samuel Watson in the New Acquisition, twenty miles below Charlotte. Then, leaving Colonel Richard Winn's troops tending bright campfires around Black-stock's, Twiggs forded the Tyger River and disbanded the militia.

Next morning Tarleton trailed Sumter to Grindal Shoals on the Pacolet. Finding that the Gamecock had again escaped him, he leisurely turned back toward Brierly's. "Sumter's wound is through both shoulders——People this instant have reported him dead," he said in his report. Lord Cornwallis accepted the rumors as true. "We have lost two great plagues in Sumter and Clarke," he wrote Balfour. "I wish your friend Marion was as quiet."

Francis Marion was far from quiet. Back and forth across Williamsburg he galloped, his patrols fanning out in all directions. Along the Santee, up the Black River, and down the Lynches River they roved, their midnight whooping and the clattering hoofs of their horses keeping the Tories in constant alarm. These frightened subjects of the King poured complaints and information upon Lord Rawdon. "I have good accounts that Marion recrossed Black River, the day after Tarleton fell back," Rawdon wrote Cornwallis on November 17. "He advanced to Gaillard's, and the next day again retired across Black River. Yesterday he lay twelve miles behind Kingstree Bridge. His numbers were accurately counted and amounted to 406."

Colonel Balfour wrote sarcastically to Cornwallis of Tarleton's cossacking along the Santee: "But after his dissipating and dispersing account of Marion, I am sorry to say that in a few days afterwards, he appeared with 500 men before Georgetown, where I am sorry to say he now is, within a few miles. However, Blacke is not allarmed and writes in perfect security. Marion's movement by Tarleton I may be remembered of——it is no joke to us."

"As to Marion," Cornwallis replied calmly to Balfour, "I do not think that Tarleton flattered himself that he had done more than stopping his immediate progress and preventing the militia from joining him and if the accounts I hear from that Country are true his visit has not been ineffectual."

But the growing power of Marion had so alarmed Cornwallis that he decided to seize Kingstree. He ordered Colonel Balfour to alert a regiment for immediate marching. By putting some military prisoners aboard ship and releasing soldiers from guard and garrison duty, Balfour assembled a corps of Hessians, Provincials, and Loyalist militia. These he attached to Major Robert McLeroth's battalion of the 64th Regiment and sent all marching toward Nelson's Ferry. On November 15 he wrote Cornwallis: "I hope that force amounting to 275 Rank and File, with two three pounders, is sufficient to give the Rebels a check."

After crossing the Santee River at Nelson's Ferry, McLeroth marched into Williamsburg. On the evening of November 20 he encamped on the village green at Kingstree. The villagers scowled at the redcoats and sent a messenger toward Black Mingo. But wariness is born of valor. Instead of mounting an attack on the British camp at daybreak, Marion hastily assembled his militia and slipped quietly away on the road to Britton's Ferry. By morning he had covered the twenty-six miles and pitched his bivouac on the bluff which forms the western bank of the Peedee. With his troops settled and his patrols hustling in and out of camp, Marion began writing his reports. He wrote Harrington about McLeroth's capture of Kingstree and begged him to send his cavalry to help drive out the invaders. But even as he wrote, he shook his head in dejection. He knew the Fabian qualities of the Brigadier. He then began struggling with his report to General Gates.

"The Bearer Captain Milton will Inform you what Difficulty I have & do now struggle with, and can give full Satisfaction of my conduct, as he has been with me ever since I left you," he wrote. "I beg leave to recommend him to you as a Brave and Worthy man, who merits much from his country; the great Distress he is in for want of cloaths, Is not in my power to prevent, for we are all poor Continentals without money." He reported his raid on Georgetown. "Since my last to you, Colo. Tarleton retreated to Camden after Destroying most of the Houses & possessions on the high hills of Santee, I marched to Murry & Nelsons Ferry along Santee river in hopes of Intercepting some of the boats of the Enemy passing to and from Camden, but finding that could not be Effected, & being told that Georgetown was garrisoned but with fifty British Invalides I marched there in hopes to have taken it. Unluckily the Evening before our arrival two hundred Torys under the command of Captns Barefield & James Lewis, got in. Those Torys came out and we scumaged with them——I killed three & took twelve prisoners drove part in the town & Disperst the others as they were cut off from the town." Without revealing his grief, he calmly reported the death of his nephew: "Our loss was Lt. Gabriel Marion & one private killed & three wounded."

"Yesterday Major McLeroth with 200 Hessians & militia from south of Santee took post at the Kingstree," he continued, "& by an Intercepted Letter from Lord Rodney who commands in Camden, to him I find they are mounting the New York Vollunteers, to send to that post for the purpose of Driving off stock & Destroying provisions." He then began a long bill of complaints. He needed everything: clothing, ammunition, medicine. "I am Greatly in want of a Surgeon, one of my wounded Bled to Death for want of one, so many is oblige to rctreat for want of Medicine, for I have not any whatever."

Finally Marion came to the matter troubling him most. Where was the American Army? "Many of my people has left me & gone over to the Enemy, for they think that we have no Army coming in & have been Deceived, as we hear nothing from you a great while, I hope to have a line from you in what manner to act & some assurance to the people of support."

At Kingstree, in the meantime, Marion's disappearance was causing dismay. The inhabitants were sullen and incommunicative, and Major McLeroth could not learn where the enemy was lurking. All day he moved around like a hunter who

expects a tiger to spring upon his back. He feared the pistol
shot that would bring a furious charge, such as the one at
Tearcoat. And so before daybreak he fled toward the Santee.

"I wrought you two days agoe since which Majr McLeroth
who took post at Kingstree, a Saturday, retreated to Murry's
ferry a Monday morning before day," Marion wrote Gates
on November 22. "I suppose the party under Capt. Barefield
was to have joined him but that party being dispersed, he
found himself too week to stay."

As a Continental officer, subject only secondarily to the
Governor of South Carolina, he continued: "I have rec. orders from his Excellency Govr Rutledge to transmit a return
of the troops under my command which I have Inclosed——
it is not often I have so many Tho I have had more." Marion
was seldom discouraged. His repulse at Georgetown and
McLeroth's capture of Kingstree, however, had disheartened
him. The independence of the militia, over whom he had
no authority but led only through persuasion and example,
worried him. "The People here is not to be depended on
for I seldom have the same set a fortnight," he confided to
Gates, "& until the Grand Army is on the Banks of Santee,
it will be the same."

Now he had a greater reason for discouragement. The
sudden departure of McLeroth had brought chaos to his
regiment. The men in homespun, fighting without pay, without medical care, without ammunition, food, and clothing,
and without recognition from South Carolina, Congress, or
the American Army, felt that they had accomplished their
purpose. They had dispersed the Tories. They had frightened the British from Kingstree. Now they wanted to go
home. Some had to rebuild the houses and barns destroyed
by the torches of Wemyss and Tarleton. Others wished to lay
in supplies of fodder, straw, and wood against the coming
winter. Some had to pen their cattle from the range. Others
said that it was time to kill their hogs. In this military de-
mocracy each knew that he was fighting for the prize of free-

dom. So each searched his conscience and made his decision. Then he rode off with or without leave from the Colonel.

Sadly, Marion watched the militia disband. His force was soon too weak to harass the British. He abandoned any idea of chasing McLeroth. With his faithful band he crossed over Britton's Ferry and disappeared in the swamps of Britton's Neck. Through his spies Lord Rawdon learned that the Swamp Fox had sought cover. On November 24 he informed Lord Cornwallis: "Marion has crossed Pedee."

CHAPTER VIII

Defeat of McLeroth

FRANCIS MARION was across the Peedee River, his regiment disbanded and his officers in hiding. Thomas Sumter lay in the New Acquisition desperately wounded, his brigade dispersed and his colonels also in hiding. Banastre Tarleton rested in his camp at Brierly's Ferry, exultant in victory and preparing for new adventures. "We are just going against the Enemy in N Carolina with a compleat & Gallant Army," he wrote his brother John Tarleton. He was readying the British Legion for the coming campaign, his farriers working day and night shoeing the mounts of the Green Horse. At the camp at Brierly's Major Archibald McArthur was also preparing his 71st or Highlanders Regiment for campaigning, and Major Timothy Newmarsh was eagerly watching the road for two hundred recruits for his 7th or Royal Fusiliers Regiment scheduled to arrive from England.

Lord Cornwallis was confident that he had subjugated South Carolina and was now preparing the British Army for its advance into North Carolina. He kept his wagon trains rumbling across the rich farming country in the Dutch Fork hauling food and forage into Winnsboro. He left the task of keeping the army supplied with clothing, ammunition, salt, rum, and other necessities to Lord Rawdon. In Camden Rawdon labored to keep supplies rolling to the front. His chief problem was keeping the long supply route to Charleston free from interference.

Lord Cornwallis still fondled the idea of forming a Loyalist militia strong enough to hold the country and guard his lines. In spite of experience, his hope centered around Colonel Tynes. On November 22 he informed Rawdon: "I shall be very glad to get Tynes exchanged." To Rawdon's surprise, Captain John Coffin, who with thirty mounted infantrymen of the New York Volunteers was riding patrol between Camden and Nelson's Ferry, notified him on November 23: "On my way down I met with Colonel Tynes who had just made his escape, with some of his officers who were with him."

Captain Coffin had been instructed to look for a place to establish a strong point in the High Hills. He became intrigued with an eminence near the Wateree known as Upton Hill. Deciding to fortify it, he sent back to Camden for help. Rawdon sent him twenty men, and with his troops and some Negro laborers from friendly plantations, Coffin threw up a redoubt. On this he mounted two small cannon. Then with his fifty men he moved in——for a few days——he informed Rawdon. "Colonel Tynes will then have his militia collected and be able to secure the post."

Major McLeroth, shaken by the disappearance of the Swamp Fox, had scarcely paused in his retreat from Kingstree. When his tired troops reached the Great Savannah, he halted and pitched camp around Sumter's house. From there he reported to Balfour. He told of his occupation of Kingstree, of his anxiety after the disappearance of Marion, and of his return to the Santee.

Nisbet Balfour, second in command of all the King's troops in South Carolina, was busy governing Charleston, looking after prisoners of war, commanding the Loyalist militia, and furnishing logistic support for the British advance. "In the movement of McLeroth, I hoped for much satisfaction, and real service to your Lordship's operations," he wrote to Cornwallis bitterly after McLeroth's retreat, "but how I am disappointed in my man——I will not now complain——nor how he has managed his matters——however he now stands in a situation where he can scarcely go wrong."

In condemning McLeroth's behavior, Balfour was influenced by the optimistic reports of the Loyalists in Georgetown. "By letters from Col. Cassells," he told Cornwallis, "I am pressed in the strongest manner to give only an opening for his people and our friends upon Little Pedee, those on the banks of Great Pedee, and the frontiers of No. Carolina, as well as those on Lynches Creek to come in to him, all which can be effected, by taking possession of Port's and Britton's ferry, upon Lynches Creek and the lower part of Pedee, which parts he means to defend with his Militia, if once given to him."

Cornwallis realized the danger in Cassels' advice more quickly than did his juniors and immediately warned Rawdon: "I tremble for McLeroth and hope Cassells will not tempt him too far."

Robert McLeroth was realistic. He dared not pit 275 infantrymen against the 500 horsemen Marion reputedly could raise with a single whistle. He knew what had happened to Lewis and Barefield. He was also humane. He had no stomach for the torch. Reared in Scotland, where hardship and poverty engendered compassion, he refused to devastate the lands of the Scotch-Irish. And so, calm and unruffled, he remained in his bivouac at Sumter's house and let his superiors worry.

"As to McLeroth, it is impossible to get him to Port's ferry as I mentioned," Balfour confessed in a worried note to Cornwallis on November 29. "I must beg Lord Rawdon to communicate with him and give him the intelligence of the enemy's movements, and direct his accordingly, as I am such a distance, and can only say that I can spare him *very well.*" Then Balfour concluded in exasperation: "But I am obliged to say, that I think the sooner he can be put into a situation

CORNWALLIS

THOMAS SUMTER

Library of Congress

Library of Congress

FRANCIS MARION

PETER HORRY

WILLIAM WASHINGTON

JOHN RUTLEDGE

HENRY LEE

LORD RAWDON

WILLIAM MOULTRIE

BANASTRE TARLETON

NATHANAEL GREENE

ANDREW PICKENS

where he has not to act for himself the better——otherwise I fear some accident to him."

Lord Rawdon wrote a similar complaint, and on December 1 Cornwallis replied: "I received this day yours inclosing the reports from McLeroth and Harrison. My apprehensions on account of the former are over. On the whole I am better pleased that he is on the Santee than on the Pedee." Two days later Cornwallis again wrote him. "I trust my dear Lord that you will have a constant eye to McLeroth, who by his letters requires much looking after," he pleaded. "A blow to any British Regiment cuts deep."

As Lord Cornwallis worried lest Marion cut up a British regiment, he made a subtle enquiry: "I do not apprehend that you want McLeroth at Camden?" After receiving a negative answer from Rawdon, he decided to take McLeroth with him on the advance into North Carolina. Since General Leslie's troops from the Chesapeake had begun arriving in Charleston, he would order Lieutenant Colonel John Watson and his 3rd Regiment of Guards to take post at Nelson's Ferry. "I know I do not make you a great present in the person of Col. W," Cornwallis told Rawdon with sardonic humor, "but as his Corps is called Light Infantry and must of course act as Light Troops there would be a constant difficulty of Command between him and Tarleton. I know your Lordship can make him obey you; his men must be as good as those of the 64th and himself as good a partisan and as intelligent a correspondent as McLeroth."

Constantly harassed by the demands upon his ingenuity, Balfour now began to fret about getting the newly arrived recruits of the 7th Regiment to Major Newmarsh at Brierly's Ferry. "Marion is too formidable to trust so near the boats, and stores, without something better than militia," he wrote Cornwallis on December 4, "and it is with great concern, I assure you, the recruits are so bad, that not above a third can possibly move with a Regiment."

While the British Lords chafed and fumed over bumble-

footed McLeroth, Francis Marion lay snug, a fox in his lair.
After he had passed Britton's Ferry, the sons of Widow Jenkins told him of a hiding place, high, dry, and inaccessible.
He followed them through the Neck until they came to Dunham's Bluff, and from there they crossed over the Peedee to
Snow's Island. They rode across the island to the plantation
of William Goddard. William, a cousin of Francis Goddard,
was about the same age as the Jenkins boys. He was an ardent
Whig, patriotic, warmhearted, and willing to turn over his
cabin, barn, and bins to the defenders of his country.

Marion found Snow's Island ideal for the headquarters of
a Partisan chief. Named for William Snow, an early settler of
Williamsburg, the island is a low ridge five miles long and
two miles wide. Along its eastern shore runs the Peedee.
Lynches River lies on the north, and along the western and
southern borders runs Clark's Creek, one of the mouths of
Lynches. To the west lie Snow's Lake and the sloughs and
morasses of Muddy Creek and Sockee Swamp.

William Goddard had built his house on the high ground
toward the middle of the island, safe above the flood waters
of the Peedee. On the ridges around his fields stood a virgin
growth of gum and oak and pine, now gray and somber
against the November sky. In the woods stood an undergrowth of bushes: dogwood, haw, and hornbeam, their
branches entangled with brambles and wild muscadine vines.
In the swamp and along the watercourses stood cypress trees
like stately sentinels, their knees bare and their features
hidden by streaming Spanish moss. On the side of the island
along Clark's Creek the undergrowth gave way to a green,
almost impenetrable, cane brake.

Marion pitched his camp in the woods near Goddard's
cabin. The ridge was dry, the drainage good, and wood and
water handy. With craft of frontiersmen, his men built crude
huts, lean-to style, to protect them against wind and rain.
For their scant stores of food and military supplies they built
storage bins. And for their prisoners they strengthened Goddard's barn and with soldiers' humor named it the Bull Pen.

To prevent surprise, the Swamp Fox drew all boats to his side of the rivers and destroyed those he did not need. To further insulate his retreat, he had his men fell trees into the fords, remove puncheon from the causeways, and break down the bridges over the creeks and branches in Williamsburg.

Marion also ordered Colonel John Ervin to throw up a small redoubt on the lower side of Dunham's Bluff, and garrison it with a guard from Captain John Dozier's company of Britton's Neck militia. Safe, well provisioned, and located in a strategic position, he then called in those militiamen who could be trusted with a knowledge of his rendezvous. As his regiment swelled, he began sending out foragers and scouts. Soon his camp was like a beehive. Far and wide his patrols ranged, their way lighted only by the stars and the moon, and soon the hoofs of their horses had worn new trails into Snow's Island.

"Since my last by Captn. Milton the Enemy under the command of Maj'r. McLeroth left Kingstree & marched near Nelson's Ferry, but yesterday I hear he was on his return to Kingstree again, he was reinforced with 150 malitia from So. of Santee," Marion wrote Gates from his new headquarters on "Linches Creek near PD." "Tynes who I had taken, with several others in the British service & sent to Gen'l. Harrington made their escape from him and is again Embodying the malitia at the high hills of Santee, with an Intention to reinforce Maj. McLeroth, this will give the Maj'r a superiority in this part of the country & I shall be obliged to retreat."

Marion was inexorable in his orders that his scouting parties refrain from violence. He would not countenance useless bloodshed. But Loyalists could be subjected to terrors, and marauding bands of Whigs committed every kind of barbarity. "Two brothers of Major Harrison's, who were ill of the Small Pox, lay at a house about eight miles in our rear," Rawdon informed Cornwallis on December 5. "Last night a scouting party of Rebels burst into the house, shot both of the sick Men in their beds, though they were incapable of making the least defense."

News of the return of Tynes and then of the murder of the Harrisons brought the Swamp Fox from his lair. With his troops he crossed over Clark's Creek and advanced to Indiantown. From there he sent Peter Horry to ride through the High Hills and reconnoiter Colonel Tynes' new position in Fort Upton.

Away galloped Horry and his troopers, before them the chance of another Tearcoat Swamp. All night they followed the high road east of the Black River. At noon next day they paused at a tavern kept by a well-known Tory. Seizing the frightened Loyalist, Horry questioned him about Tynes. But the publican's wife was not frightened. During the interrogation she beckoned to a soldier and led him to a storehouse. There she pointed to a barrel of apple brandy. The thirsty trooper helped himself. He then called his comrades. They swigged and twigged and filled their canteens.

As they rode forward that afternoon, Horry noticed the high spirits of his men. They were constantly pulling on their canteens. "What the plague have you got there, boys, that you are so eternally drinking?" he finally asked.

"Water, sir, water! Nothing but water," they answered.

"But I might as well of talked to a troop of drunken Yahoos," Horry said. "For some of them grinned in my face like monkeys; others looked as stupid as asses; while the greater part chattered like magpies.

"Indeed our guide, a fat polter-headed fellow, fetching one of his heavy lee lurches, got so far beyond his perpendicular, that he could not right himself again; but fell off, and came to the ground as helpless as a miller's bag. In short, among my whole corps there was but one sober man, and that was Captain Neilson."

To have led men in such condition into action would have been murder. "I therefore instantly ordered a retreat," said Horry, "which was made with all the noise and irregularity that might have been expected from a troop of drunkards, each of whom mistaking himself for Commander-in-Chief, gave orders according to his own mad humor; and whooped

and halloed at such a rate, that I verily believe no bull drivers ever made half the racket."

When a crestfallen Horry returned to Witherspoon's
Ferry, Marion asked: "Well, where is Colonel Tynes?"

Peter Horry told his ludicrous story. Marion chuckled.
"Well, you did right to retreat," he finally said. "But pray
keep a careful eye on the apple water next time."

Horry's comic foray was, however, as effective as a battle.
His whooping, drunken troopers, raging like bull drivers in
a hassle, terrified the Loyalists along the Black River. "Colonel Tynes arrived here this evening exceedingly frightened,"
Lord Rawdon wrote Cornwallis on December 8. "His militia,
upon some vague report of Harrington's approach, except
twenty, deserted his new fort. He thought the twenty who
remained too small a garrison and therefore deserted them.
He says that he is convinced he can do nothing with the
Militia, and on that account begged leave to resign his command. I accepted his resignation."

With all the disgust of an English nobleman for cowardly
provincials, Lord Cornwallis wrote Balfour: "I find Tynes's
Militia has again squandered."

From Charleston, in the meantime, Balfour had sent the
motley recruits of the Royal Fusiliers marching toward
Winnsboro. "I have therefore proposed, that the recruits
shall cross at Nelson's, be joined by Major McLeroth at
Sumpter's House," he reported to Cornwallis, "and by his
Corps be conducted as far as the high hills of Santee, where
a mounted party from Camden might be sent to meet them."
Learning from his spies that the recruits had marched from
Charleston, Marion issued a call for the militia to assemble.
Times were slack and most men idle, and so they came troop-
ing in. When the Colonel mounted Ball and turned his head
toward Nelson's, he had seven hundred horsemen at his back.
Leisurely he rode across Williamsburg, but from Murry's he
went charging up the Santee Road. By December 12 he had
passed Nelson's. Just above Halfway Swamp, some twenty

miles beyond the ferry, he overtook unsuspecting, dawdling
Major McLeroth, patiently herding the recruits of the 7th
Regiment along toward Camden.

Marion immediately drove in the British pickets. He dispatched riflemen to skirmish with the rear guard. Then,
wheeling his horsemen around McLeroth's flank, he began
a direct attack. The veterans of the 64th squirmed and
skirmished and finally reached a field enclosed by a rail fence.
Into the enclosure they scrambled, dragging in the frightened recruits behind them. They then posted themselves behind the fence jams and defied the horsemen. On the east of
the Santee Road, just beyond range of the British guns, lay
a dark, boggy cypress pond, its shoreline stretching off toward
Halfway Swamp. Here Marion drew up his troops and waited.
Soon Major McLeroth sent a British officer under a flag of
truce. The redcoat protested vehemently against the Americans shooting British pickets. He argued, and argued. He
swore that shooting pickets was contrary to all the laws of
civilized warfare. With the fervor of wronged innocence, he
dared the Americans to come out of the woods and fight in
the open field.

Marion replied as vehemently. He maintained that burning the houses of patriots was more indefensible than
shooting armed pickets. He cited the forays of Wemyss and
Tarleton. As long as the British burned houses, he would
continue to shoot pickets. "I consider the challenge that of a
man in desperate circumstances," he concluded. "But if
Major McLeroth wishes to see mortal combat between teams
of twenty men picked by each side, I will gratify him."

McLeroth accepted. After British and American deputies
had selected a battleground near an old oak tree that stood
in the field, he chose twenty sharpshooters and sent them to
their post. Marion chose Major John Vanderhorst to command his team. Second in command he placed Captain Samuel Price of All Saints. Then he began slowly, deliberately
choosing his marksmen. As he decided on a man, he wrote
his name on a slip of paper. The first of these he handed to

Gavin Witherspoon. He chose only the bravest, and none refused the ordeal.

"My brave soldiers!" Marion exclaimed, after Major Vanderhorst had formed his men. "You are twenty men picked this day out of my whole regiment. I know all of you, and I have often witnessed your bravery. In the name of your country, I call upon you once more to show it! My confidence in you is great, and I am sure you will not disappoint me. Fight like men! Fight as you have always done, and you are sure of victory."

Vanderhorst then turned to Witherspoon and asked: "What distance would you choose as the surest to strike with buckshot?"

"Fifty yards for the first fire," replied the sharpshooter.

"Then, when we get within fifty yards, my boys," the Major told his men, "as I am not a good judge of distances, Mr. Witherspoon will tap me on the shoulder. I will then give the word, and you will form on my left opposite those fellows. As you form, each man will fire at the one directly opposite him, and on my word few will be left for a second shot."

Vanderhorst advanced boldly to within a hundred yards of the British, but as he was closing to fifty, an officer passed hurriedly along the enemy line. At his command the redcoats shouldered their muskets and retreated in quick step. After giving three cheers, Vanderhorst and his men returned to their comrades.

McLeroth pronounced his name Mackclroth. James spelled it McIlraith, and Horry called it Muckleworth. The young British colonels undoubtedly called him mucklehead. But the Major had a Highlander's canniness. He was only stalling. As soon as he had seen Marion's advance guard, he had sent couriers racing for help. They met Captain Coffin and one hundred and forty mounted infantrymen sent to escort the recruits. But instead of galloping to rescue McLeroth, Coffin turned back and lodged his troops behind Swift Creek.

"I understand that McLeroth sent to Coffin for reinforcements. In that case he had either beaten off the enemy, or was only skirmishing with them. Otherwise his messenger could not have gotten through," Rawdon advised Cornwallis. "Information was given Coffin that he was to be attacked in the night and a large body of the Enemy approached very near him in the evening. Under these circumstances Coffin judged it best to retire."

During the night McLeroth's troops lighted huge camp-fires. They burned fence rails and heaped on logs. They shouted and they sang. Toward midnight they began to quiet down. Then, abandoning their baggage, veterans and recruits slipped noiselessly away on the road to Singleton's Mills. At daylight Marion discovered the ruse. Immediately he dispatched Major Hugh Horry and a hundred horsemen to beat McLeroth to Singleton's. Horry soon realized that he could not overtake him. Detaching Major James and a squadron with the fleetest horses, he told them to ride around the millpond and seize Singleton's houses.

James outraced the British. He circled the pond and swept up Singleton's Hill just as McLeroth's runners reached the foot. His troops seized the buildings and from their safety delivered one fire. Then, to the amazement of their enemy, they remounted their horses and fled as if from the devil.

The Singleton family was down with smallpox!

"I have just received an express informing me Major McLeroth was attacked this day by seven hundred Rebels," Captain Coffin informed Rawdon on December 13. "The Attack began at twelve o'clock at Singleton's Mills——he has sent for a reinforcement which I understand is at hand, and shall proceed with an expedition."

After Coffin's note there was silence. "Not even a rumor has reached us," Rawdon complained to Cornwallis on December 14. All next day he waited for word from the troops at Singleton's. "I began to be uneasy at not hearing from McLeroth when to my great surprise, I saw him enter the room," Rawdon wrote Cornwallis on December 16. "The

matter has been as I expected: Marion had been reconnoiter-
ing him and there has been some loose firing at his outposts.
Capt. George Kelly and two privates of the 64th were
wounded. The Rebels lost ten or a dozen. Coffin joined Mc-
Leroth near Singleton's; but no pursuit of the enemy was
undertaken. Marion (whose force is about 600) lies between
Nelson's Ferry and the 64th, sixteen miles from the latter."
Then, with a show of resolution, he concluded: "I must drive
Marion out of that Country; but I cannot yet say what steps
I shall take to effect it."

Next day Marion moved back down the Santee Road. His
show of force had ended in a petty stroke, but unknown to
him it had ended the military career of Robert McLeroth.
"I must immediately dislodge Marion," Rawdon informed
Cornwallis that morning. "But as McLeroth has not quite
enterprise enough, I shall let him go to Charleston (which
he wishes)."

Robert McLeroth was being cashiered. He had not been
vigorous enough with the sword and the torch. But William
James, who had ridden with Marion during the chase, testi-
fied to the humanity of the Major: "It has been currently
reported that he carried his dislike of house burning so far,
that he neglected to carry into effect the orders of his commander-in-chief on that point to such an extent as to gain
his ill will and that of many other British officers."

Colonel Peter Horry was also in the running fight with
McLeroth. He said that during the skirmishing between
Halfway Swamp and Singleton's Mills, after each side had
several wounded, McLeroth left them in a tavern under a
flag of truce. When Marion alighted at the tavern, the old
woman who ran it exclaimed: "If I ain't down right sorry
to see you, then I'll be hanged. You are chasing the British
to kill them. Ain't is so now, Colonel?"

"That is indeed my business," Marion told her grimly.

"Well, dear me, now! And did I not tell you so? But pray
now, my dear Colonel Marion, let me beg of you, don't you

do any harm to that dear good man, that Major Muckle-worth, who went from here a little while ago. For, oh, he's the sweetest-spoken, mildest-looking, noblest-spirited Englishman I ever saw in all my born days."

The old crone led Marion into the cabin. On pallets on the floor lay several wounded men. Attending them was a well-dressed middle-aged man. To Marion's greeting he replied calmly: "I am a surgeon in the service of his Britannic Majesty." As Marion nodded, the doctor continued: "I was left by Major McLeroth to take care of the wounded, of whom Sir, I believe that nearly one-half are your own men."

All the time the old woman chattered away, rattling the English guineas that McLeroth had paid for a fortnight's lodging for the wounded. "And now, Colonel, would it not be a burning shame to kill such a dear good gentleman as that?"

After leaving the tavern, Marion rode a long while in silence. Then, turning to Horry, he said: "Well, I suppose I feel now very much as I should feel were I in pursuit of a brother to kill him."

When Marion called off his troops and returned from Singleton's Mills, many of them said that the Major's generosity to their comrades had so won their hearts that they had none left to fight him. "From the effect produced on our troops, by this amiable officer's conduct," said Horry, "I have often been led to think favorably of a saying common with Marion: 'Had the British officers but acted as became a wise and magnanimous enemy, they might easily have recovered the revolted colonies.' "

To the High Hills of Santee to take command of McLeroth's 64th Regiment, Lord Rawdon sent Major John Campbell. "In justice to McLeroth," the young Irish Lord then secretly reported to Cornwallis, "I should mention that his mild and equitable behaviour to the inhabitants of that country has been of great Service."

CHAPTER IX

Lair on Snow's Island

SLOWLY, unhurriedly, Marion returned from Singleton's. For a week his troops lay boldly across the British supply route. They blocked all traffic on the Santee Road; they also stopped all traffic on the Santee River. With his wonted pessimism, Colonel Balfour ordered the wagon trains to follow the longer, harder route from Moncks Corner to Friday's Ferry on the Congaree. He also sent word for the captains of the supply boats to remain below Murry's Ferry. But the captain of the boat coming down from Camden, unwarned of the blockade, docked at Nelson's on the morning of December 14. Before the startled crew realized their danger, Marion's men had swarmed aboard and seized the vessel. After removing the stores, sails, hardware, and everything else of military value, they applied the torch.

Four days later Major John Campbell reported to Lord Rawdon that Marion still lay at Nelson's Ferry, his regiment of horsemen too powerful for the 64th. For the next several days Campbell and Marion lay watching each other, their troops contented with an occasional random shot. Both realized that their skirmishing was only the entr'acte in a vast drama moving toward its climax. The main actors on both sides were resting, waiting for reinforcements, and girding for the final struggle for the American continent.

After Lord Cornwallis had destroyed Gates' army at the

Battle of Camden, the congressional delegates from the Southern states had demanded a new commanding general. Under their prodding, on October 5, Congress passed a resolution requesting General Washington to appoint a commander in the place of Gates. John Mathews of South Carolina suggested Major General Nathanael Greene, friend and confidant of the Commander in Chief. On October 22 Washington wrote Greene, telling of the resolution and saying: "I have thought proper to choose you for this purpose."

Washington then wrote Congressman Mathews: "You have your wish in the officer appointed to the Southern command. I think I am giving you a general, but what can a general do without men, without arms, without clothing, without shoes, without provisions?"

Soon after receiving Washington's memorandum, General Greene started toward the South. Although he dreaded the perils of his new assignment, he was enthusiastic about it. He realized that the operations in the Carolinas were almost a separate war. He would have to win the confidence of new civic and military leaders. He would face challenging questions of strategy and difficult problems of logistics. So he paused in Philadelphia to learn from the Southern delegates in Congress what he might expect in men and materiel.

Satisfied with his conferences, even though he had learned that he could expect very little, on November 23 Greene set off for Hillsboro, headquarters of the Southern Army. But when he arrived, he was disappointed. General Gates had marched to Charlotte. Greene reached Charlotte on December 2, but waited until December 4 to take command of the army. Afterward he spent the day conferring with officers and listening to reports. He had a long interview with Governor Rutledge and persuaded the Governor to call out all the South Carolina militia. After a busy day reorganizing his forces, he turned to his correspondence. Among the unanswered letters in Gates' file was the report written by Marion on November 22. After a chat with Captain Milton, Greene began his first letter to Marion.

"I have not the honor of your acquaintance," he wrote, "but I am no stranger to your character and merit. Your services in the lower part of South Carolina, in awing the tories and preventing the enemy from extending their limits, have been very important. And it is my earnest desire that you continue where you are, until further advice from me."

After intimating that the Grand Army would not soon stand on the banks of the Santee and that the dull, savage bushwhacking would have to go on indefinitely, without hope, reward, or succor, Greene assigned Marion a specific task. "Spies are the eyes of an army. . . . At present, I am badly off for intelligence. It is of the highest importance that I get the earliest intelligence of any reinforcement which may arrive at Charleston."

With the hunger, illness, and tatters of his own army depressing him, Greene turned to Marion's request for supplies. "I am sorry to have it not in my power to order a supply of clothing to Captain Melton, but there is none with the army. Ammunition I am told is gone to you since you wrote. I am too little acquainted with the medical department to give any answer respecting a surgeon; but if it is possible to comply with your wishes it shall be done."

Upon his return from Charlotte, Captain Milton found Marion and his men encamped at Benbow's Ferry, drawing food and forage from the Whigs along the Black River. In Greene's letter the Swamp Fox read the first words of encouragement or command that he had received in two months. Alone and almost forgotten, he had been waging an isolated campaign in the narrow country between the Peedee and the Santee. Now he was again in the van of the struggle for Liberty. How his dark cheeks must have glowed and his spirits soared as he read the words of approbation from his new commanding officer.

"I received yours b'y Captain Milton," Marion answered on December 22, "and shall Indeavour to procure Intelli-

gence as you desire but shall meet with great Difficulty as
nothing but gold or silver passes here and I am Destitute of
Either. The enemy is so Suspicious they will not permit any
man to pass on the South of Santee without the Strictest Ex-
amination and they have patroles along the river & guards at
several passes." The British guard on the western side of
Nelson's Ferry consisted of eighty Hessians, reinforced on
December 18 with 150 fresh troops from Charleston. "They
report that Genl. Lesley is arrived in some part of This
State, but I have sertain Intelligence they are not in Charleston," he wrote. "I was in sight of Nelson's ferry Tuesday,
agoe, when the Enemy attempted to Cross but my party being seen, prevented them."

The former Commandant of the Second Regiment of
South Carolina Continentals respected the men of the militia. They were brave, willing, devoted to liberty, and ready
to die defending their homes. But he knew their limitations,
and he longed for a corps of disciplined regular troops. To
Greene he now confided: "If I had a few Continental Troops
I should be able to do much more than I am at present by
their awing the militia who act with diffidence, 100 would
be sufficient for this purpose."

Alert, restless, never remaining at any spot long enough
for the Tories to guide the British to his camp, Marion left
Benbow's Ferry on December 24 and marched back to the
Santee. The weather was mild and the countryside a wintry
gray, soft and pleasant. He was genial and his troops were
in good spirits. Everyone had a consciousness of sacrificing
self-interest for a noble cause. Instead of returning to their
homes to spend a warm yuletide with their families, the
horsemen spent Christmas Day patroling the long, winding
road between Murry's and Nelson's Ferries. After satisfying
himself that there was no new invasion of the territory he so
zealously guarded, Marion called in his riders and returned
to the security of Snow's Island.

But there was an important movement afoot, even though

the Swamp Fox had failed to learn about it. On December 24 Cornwallis wrote Lord Rawdon: "I am anxious to know what Campbell has done with Marion."

"Marion has fallen back without doing other mischief than firing the supply boat," Rawdon answered. Next day he relayed the latest report from Major Campbell: "Marion is across Black River."

"I received yours of yesterday and am glad Marion has left the coast clear," Cornwallis replied cryptically.

All day on December 26 there was excitement and activity among the British troops along the Santee. Major Campbell and the 64th Regiment lay under arms at Sumter's house. From daylight until dark Captain Coffin and his mounted infantry swept the Santee Road. On both sides of Nelson's Ferry the Hessian guards were alert and ready to meet any surprise attack by Marion. All Christmas night Lieutenant Colonel John Watson had been marching the 3rd Regiment of Guards relentlessly along the road from Moncks Corner to Nelson's Ferry. The ferrymen were now rowing Watson's famed Buffs across the flooding Santee.

Instead of rushing down the Santee Road, threatening destruction to any rebels found in Kingstree, at Indiantown, or on Snow's Island, Colonel Watson moved slowly, cautiously. He decided——perhaps at General Leslie's insistence, for the General had ridden with him to Nelson's Ferry to inspect the facilities for moving his army across the Santee ——to assure better protection to the troops and provisions moving toward Camden. He realized that Sumter's house was unsatisfactory for a strong point. So with Harrison as guide, he marched to Wright's Bluff on Scott's Lake, some ten miles above Nelson's. There Watson selected an Indian burial mound, a kind of tumulus thrown up by the ancient Santees, and turned it into a bastion. Around the base of the mound, with principles copied from fortifications in the Old World, he threw up a formidable redoubt, complete with fosse, parapet, abatis, and ports for his two cannon. On top of the eighty-foot mound he scooped out a nest for his sharpshooters. Then, in honor of John Watson Tadwell-Watson, Lieutenant Colonel of his Majesty's 3rd Regiment of Guards, he named the post Fort Watson.

Captains Mitchell and Waties, bearing Marion's letter of December 6, followed the trail of Captain Milton to Charlotte. They found great excitement, vigor, and hope at Greene's headquarters. The General was readying his army for campaigning. Governor Rutledge was stirring up the Whigs. Even though wracked by excruciating pain, General Sumter, with the courage of a lion, had ridden to Charlotte for a conference with Greene. The Gamecock reported that Lord Cornwallis had probably no more than five hundred effectives at Winnsboro and urged Greene to strike directly at the British Army. Realizing that the bulk of his troops needed training and conditioning, Greene refused the hazard, but he was so impressed by Sumter's account of the valor of the militia that he decided to make a daring strategic move.

"You are appointed to the command of a corps of light-infantry of 320 men detached from the Maryland line, a detachment of Virginia militia of 200 men, and Colonel Washington's regiment of light-horse, amounting to from sixty to an hundred men," he wrote General Daniel Morgan on December 16. "With these troops you will proceed to the west side of the Catawba River, where you will be joined by a body of volunteer militia under command of General Davidson of this State, and by the militia lately under the command of General Sumter." Greene then placed the main army under Brigadier General Isaac Huger, with orders to cross the Peedee and go into camp at a site chosen by Colonel Thadeus Kosciusko. On December 20 both General Morgan and General Huger evacuated Charlotte. Each marched his corps to its assigned quarter. Morgan hastened across the Catawba and the Broad and finally halted on the Pacolet River. Huger moved more slowly. He crossed the Peedee, and on December 26 encamped the army on Hicks Creek, nearly opposite Cheraw.

Greene's strategy was sound. He wished to supply his army with food from the unravished plantations in the eastern Carolinas. He wished to station his army behind an unfordable river, with its protection and potential for water transportation. But most of all he desired a pivot from which he could apply pressure against the British in Camden or Winnsboro or Ninety-Six. "It makes the most of my inferior force," he wrote friends, "for it compels my adversary to divide his, and holds him in doubt as to his own line of conduct. He cannot leave Morgan behind him to come at me, or his posts of Ninety-Six and Augusta would be exposed, and he cannot chase Morgan far, or prosecute his views upon Virginia while I am here with the whole country open before me."

Greene also wished a short, strong line of communication with Colonel Marion. With his small army, ill-equipped and ill-supplied, and with small likelihood of greater support from Congress, he would have to depend largely upon the state troops and the militia of the Southern states. The Swamp Fox led the most numerous, active, and successful corps still in the field in South Carolina. The militia from the Scotch-Irish along the Peedee and Black Rivers and from the Huguenots along the Santee was the most ardent in the state, and Greene wished to give them all possible moral and logistic support.

Lord Cornwallis grasped the implications of Greene's strategy immediately. Accordingly he made his countermoves. He ordered Colonel Tarleton to prepare for a campaign to drive Morgan from the British left flank. He next ordered Colonel Balfour to drive Marion from the supply line.

Nisbet Balfour, the dour Scot upon whom fell so much of the drudgery of the operations in South Carolina, responded quickly. He sent Lieutenant Colonel George Campbell with the King's American Regiment to Georgetown. He also sent fragments of several regiments caught up and brought south in the draft of reinforcements under Leslie. Among these was Captain John Saunders' troop of the famed Queen's Rangers, a green-coated regiment of Tories commanded by Lieutenant Colonel John Graves Simcoe. Instead of obeying Balfour's orders, Saunders sent his horsemen to Georgetown under the command of Cornet Thomas Merritt, while he rode on to Winnsboro to try to persuade Lord Cornwallis to send him and his men back to their regiment in Virginia. Balfour also called out Major Ganey and his Tories and sent them to Georgetown.

With his deployment completed, Balfour began pushing his offensive. He ordered Colonel Campbell to prepare to march up the Peedee and seize Kingstree. He also ordered Colonel Watson to get ready to move against Marion. "Major Campbell writes me that Marion lies on this side of Black River and that he means to press Watson to push him directly," Lord Rawdon wrote Cornwallis on December 28. "Should the movement specified in Benson's letter take place, Marion may be in a scrape."

But Francis Marion had been in scrapes before. Somehow he seemed to thrive on danger and he always escaped. This time he outfoxed both Rawdon and Balfour. "I left the banks of Santee yesterday," he wrote Greene from Indiantown on December 27. "Emagining the Enemy had an Intention to cut my Retreat off from Pedee is the reason I have retreated from Santee."

From his spies Marion had learned of the arrival of the British reinforcements. "Genl. Lesley landed in Chas. town last Thursday, by the best Information he had not Two Thousand Men, on Sunday his troops was at Moncks corner on their way to Nelson's ferry." He then concluded: "Five hundred Men crossed Lenew's ferry near the mouth of Santee river, intended for Georgetown, this last wants confirmation which I shall be sertain of the truth tomorrow & will send you by express."

To ascertain the strength of the enemy in Georgetown, on December 27 Marion told Peter Horry to muster a troop of horsemen for a probing raid. At dusk Colonel Horry, Captain Baxter, and Sergeant McDonald and thirty men galloped from Indiantown. Swiftly they rode through the Whig communities of lower Williamsburg. About midnight they crossed the Black River at Potato Ferry and raced on to The Camp. There they hid in an ambush.

About midmorning Cornet Merritt and another officer, elegantly mounted on Virginia thoroughbreds, escorted a carriage with two young ladies past Horry's ambuscade. While only a courting party on the way to dine with friends, the officers decided that all would be safer if protected by a squad of the Queen's Rangers. Back they turned to the village and the young women drove on into the country. Soon afterward Horry and his men decided to seek a late breakfast at the home of a well-known Whig. Upon entering his friend's home, Horry saw the Tory belles.

"What business do you have here?" one of them asked pertly. "The gentleman of the house is not at home. There are no provisions here for you, and to be sure you are too much of a gentleman to think of frightening a family of poor helpless women!"

But the wife of the Whig slipped out of the room and beckoned Horry. "Go back into the house," she told him. "When I return, you must demand provisions. I will deny that I have any. You then get into a violent passion and swear you will have them or set the house on fire."

The Colonel understood that the patriotic Whig was afraid of her Tory visitors. He acted out the little charade and took the keys when she threw them on the floor. From the barn he scrounged corn and fodder for his horses. In the smokehouse he found milk, eggs, butter, and bacon enough to provide breakfast for his troops. The good-natured Negro women soon cooked a meal, and the hungry soldiers sat down with a "God be praised!"

As Horry's men finished eating, they heard the vedettes fire a warning. "To horse! To horse!" cried Horry. While his troops were mounting, the sentinels dashed in with Merritt and the Queen's Rangers hard at their heels. "Charge!"

shouted Horry, and his cavalry turned on the Rangers. There were flashing sabers, war cries, and groans from the wounded. Down the lane fled the Rangers and never stopped until they were safe in Georgetown.

When his comrades took flight, young Merritt headed into the swamp and in the heat of the chase escaped his pursuers. "But will you believe me," he afterward told his friends in New York, "when I assure you that I went out that morning with my locks as bright an auburn as ever curled upon the forehead of youth. By the time I had crawled out of the swamp into Georgetown that night, I was as gray as a badger!"

Horry's horsemen drove the outnumbered British cavalry into Georgetown. As the Rangers retreated to safety, Major Ganey's Tories dashed out to meet the challenge. At their head galloped the Major. "A stout officer-looking fellow he was, too," exclaimed Horry, "and most nobly mounted." With the courage of the Scots, red-headed Sergeant McDonald charged to meet him. In the shock of battle, as cavalry sabers clanked against homemade swords and horses whirled and bolted, Ganey's troopers again deserted him. As at the Blue Savannah, Ganey turned back—with McDonald chasing him. For two miles the Sergeant and the Major raced, their horses' hoofs ringing on the cold ground. "Never on earth did two horses or two horsemen make greater exertions," said Horry, "fear impelling the one, fury urging the other!"

Into the edge of the village they galloped. As they turned Richmond Corner, McDonald's powerful horse Selim brought him almost abreast of Ganey. Realizing that the distance was still too great for his sword, the Scotsman seized his carbine, raised himself in his stirrups, and lunged. His bayonet plunged into the back and out through the chest of Ganey. When the Sergeant attempted to draw back his gun, it twisted, loosed the bayonet, and left it driven up to the hilt in the Major. Screaming and clawing at his side, with blood streaming fore and aft, Ganey rode up to the redoubt, "prodigiously to his own and to the mortification of his friends the British and the Tories," said Horry.

"I hear Ganey is near death," Marion reported soon afterward to Greene.

As soon as Horry had returned from his raid, Marion left Indiantown, crossed Clark's Creek, and again encamped around Goddard's cabin. As his men rested, he began catching up with his correspondence. "Yours of the 24 Inst. just received," he wrote Greene from the "Mouth of Linches Creek near Pedee" on December 28. "I wrought you two days ago since which I find the Enemy in Georgetown is reinforced with two hundred men, their strength there is near three hundred men Including twenty horsemen well mounted; they have two Galleys & have brought three 9 pounders for their redoubt which incloses a Brick Building, a small party sent there was pursued and wounded a Captn lost one man."

As the eyes of Greene's army, Marion reported that "Genl. Lesley was on Thursday crossing his troops at Nelson's ferry." He confessed that he could not learn the strength of the reinforcement, but continued: "I have sent three men over Santee, when they return I shall acquaint you with the particulars of their Intelligence." In the security of his lair on Snow's Island he concluded his report, "The Enemy reported they Intended an attack on a small post I had here which is the reason of my retreat to this place," he said. "Should they attempt it I hope my Situation will give me an Advantage, I shall remain here a few days to rest my horses when I will again advance to Black river."

But the Swamp Fox did not rest long. As soon as Horry's troopers had left Georgetown, Colonel Campbell sent Cornet Merritt with the Queen's Rangers on a sweep through southern Williamsburg. Early on the morning of December 30 Marion's scouts dashed in with news of the raid. Immediately the Swamp Fox was in the saddle. All forenoon he followed the trail of the Rangers. In the afternoon he turned his jaded horses back toward Snow's Island. To Greene he reported dejectedly that the enemy "made so much haste in returning I could not catch up with them."

That evening Marion called in Captain John Postell and handed him a set of orders:

Snow's Island, Dec. 30, 1780.

Sir:

You will proceed with a party down Black river, from Black Mingo to the Mouth of Pedee, and come up to this place; you will take all the boats and canoes from Euhaney up, and impress negroes to bring them to camp; put some men to see them safe; you will take every horse, to whomsoever he may belong, whether friend or foe. You will take all arms and ammunition for the use of our service. You will forbid all persons from carrying any grains, stock or any sort of provisions to Georgetown, or where the enemy may get them, on pain of being held as traitors and enemies to the Americans. All persons who will not join you you will take prisoners and bring to me. You will return as soon as possible. Let me know any intelligence you may gain of the enemy's strength or movements.

I am, your obedient servant,

Francis Marion.

Adjt. Postell.

N. B.——You will bring up as much rice and salt in the boats as possible.

John Postell had been reared on a plantation above Georgetown. He knew every creek, path, and roadway along the Lower Peedee. He was acquainted with every Whig and Tory in the district. As he enquired about salt, he learned from friends of an unguarded treasure on Waccamaw Neck. He reported his discovery to Marion. "Have heard of 150 Bushels of Salt on Waccamaw which the Enemy intend to make use of to salt 60 head of cattle they have collected," Marion laconically informed Greene: "I have sent a party to bring it off."

What a precious commodity was salt! The manufacturers in All Saints Parish on Waccamaw Neck extracted it from sea water in huge evaporation vats and sold it for ten silver dollars a bushel. As few Whigs or Tories had gold or silver, their families ate unsalted meat and unsavored bread. With the instincts of a guerrilla chief, who somehow provides necessities for his people even when he denies his troops, Marion sent a detachment with wagons and sumpter horses to bring off those 150 bushels. "As soon as Gen. Marion could collect a sufficient quantity of this desirable article at Snow's Island," James afterward wrote, "he distributed it out in quantities, not exceeding a bushel for each Whig family; and thus endeared himself the more to his followers."

CHAPTER X

Repulse at Georgetown

"I HAVE APPOINTED Col. Marion a Brigadier and thrown all the Regiments eastward of Santee, Wateree and Catawba into his Brigade," Governor Rutledge wrote the South Carolina delegates in Congress on December 30, 1780. A courier with a letter from the Governor, posting rapidly down the Peedee from Thomas' Plantation nearly opposite Cheraw Hill, reached Snow's Island on New Year's Day. Marion opened the letter from the Governor. His dark eyes lighted up, and a smile spread over his swarthy face. He handed the paper to Peter Horry. "As soon as I came to his new title 'Brigadier General,'" said Horry, "I snatched his hand and exclaimed, 'Huzza! God save my friend! My noble General Marion!'"

Governor Rutledge had appointed Francis Marion Brigadier General because of his rare abilities. As a Continental officer he had rallied, inspired, and led the militia to victory after victory. He was a sound strategist, a keen tactician, and a savage fighter. He had surpassed every other leader in spreading terror among the Tories between the Santee and the Little Peedee.

He was a stern disciplinarian, observing and demanding the highest standards of military efficiency. And yet he was kind, humane, and thoroughly sympathetic to his suffering, ill-equipped followers. Since they had no tents, he also slept in the open. He was bold to the verge of audacity, and yet he took no unnecessary chances, protecting his men and himself from all avoidable hazard. They followed him with admiration and devotion.

Excitement soon spread through the woodland camp at Goddard's. Brigadier General Marion had begun organizing his Brigade. From his band of heroes he appointed Captain John Milton his aide, and for junior aides chose Captain Lewis Ogier and Captain Thomas Elliott. Captain Elliott took charge of the General's correspondence, and from that time the contacts with General Greene, Governor Rutledge, and the Whig leaders became firm and regular.

General Marion appointed Colonel Hugh Ervin, the senior officer of the militia, second in command of the Brigade. He gave Colonel Peter Horry command of his cavalry, and Horry formed his regiment of the troops commanded by Major Lemuel Benson and Captains John Baxter, John Postell, Daniel Conyers, and James McCauley. Marion also gave the regiment nominally commanded by Colonel Adam McDonald, then a prisoner on parole, to Lieutenant Colonel Hugh Horry. Hugh Horry's subordinates included Major John James, Captain John James, Captain James Postell, and Captain James Witherspoon.

Then, with Colonel Hugh Horry and Captain James Postell, trusted Huguenot counselors, Marion formed a mess. For his mess sergeant he detailed Sergeant Davis whom he had rescued at Sumter's house. Aided by faithful Oscar, Davis became an enterprising caterer. To the almost constant diet of cornbread, beef, fresh pork, peas, and sweet potatoes, he added fish and game from the surrounding rivers and swamps.

As soon as the flurry over the organization of the Brigade had settled, General Marion turned to routine duties. His failure to obtain powder, flints, or cartridge paper from Harrington or Greene, or to capture any from the British supply boats, had disarmed half of his men. Because of this constant shortage of ammunition, he had decided to convert part of his infantry into cavalry. Commandeering every whipsaw in Williamsburg, he set the blacksmiths hammering out broad swords. Soon his horsemen were armed with long, keen, deadly weapons.

He then began recruiting. As his brigade increased, many of the Tories laid down their arms. Lukewarm patriots re-affirmed their allegiance, "again to reconcile themselves to the cause they had first adopted and deserted with the utmost reluctance," William James noted, "and became confirmed in their views, by his apparent abilities and successes."

The General also began collecting provisions for his troops. Upon their return to Snow's Island the salt-collecting detachment had reported that the plantations in All Saints were still unravished. The barns, cribs, and smokehouses were overflowing. Calling in Colonel Peter Horry, who knew every bypath on Waccamaw Neck, Marion concerted a plan to fill his larder. Writing out a set of orders similar to those given Captain Postell, he handed them to Horry. Then he reported to Greene: "I sent a detachment of 40 men under Peter Horry to collect boats and drive off cattle."

Colonel Horry, Captain Clarke, Sergeant McDonald, and their troops crossed the Peedee near the house of Widow Jenkins, cut through the Back Swamp, and crossed the Little Peedee at Potato Bed Ferry. Before noon they crossed the Waccamaw below Kingston and cantered down into the Neck. As they were passing along Socastee Swamp, Sergeant McDonald spotted a splendid charger hidden in the swamp. Surrounding the horse with his squadron, he seized him. Presenting him to Colonel Horry, he begged him to spare his own Janus.

As the detachment rode down Waccamaw Neck, whooping, halloing, and frightening the Tories, the advance patrol captured a man from the plantation of Captain William Allston. After questioning him, Horry placed him under guard. Soon afterward the party bivouacked near the Allston Plantation. During the night Captain Clarke, who knew the slave, cut his bonds and sent him home. "Behold a militia captain releasing a prisoner confined by his colonel commandant," exclaimed Peter Horry wrathfully, "and see the consequences!"

Unknown to Horry, there was a troop of enemy horsemen on Waccamaw Neck. Angered by the recent salt raid, Colonel Campbell had sent sixty-five of the Queen's Rangers across Winyah Bay. As the Negro was slipping back to Allston's about sunrise, these Rangers picked him up. Frightened by their threats, the captive betrayed the presence of Horry's troops. Campbell immediately headed for their camp. But Peter Horry was vigilant. He was already moving forward and had sent Captain Clarke and five troopers ahead as advance guard. Spotting them, Campbell blew his horn.

"Stop!" cried Clarke to his men. "Wait and you will see the deer, dogs, and huntsmen as they cross the road!"

Before the hapless militia Captain recovered from his dream of chasing deer, some twenty of Merritt's veterans had put his party to flight and were hacking at his head. He surrendered. Colonel Campbell treated him with great courtesy and took his parole, only to see him take to his heels and disappear behind the brambles and jessamine vines of Waccamaw Swamp.

Alarmed by the noise of the scuffle, the rest of Colonel Horry's troops dashed up. They gave the Rangers a scattering blast of swan shot. At the sound, the captured horse bolted and threw Horry. Before he could run, a British sergeant bore down upon him with drawn sword. Fortunately, Horry's Continental uniform looked so much like that of a British lieutenant colonel that the Ranger gave him a puzzled look, lowered his saber, and left him unscathed. The green-coated Rangers then galloped away, and Horry supposed himself master of the field. Quickly he sent a detachment off with the prisoners. But to the Colonel's surprise, Campbell dashed up with his entire command. Before Horry could catch his horse and mount, his men had scampered. Sergeant McDonald, seeing his commanding officer unhorsed, gave him his pony and then sprang into the somber morass of Socastee. "The

Enemy had three men and four horses killed, and we took
two prisoners which proved to be the Queen's Rangers, we
had one man slightly wounded and two horses killed," Marion reported to Greene on January 14. "I have sent reinforcements to Col. Horry."

Colonel Campbell, who had planned to establish a post
near Bull Island in order to control the Waccamaw and the
Lower Peedee, returned to Georgetown. Horry trailed him
to Sand Hill Plantation. Finding himself among wealthy
Whigs with ample provisions, he paused and threw up a
small redoubt. But Marion recalled him. "He wrote me,"
said Horry, "that the open field was our play, that the enemy
knew better how to defend forts and entrenched places than
we did, and that if we attempted it, we should soon fall into
their hands."

The daring activity of Captain John Postell in impound-
ing rice, driving off livestock, and collecting horses nettled
Colonel Campbell. To end the rankling he sent handsome
young Captain James DePeyster, of the King's American Regiment, with twenty-nine grenadiers, to drive Postell from the
Lower Peedee. Captain Postell's father, seventy-year-old Captain John Postell, had been captured in the fall of Charleston. He had signed a parole, returned home, and since then
had lived quietly upon his plantation. As a salutory example,
DePeyster seized the Postell mansion, and his men stripped
the plantation. "My honor is all I have left," old Captain
Postell wrote Marion on January 14. "My family has been
reduced to beg their bread."

Instead of recalling young Captain Postell, Marion sent
Lieutenant King and fifteen men to reinforce him. "I would
have all the flats and boats you can collect, loaded with rice,
and sent to Mr. Joseph Alston's plantation, on Bull's creek,"
he said in supplementary orders carried by King; "and the
rice is there to be stored, and the boats kept going until all
that is beat out in your district is carried. From there I will
send for it up higher."

He then requested that Captain Postell obtain fifty slaves for General Greene. He ordered that all persons suspected of dealing with the enemy be arrested and sent to him for interrogation and judgment. "I beg you would give me intelligence of the movements of the enemy in Georgetown," he wrote with great objectivity, "and, if possible, their particular strength: what corps of horse and foot, and how many militia, and if there are any cannon mounted on their redoubt, and whether they are making any new works."

There was a secret reason for Marion's request for specific information about Georgetown. While the Swamp Fox had been harassing the enemy in eastern Carolina, two movements had gotten under way elsewhere. Each seemed routine in its inception, but they proved to be of vast strategic consequence in the dénouement of the American struggle for independence.

At his headquarters in Winnsboro, Lord Cornwallis was vigorously pushing his preparations to invade North Carolina. In order to drive Daniel Morgan back from the Pacolet River and remove the danger of an attack on Ninety-Six, on January 1, 1781 he sent Colonel Tarleton and twelve hundred men across the Broad River. With his usual impetuosity Tarleton started floundering through the creeks along the Enoree and Tyger Rivers, hoping to catch Morgan before he could escape across the Broad River. In loose coordination with Tarleton's advance, Cornwallis evacuated Winnsboro on January 8 and began marching the British Army slowly toward King's Mountain. He expected Leslie to overtake him with the reinforcements brought down from the Chesapeake.

The second movement was the approach of Lieutenant Colonel Henry Lee and his Legion.

"I have put Major Lee's corps under marching orders," Washington wrote Greene in October when he ordered him to the command of the Southern Department, "and as soon as he is ready, will detach him to join you."

After outfitting his Legion in elegant style, Henry Lee,

promoted to Lieutenant Colonel by Congress, started creeping southward. He lingered in Richmond until December 15. Then, by easy marches averaging about ten miles a day, he passed along the wintry roads of North Carolina. "Colonel Lee is near at hand," Greene wrote Marion on January 4, in guarded reference to their secret plans. "I beg you to have collected all boats fit for transportation, down as low toward Georgetown as you may think it safe to send for them, and to keep them in readiness until you hear further from me."

Light Horse Harry and his Legion arrived at Camp Hicks on January 9, officers and men looking as if they had just come from a parade. "Col. Lee arrived yesterday, with his Legion, about 260," Rutledge wrote the South Carolina delegates. "I like him very much and expect great service from his corps."

Greene wrote Marion: "I wish your answer respecting the practicability of surprising the party near Nelson's." Then in routine fashion, he reported: "By the last accounts Lieut. Col. Tarleton was in motion, with about one thousand troops, towards Gen. Morgan, who is in the fork of Broad river."

At last able to spare the Continentals that Marion needed to stiffen the morale of his militia, Greene hustled off Colonel Lee down the Peedee. But the green uniform of his legionnaires, almost identical with those of Tarleton's Green Horse and Simcoe's Queen's Rangers, frightened the Whigs. They would tell him nothing about Marion's camp. So the Colonel halted at Bass' Mill on Catfish Creek and sent Major John Rudolph with a squadron to locate the elusive Swamp Fox.

As Lee's famed Continentals approached Snow's Island, Marion became perturbed. He realized that campaigning with young Harry Lee would raise delicate problems of command. The Carolina militia, with their loose discipline and their disdain of the regulars, would not take orders from the Virginian. And so, while Lee was still at Bass' Mill, the

Brigadier General settled the question of seniority. "Should I join in duty with him," he replied to a memorandum from Greene, "I expect to command, not from the Militia Commission I hold, but from an elder Continental Commission."

As Lee drew near, Marion sent an officer under a flag to Georgetown. His mission was ostensibly to return some letters captured from Major Irvine and to arrange a prisoner exchange. But his instructions were to spy out conditions in Campbell's headquarters and to observe the state of the British garrison. Colonel Campbell received him civilly. "A Captain Clark of yours fell into my hands at the Waccamaw," he wrote Marion. "I have a right to expect he will come and surrender himself as a prisoner of war; if he has any spark of honour, he must, from my own generosity to him, think it a duty."

Lord Rawdon was alarmed by Colonel Lee's march from Camp Hicks with the finest combat team in the American Army. He feared that the maneuver foreshadowed an attack upon Camden. With Tarleton beyond recall and Lord Cornwallis drawing away toward King's Mountain, he begged Leslie to remain with him for a few days. This delay in the march of the reinforcements had startling consequences. Instead of rushing on and cutting the Cherokee Road, thus forcing Morgan to retreat, Cornwallis waited for Leslie at Hillhouse Plantation on Turkey Creek. "I fear Morgan has too much the start of you," he wrote Tarleton on January 16. "Leslie will join me tomorrow or Thursday."

Unaware that Cornwallis had changed their plans, Tarleton was vigorously pushing his corps westward. By swimming his horses and passing his men on foot logs, he crossed the swollen Enoree and Tyger Rivers. Crossing the Pacolet at Easterwood Shoals, before breakfast on January 15 he struck the American camp. Morgan immediately retreated to Burr's Mill on Little Thicketty Creek. On the night of January 16 he camped on an eminence known as the Cowpens.

At two o'clock on the morning of January 17 Tarleton be-

gan a rapid advance toward the Cowpens. Just before day
an American patrol discovered his approach and dashed
away to warn General Morgan. The General began forming
his lines of defense. Near the foot of the hill he established
a cordon of skirmishers. About 150 yards above them he
posted Colonel Andrew Pickens and his Carolina militia.
Among the oaks and the chestnuts across the ridge of Cowpens he stationed the Continentals commanded by Colonel
John Eager Howard. And in a depression behind the ridge
he hid Colonel William Washington and his dragoons.

Tarleton reached Cowpens about sunrise. Immediately he
began marshaling his troops, the blended redcoats and green-
coats forming a colorful line. On his far left stood Major
Timothy Newmarsh's 7th Regiment. The two hundred recruits that the Swamp Fox had frightened so badly, while
Major McLeroth was shepherding them through Santee
Swamp, were nervous and trembling. At Tarleton's command the British line began advancing, while their two cannon sprayed the hillside with grapeshot. Uphill they charged,
their officers shouting: "Give them the bayonet!" After Pickens' militia fell back, Tarleton ordered Major McArthur's
Highlanders to turn Howard's right flank. In wheeling to
meet McArthur's attack, the Continentals fell into confusion. They then began retreating. Sensing victory, Tarleton
threw everything into action, his infantry surging toward
the Americans, his line straggling in tumultuous disorder.

Morgan chose a new position and, as the Continentals
reached it, Howard shouted: "Face about! Give them one fire
and the day is ours!"

The Continentals came sharply about. They loosed a with-
ering blast of buckshot from the hip. Shouted Howard: "Give
them the bayonet!"

Panic seized the British line. The recruits of the 7th Regiment threw themselves on the ground and bellowed for quarter. Howard's troops charged through the hole they left in
the line and began rounding up the British infantry. They
captured both Newmarsh and McArthur, with their entire

regiments. Banastre Tarleton saved only his Green Horse from the debacle.

"I have the particular pleasure to congratulate you on the entire defeat of the enemy under Lt. Col. Tarleton," Greene exultantly wrote Marion on January 23. "Major Giles this moment arrived, brings the glorious intelligence."

Greene requested Marion to forward "this important intelligence" to Colonel Lee. "If he has not attacked Georgetown, I wish he could transmit it to the garrison." But even while the General was writing, Light Horse Harry and his Legion were moving toward Georgetown. On the evening of January 22 Captains Patrick Carnes and Michael Rudolph camped beside the militiamen on Snow's Island. At dawn they embarked ninety men in the flat-bottomed boats confiscated by Captain John Postell and, guided by Marion's rivermen, set off down the Peedee, with ninety miles of winding, icy river between them and Georgetown. All day and night they paddled and rowed and drifted. Before day on January 24 they reached the mouth of the Peedee River and concealed themselves on a small island at the head of Winyah Bay.

As soon as the water-borne contingent was under way, Marion began calling in his scouts, patrols, and detachments. "Particular circumstances make me desire that you will immediately march all the men under your command to join me at the Kingstree," he wrote Captain Postell; "you must proceed by forced marches until you come up to me, for no time is to be lost."

Having collected his men, on the evening of January 24 Francis Marion, with Henry Lee beside him, galloped down the road from Kingstree. But because of the bad roads they were late in reaching Georgetown. Before their arrival the infantry had begun operations. About midnight Captains Carnes and Rudolph left their island hideout, crossed the bay, and went ashore at Mitchell's Landing. Dreading delay and the danger of discovery, they raced along a rice field dam until they came to the edge of the village. But instead of charging directly against the silent redoubt, the Captains made the mistake of deploying their troops on lesser objectives. Captain Rudolph posted his men along an adjacent street to prevent entrance to or exit from the fort. And Captain Carnes dashed toward headquarters to capture the British officers.

The surprise was perfect. Carnes found Colonel Campbell in bed, fast asleep. He shook him. The Tory officer opened his eyes sleepily, blinked, and then stared at the American soldier standing over him, his bayonet poised at his chest. Campbell stammered a surrender and Carnes took his parole.

While Carnes was securing the Commandant, Lieutenant James Cryer and his militia charged on after the other officers. They found Adjutant Crookshanks and Major Irvine "sound asleep," as Horry noted, "at a tavern belonging to a genteel family, with whom they had spent the evening with great hilarity." Hearing the noise made by the soldiers surrounding the tavern, Major Irvine sprang from bed, grabbed his pistol, and ran out on the piazza. He fired once. Then, as he was raising his hands in surrender, Lieutenant Cryer spitted him on a bayonet. Cryer had never forgotten the five hundred lashes he had received on orders from Irvine.

Cryer jerked his bayonet free and started in pursuit of Crookshanks. But the daughter of the tavern keeper, having heard the shooting and cursing and struggling, ran out on the piazza, threw her arms around the Major's neck, and screamed: "Save Major Crookshanks!" Mercifully, Cryer lowered his bayonet and accepted the Major's surrender. He then left the lovers in trembling embrace.

As soon as Marion and Lee arrived with their cavalry, they dashed into the village. Everything was orderly and going according to schedule. Captain Carnes had achieved his objective. Captain Rudolph had his men correctly posted. But not one British soldier had appeared. None had come to the rescue of the Commandant. None had tried to gain entrance to the redoubt. The little fort, its fraise and palisade menacing in the half-light, looked impregnable. Without battering rams and scaling ladders, the assailants were helpless. Lee did not wish to sacrifice his infantry in direct assault. Marion knew better than to try to storm a fort with his militia. And so, with daylight breaking and their men becoming targets for sharpshooters, Marion gave the signal to withdraw.

"My force was inadequate to the assault of the enemy's enclosed works," Lee reported to Greene next day. Soon after their troops had gone into bivouac at Murry's Ferry, Marion reported: "Colonel Lee informed you yesterday by express of our little success on Georgetown, which could not be greater without artillery." Then, in fraternal admiration, the Swamp Fox wrote: "Col. Lee's Interprizing Genius prom-- ises much."

The crushing defeat of Tarleton stirred Greene's imagination. He thought of cutting boldly across the trail of Cornwallis and attacking Ninety-Six. "I wish to have your opinion upon the practicability of crossing the Santee with a party of three or four hundred horse, and whether they would be much exposed by being in the rear of the enemy," he wrote Marion on January 25, seeking the Partisan's help in the enterprise.

Marion thought the idea of crossing the Santee, riding around the enemy while cutting his lines and disturbing his rear, and then meeting the army for an assault on Ninety-Six, too daring to try with his militia. They were good at patroling and excellent on forays, with their thrust, parry, and escape. But if taken on long campaigns, beyond the known and loved, they would simply desert.

Instead of encouraging Greene's idea, the Swamp Fox decided that he could do greater damage with his militia if they remained near the Santee. "You will cross Santee river with twenty-five men, and make a forced march to Watboo Bridge, there burn all British stores of every kind," he wrote Captain John Postell in an order dated January 29 at Cordes' Plantation. He also ordered the Captain to burn the stores and wagons at Moncks Corner on his return from the Lower

Cooper. With merciless candor he wrote, "bring no prisoners with you." Then, calling in Major James Postell, he gave him a similar order to select about forty men, cross the Santee, sweep northward, and burn the stores accumulated at Colonel William Thomson's Plantation on the Congaree River.

While awaiting the return of the Postells, Marion and Lee began planning to attack the weak garrison at Fort Watson. But they were courting disappointment, for Greene suddenly changed his entire strategy. Instead of threatening Camden or developing his plans for capturing Ninety-Six, on the morning of January 28 he called in all of his field detachments and turned the command of the army over to General Huger. Then, with a guide, a sergeant, and three mounted militiamen, he rode off to the Catawba, to join Morgan who was retreating ahead of Cornwallis.

Greene's recall found Lee at Cordes' Plantation. Immediately Light Horse Harry put his Legion under marching orders. Early on the morning of January 31, without learning the outcome of the raids of the Postells, he set out in pursuit of the Amerian Army moving northward from Camp Hicks. Francis Marion watched Henry Lee march off on the road to Kingstree. He liked the Virginia cavalier. He envied him his Legion, with its discipline, its smartness, and its zeal. He had expected great accomplishment from their cooperation. Now he felt frustrated. The Continentals were gone. Nor was the Grand Army ever likely to stand on the banks of the Santee.

But he did not mope long. The Postells returned from their raids across the flooded Santee. They had acted with great gallantry. Major Postell had burned a large quantity of military stores at Manigault's Ferry, five miles above Nelson's. Captain Postell, after destroying the stores at Wadboo, had surprised the depot at Keithfield, near Moncks Corner, and burned fourteen wagons loaded with clothing. Warmed by the success of the brothers, Marion wrote a cheerful report to General Greene. "Give my particular thanks to Major and Captain Postell, for the spirit and address with which they executed your orders over the Santee," Greene wrote from Guilford, North Carolina, on February 11. And then, basing his decision upon the tradition of seniority, he continued: "General Sumter is desired to call out all the militia of South Carolina and employ them in destroying the enemies' stores and perplexing their affairs in South Carolina. Pleased to communicate and concert with him your future operations."

CHAPTER XI

Blood on the Sampit

SOON AFTER the departure of the Continentals under Light Horse Harry Lee, the Swamp Fox dismissed most of his militia and, with the nucleus of his Brigade, retired to Snow's Island. Here he waited further word from Greene. Instead of orders from the Commander, however, he received an unexpected letter from General Sumter. The ailing Gamecock had lost no time in obeying Rutledge's orders to call out the militia in South Carolina. He believed that a swift move to the Congaree and the capture of the British depot at Fort Granby would provide supplies for a campaign. A foray down the Santee would raise the standard of a general revolt. And so on February 16 he and his Brigade marched toward the Congaree.

"Hurry of business obliges me to be laconic," Sumter wrote Marion from his camp in front of Fort Granby on February 20. "I arrived at this place yesterday morning about four o'clock. Shortly after, attacked the fort, with which I have been ever since engaged. Everything hitherto favorable, and have no doubt but I shall succeed, if not interrupted by Lord Rawdon, who, I know, will strip his post as bare of men as possible to spare, to obviate which, as far as may be in your power, it is my wish that you would be pleased to move in such a direction as to attract his attention, and thereby prevent his designs."

Francis Marion was not enthusiastic about Sumter's strategy. From information gathered since the raids of the Postells, he knew that Balfour had reinforced the posts and that it would take more than Sumter's militia to collapse the British supply line. But as the junior Brigadier, he obeyed the orders of the senior. Moving his camp to Indiantown, he sent his scouts to collect the militia. They, too, were less than enthusiastic and few heeded the call of the Swamp Fox.

In the meantime Lord Rawdon sent Colonel Welbore Ellis Doyle and the New York Volunteers to the relief of Fort Granby. At the approach of the British, Sumter called off his men and retreated down the Congaree. Next day he surprised the post at Belleville, Colonel Thomson's plantation thirty-five miles below Fort Granby. After cutting all approaches and seizing the boats, he tried to carry the stockade by assault. The defenders drove off his men. Leaving a strong detachment to continue the siege, the Gamecock marched on for two miles and went into bivouac at Manigault's Ferry. But Major McIntosh, with a fresh detachment from Camden, crossed the Congaree and drove Sumter's men from Belleville. As pressure mounted, Sumter decided to cross the Santee. Putting his men in canoes and swimming his horses, he escaped to the eastern bank. On February 28 he wrote Marion: "Passed the river last night at Mrs. Flud's."

The Gamecock immediately moved against Fort Watson. Rashly, without proper reconnaissance, he struck at high noon. As his militia charged through the fennels and the hawthorn bushes, the defenders opened with their muskets. Man after man tumbled into the stubble. When the survivors began to falter, Sumter called off the attack. Hastily retreating to Farr's Plantation, he encamped near his own home at the Great Savannah.

"I think it advisable that we form a junction, or at least approach so near each other as to cooperate upon the shortest notice," Sumter wrote Marion from his camp at Farr's. ". . . I hope it will not interfere with any plan that you might have laid to come this way. From the idea I have of the state of things in this quarter, I think it expedient for you to proceed to this place. I shall wait impatiently for the happiness of an interview with you."

But on March 1 General Sumter learned that Colonel Watson was mobilizing overwhelming forces at Fort Watson for the purpose of removing him from Farr's. Without waiting for the laggard Swamp Fox, the Gamecock abandoned his camp. Resolute and daring, he then began a desperate venture. Swinging clear of Fort Watson, he led his troops to his plantation in the High Hills. Boldly he set about bringing off his wife and son. Young Thomas was able to ride with the men, but Mary Sumter, eight years her husband's senior, had been a paralytic for years. Undaunted, Sumter strapped a mattress across the back of a horse, set her on it, and seated a Negro woman behind her. He then headed across forty miles of pine barren to the Bradley Plantation beyond the Black River.

"Yours of the 2nd instant has this moment come to hand, I am very sorry to be so far out of the way of meeting with you at a time when there is the greatest occasion for it," Sumter replied to a letter from Marion on March 4. "I shall therefore remain at or near this place for that purpose, and beg that you may come this way with all possible speed, if not convenient with all your men to facilitate an interview, please to come with a few."

All next day Sumter waited impatiently. Early on the morning of March 6, having given up hope of seeing the junior Brigadier, he started moving northward. As his entourage was passing between Scape Hoar Creek and Ratcliffe's Bridge over Lynches River, they stumbled upon the troops of Major Thomas Fraser of the Loyal South Carolina Regiment. Both sides began firing. Never was a militia brigadier in a worse dilemma. His men began retreating and his wife and son were caught between the lines. He shouted encouragement to his men. He drew Mary out of the line of fire. And he made the woods ring, bellowing: "Lie down, Tom! Lie down!"

"Frazer yesterday fell in with Sumter (who was advancing this way) between Scape Hoar and Radcliff's Bridge," Rawdon informed Watson on March 7. "A smart action ensued, in which the enemy were completely routed, leaving ten dead on the field and about forty wounded. . . . Sumter fled across Lynch's Creek and continued his retreat northward."

Lord Francis Rawdon, field commander of the King's forces in South Carolina since the departure of Lord Cornwallis, decided that the time had now come to crush Marion. For this he initiated a double-pronged drive. He ordered Colonel Watson to march down the Santee and attack Marion in front. At the same time he sent Colonel Doyle to the eastward, with orders to march down the Peedee, cross Lynches River, and cut off Marion's retreat.

Early on the morning of March 5 Colonel Watson, with his regiment of Guards and Harrison's Provincials, marched from Fort Watson. Soon he turned down the Santee Road. In late afternoon he went into bivouac below Nelson's Ferry. But that evening Captain Zach Cantey spotted the camp, reconnoitered it, and galloped away to warn Marion.

General Marion had already passed Murry's Ferry on his way to meet Sumter. He realized that this was the supreme attempt of the British to drive him from the Low Country. He knew that Watson's Buffs was one of the crack regiments of the British Army. His militia would now have the bloodiest kind of fighting, man to man, gun to gun, sword to sword. They would be entirely on their own, for there was no chance of any reinforcements. Colonel Lee was with Greene far to the north. General Sumter was on his way back to the Waxhaws.

But Francis Marion did not hesitate. His men would be fighting to prevent the enemy from overrunning their farms and plantations, destroying their homes, and leaving their families destitute. In such circumstances even raw levies will fight heroically. So he ordered an immediate advance. Next morning he ambuscaded his troops at Wiboo Swamp, a difficult pass on the Santee Road about midway between Murry's and Nelson's Ferries.

Soon the British marched into view. Always suspicious, they halted to reconnoiter. Out rode Watson to survey the scene of the coming struggle. Out rode Marion to face his opponent. Here, across a quarter mile causeway spanning the muck and morass of Wiboo Swamp, were arrayed in symbol the powers of the Old World and the New. Watson, towering and majestically uniformed, sitting a splendid charger, and backed by a disciplined regiment of Britain's finest soldiers, faced a little smoke-dried Huguenot, thin and ragged, sitting a sorrel gelding he had taken from his enemy, and backed by untrained, poorly armed men in homespun.

Watson opened the battle. Ordering Colonel Henry Richbourg forward, he sent him and his Loyalist horsemen thundering over the causeway. Expecting this maneuver, Marion ordered Peter Horry and his horsemen to meet them. After a brief skirmish on the narrow roadway, both sides recoiled. Throwing the rest of his troops across the highway, Marion again ordered Horry to charge. Watson's regulars held. His artillerists unlimbered their field pieces, and a fusillade of grapeshot sent Horry's cavalry reeling backward. At that moment Watson threw in the Tory dragoons under Major Sam Harrison.

Gavin James, powerful of frame and fierce of courage, turned back to dispute Harrison's passage. Mounted on a gray horse and armed only with musket and bayonet, he threw himself directly in the path of the dragoons. Their foremost man he dropped with buckshot. Before he could reload, a dragoon rushed him with his saber. James slew him with his bayonet. Another, charging to aid his comrade, received the same dripping bayonet. In falling he seized the barrel of James' gun, and for fifty yards in his retreat Gavin dragged the dying Tory.

As Harrison's dragoons had now crossed the causeway, Marion threw in the rest of his cavalry. Led by Captains Conyers and McCauley, they drove the Tories back across the

Wiboo. In hand-to-hand fighting Captain Conyers slew Major Harrison. Seeing his horsemen beaten off, Watson ordered the Guards to clear the passage. Forward they stepped, towering, silent, their helmets set, their red coats shining, and their bayonets glittering. Knowing that his men could not stand before such veterans, Marion called to them to mount and follow him in quick retreat.

Before Marion could break camp at Cantey's Plantation next morning, he received a bundle of correspondence forwarded from Snow's Island by Colonel Hugh Ervin. In it was a letter from Captain John Saunders, of the Queen's Rangers, who had succeeded Colonel Campbell as the Commandant in Georgetown. According to Marion's instructions, Ervin had released four prisoners from the Bull Pen at Goddard's, and sent them to Georgetown with an escort under Captain John Postell and Lieutenant William Futhey. This was a mistake. Postell had broken his parole given at Charleston and the British were eager to capture him. In spite of the flag of truce, Saunders ordered an armed guard to seize Postell; Futhey outran the party and escaped.

"Captain John Postell being a prisoner of ours, cannot receive orders from you, and he has forfeited all claim to lenity by a violation of his parole," Saunders wrote Ervin on March 6. "I cannot indulge him in returning to the country until I receive directions."

Marion read Saunders' letter with growing anger. He would allow no mistreatment of his officers and men as long as he could exact retaliation. He decided to make his position and future policy clear to his enemies. To Captain Saunders he wrote:

March 7th, 1781

Sir:

By my orders, Lieut. Col. Irvin sent Capt. John Postell with a flag to exchange the men you agreed to, and am greatly surprised to find you not only refused to make the exchange, but have violated my flag by taking Capt. Postell prisoner

contrary to the laws of nations. I shall immediately acquaint
the commandant at Charles Town, and, if satisfaction is not
given, I will take it in every instance that may fall in my
power. I have ever used all the officers and men taken by me
with humanity; but your conduct in closely confining Capt.
Clark in a place where he cannot stand up, nor have his
length, and not giving him half rations, will oblige me to retaliate on the officers and men which are, or may fall in my
hands, which nothing will prevent but your releasing Capt.
Postell immediately, and using my officers as gentlemen and
your prisoners as customary in all civilized nations.

I am, sir, your obedient servant,

Francis Marion, B.G. Militia.

Believing that Saunders had overstepped his authority,
Marion reported the affair to Lieutenant Colonel Balfour,
the senior British officer in South Carolina. "I sent Capt.
John Postell with a flag to exchange some prisoners, which
Capt. Saunders, commandant of George Town had agreed to,
but contrary to the laws of nations, he seized Capt. Postell
and detained him as a prisoner; as I cannot imagine his conduct will be approved of by you, I hope you will give orders
to have my flag discharged, or I must immediately acquaint
Congress of this violation, the ill consequences of which is
now in your power to prevent. . . . Lord Rawdon and Colonel
Watson have hanged three of my Brigade for supposed crimes,
which will make as many of your men in my hands suffer."

Marion decided that the safest way to have his letter delivered to Balfour was to send it to Colonel Watson. Although
his messenger rode under a flag of truce, the Swamp Fox sent
a heavily armed party to escort him to the Wiboo.

He wrote:

Inclosed is a letter which I wish may be forwarded as soon
as possible. I make no doubt but you will be surprised to see
a flag sent at the head of an armed party. The reason of it is
that Capt. Saunders, commandant of George Town, has violated the laws of nations, by detaining, taking and imprison-
ing Capt. Postell who carried prisoners to exchange, which

was agreed to by him. The hanging of men taken prisoners, and the violation of my flag will be retaliated, if a stop is not put to such proceedings, which is disgraceful to all civilized nations. All your officers and men which have fallen in my hands have been treated with humanity and tenderness; and I wish sincerely, that I may not be obliged to act contrary to my inclinations, but such treatment as my unhappy followers whom the chance of war have thrown in my enemies' hands meet with such; such must those experience who fall in my hands.

Without deigning to reply, next morning Colonel Watson resumed his march down the Santee Road with Marion slowly backing away just beyond the range of the cannon. Reaching the Cantey Plantation, he turned aside and encamped. Mortified by Marion's charges and resentful of his threats, he began a spirited letter. He, too, would make his own position and that of his Majesty's Army clear to the rebels.

It is with less surprise that I find a letter sent by you in all the apparent forms of a flag of truce, attended by an armed party who concealed themselves within a certain distance of a place that pointed itself out for the delivery of it, than to see the contents of it exhibit a complaint from you against us for violating the law of nations. I believe, sir, it would be as difficult for you to name an instance of breach of it in his Majesty's troops, as it would for them to discover one where the law of arms or nations has been properly attended to by any of your party. . . . You say it was agreed that an exchange of prisoners should take place at George Town, and that Capt. Postell went with a flag for that purpose, in consequence of that agreement. But I conceive it was not agreed that a man on parole to us should become our enemy. Capt. Postell was, I understand, taken at Charles Town, and admitted to the country on parole, if so, his detention, with all its consequences, is justifiable.

"Marion made him no reply," said William James, "but gave orders to his nightly patroles, to shoot his sentinels and cut off his pickets. Such retaliation was to be expected; and thus raged the civil warfare."

After resting and reorganizing his corps, Colonel Watson started slowly forward, Harrison's Tories in the lead, followed by the Guards in column. Marion was waiting, his horsemen already backing off along the Santee Road. At Mount Hope Swamp he broke down the bridge and left Hugh Horry and McCottry's riflemen to prevent any crossing. Watson's artillerists swept them from the opposite bank with grapeshot, and the Guardsmen plunged across the stream.

Down the road crept the pursuer and the pursued. Marion crossed the road leading from Murry's Ferry to Kingstree, and Watson plodded relentlessly after him. Marion ignored the road leading to Lower Bridge, only twelve miles away, and retreated on toward Georgetown. Watson followed. But as the Swamp Fox had expected, the crafty Briton soon wheeled his column back to strike at Kingstree.

This was the decisive moment of the campaign. If Watson's troops should cross Lower Bridge, they would hold the heartland of the Whig resistance in their grasp. Calmly Marion called Major James. After some instruction, he dispatched the Major with seventy men, thirty of them McCottry's sharpshooters, to hold the bridge. Away James galloped, and by taking short cuts through fields and woods he soon outdistanced Harrison's dragoons. Crossing the Black River at a ford below the bridge, he seized the prize. In a few minutes he and his men had removed the planks from the middle span and set fire to the stringers on the eastern end. He then posted McCottry's riflemen at the abutment so that they could shoot directly across the ruined bridge. He posted the musketeers upon the flanks, to support the marksmen and defend the ford. By the time Major James had finished deploying his men, Marion and the remainder of his Brigade had come up and forded the river. The Swamp Fox was highly pleased with James' tactics. He sent Captain Thomas Potts and his Peedee company to reinforce the defenders.

With the rest of his troops he took his place some distance in the rear and silently awaited the approach of the enemy.

At Lower Bridge the east bank of the Black River was low and swampy. The west bank was a high bluff, and the roadway descended through a ravine to the bridge. As the river was only fifty yards wide, just the proper distance for a sharpshooter, Watson would not send his men into the defile. Instead, he ordered his artillery to clear a passage across the ford. But the gunners could not depress their guns enough to cover the east bank. The grapeshot whistled harmlessly through the air or struck about midway the trunks of the pine trees. When the gunners attempted to wheel their cannon to the edge of the bluff, McCottry drove them back in disorder.

John Watson had the blind courage of a Guardsman. Forming his troops in column, he sent them toward the ford. At their head marched a captain, his sword waving encouragingly. As the Briton reached the ford, Captain McCottry sprang up, took careful aim, and fired. Four men ran to bear off their captain. All four shared his death. Baffled, with his tired troops huddled around him, John Watson remained in the field above the ford until evening. Then he moved to John Witherspoon's plantation, a mile above the bridge. He established his headquarters in the Witherspoon home. To his unwilling Whig hostess he confessed: "I have never seen such shooting before in my life."

Francis Marion went into bivouac among the saplings on the ridge below the ford. He knew that the struggle for Lower Bridge had been only a skirmish, brief and hot, but with less than a dozen killed and wounded. Only fifty yards of shoulder-deep black water separated the Guards from the conquest of the Santee country. But neither courage nor heroism beyond the call of duty could have driven the Williamsburgers from Lower Bridge. Simple countrymen in blue jeans, armed with squirrel rifles, fowling pieces, and homemade swords, they had thrown back one of the finest regiments of the British Army.

Before daybreak the Swamp Fox was up, rousing and deploying his troops. He pushed Captains McCottry and Conyers across the Black River with orders to pick off Watson's pickets and sentinels. All day the mounted riflemen and musketeers hovered around Witherspoon's, just out of range and yet keeping the enemy in an uproar. Red-headed Sergeant McDonald set a mark for the snipers. Climbing unperceived into one of the large oaks that lined the avenue to Witherspoon's house, at three hundred yards he put a rifle ball through the knee of Lieutenant George Torriano of the Guards.

Captain Daniel Conyers was no less heroic. In love with Mary Witherspoon, he circled around the plantation full of jealous fear as well as patriotic fervor. Mary followed his every movement with beaming eyes. John Watson was a gentleman, humane and chivalrous; but after the wounding of Lieutenant Torriano, some of his officers became insolent and insulting. One of them made sarcastic remarks about Conyers. Having no other weapon, Mary pulled off her heavy walking shoe, smote him in the face, and cried: "There's Captain Conyers now. Go out and fight him, you coward!"

That afternoon Colonel Watson moved half a mile farther up river and encamped in a large open field on the Blakely Plantation. Even here, without trees and buildings to conceal them, Marion's snipers kept the British regulars in a panic. Thus besieged, with his wounded suffering from lack of medical attention, the Colonel shelved his pride and wrote a letter to Marion:

Blakeley's, March 15th 1781.

Sir:

The very extraordinary method you took of sending the letter I received from you, makes it rather difficult to guess in what way you mean to carry on this war, and therefore induces me to take the mode of addressing you through a neutral person. The bearer is a little boy of John Witherspoon's. We have an officer and some men wounded, whom I should be glad to send where they could be better taken care of. I wish therefore to know if they will be permitted to pass without interruption from any of your parties to Charles Town.

I am, sir, your very humble servant,

John Watson

Francis Marion was thoroughly angry over the Postell affair. He resented Watson's "in what way you mean to carry on this war." But still he believed in being humane. He scribbled a reply and sent it back to Blakely's by young Witherspoon.

Sir:

Yours of this day's date I received. In answer, I wish to carry on this war as usual, with all civilized nations. The violation of my flag is a good reason to believe it may a second time be done, and oblige me to act as I did; when my flag is released, I will have faith, and act in the usual way. If Capt. Postell was a prisoner, it was no reason for the violation of my flag, especially when it was sent to exchange prisoners agreed to by Capt. Saunders; but this matter I expect Lord Rawdon will set to rights. The enclosed letter gives me reason to believe it, and you may be assured I will not act in any other way, than what I find is done by the British Troops. If you will send me the number of wounded you wish to send to Charles Town, I will send you a pass for them.

I am, sir, your obedient servant.

Francis Marion

Watson answered immediately, sending the name of Lieutenant Torriano ". . . wounded, 3 soldiers and a Negro servant to attend the Lieutenant; 6 soldiers wounded, and 2 soldiers to attend to the wounded soldiers." He, too, was angry, and he detailed some of the atrocities committed by members of Marion's Brigade. In his renewal of the epistolary war, he complained that one Maynard and several companions had whipped a number of Tories. He said that Captain Conyers had whipped Thomas Wise and John Stillwell almost to death.

Next morning General Marion wrote a pass, saying: "One officer and six wounded men with six attendants of the

British troops, are permitted to pass to Nelson's Ferry, from thence to Charles Town unmolested." In his letter of transmittal he launched into his favorite themes: the barbarity of British house-burning and the villainy of Tory plundering.

"Your mentioning that you wished to carry on the war as usual with civilized nations led me to mention the circumstances I did," replied Watson. . . . "The burning of houses and the property of the inhabitants who are our enemy is thought right and is customary in all countries."

"I have received your letter of the 7th instant, respecting the retention of Capt. John Postell, when charged with a flagg of truce to George Town, and complaining of the same as a breach of the law of nations," Colonel Balfour wrote Marion on March 12. "The best answer I can return to which is transmitting you his parole. . . . I therefore trust when you represent this case to your Congress, you accompany it with so essential a document as the enclosed."

Balfour sent his letter to Captain John Saunders for delivery. "As to Postell you have done perfectly right," he wrote Saunders. He advised the Captain in delivering the letter "to be careful who you send; a non-commissioned officer will be best, for fear he detains the person sent on account of Postell."

Instead of heeding Balfour's warning, Saunders called in Cornet Thomas Merritt and asked him to deliver the letter. In uniform and bearing a white flag, the Cornet rode off to find Snow's Island. At Britton's Ferry he asked the ferryman to serve as his guide. On their way through Britton's Neck the two stopped at Widow Jenkins'. As they chatted, not suspecting that Merritt was a Tory, for Light Horse Harry Lee's troops also wore green uniforms, the widow asked her cousin if it would be safe for her sixteen-year-old son James to go down into Waccamaw Neck for salt.

"No, madam," exclaimed Merritt, "for we have a great big thing there we call a galley."

Elizabeth Britton Jenkins was proud of the fact that when

she was a girl her father had sent her to school in Charleston. "Sir, I suppose you think you have got so far back in the country that no one here ever saw a galley but you," she snapped. "I'll have you know, Sir, that I have been as well raised as yourself."

As the Cornet reached for his cap, Elizabeth turned upon the ferryman. "Cousin Britton," she said angrily, "if you cannot bring any better company with you than this, you'd better keep away."

She slammed the door, and the two men sheepishly rode off toward Dunham's Bluff. Upon their arrival, the Captain of the Guard invited Merritt into the redoubt. He immediately sent a messenger across the Peedee to Colonel Hugh Ervin. A short time later the Colonel and an armed party shot across the river in canoes. Before the astonished Cornet understood what was happening, he had been tied up and was on his way to Snow's Island.

"I am greatly astonished to find you should have detained an officer of ours sent out with a flagg of truce to you, and acting under its sanction," Balfour wrote Marion on March 21. "This is an impaction of the laws of nations and of war, as you complain in the case of Captain Postell; and such a one as if not immediately addressed, I shall be obliged to punish in the most exemplary manner by the severest retaliation."

Marion never replied. He had made it perfectly clear that if the British injured one of his officers, he would inflict a similar injury upon a British officer. Should they hang Captain Postell, he had Cornet Merritt ready for a similar hanging.

While Marion had been contending with Saunders and Balfour, Colonel Watson had continued quietly at Blakely's, his men slaughtering the hogs and cattle and his horses eating the corn and fodder from the neighboring plantations. But he was in one of the regions of America most hostile to England. Almost every thicket concealed an enemy scout and every plantation housed a spy, either white or black. Daily he expected to hear of the approach of Colonel Doyle, but messengers could not break through Marion's cordon. As his situation was becoming desperate, he decided to retreat.

"I shall be this afternoon with the corps under my command at George Town, or very near it, and will be obliged to you to have some forage ready for us, rum, salt and flour, if you have it, we shall want to take with us," he wrote Saunders on March 28. He then sank his dead in an abandoned rock quarry, loaded his wounded on wagons, and marched his troops off at double time down the road to Georgetown. At Ox Swamp, seven miles below Blakely's, Watson found the bridges destroyed and trees across the causeway. With his passage blocked and a boggy swamp on either side of the roadway, and with Marion closing rapidly upon his rear, the Colonel had to fight or run. He chose to escape. Wheeling abruptly to the right, he sent his troops racing across fifteen miles of pine lands to the Santee Road.

"We followed close in the rear," said Peter Horry, "constantly firing on them from every thicket and swamp; and often, in spite of their field pieces, making false charges. Never did I see a body of infantry ply their legs so briskly! The rogues were constantly in a dog trot, except when they occasionally stopped to give us a blast, which they did from their whole line."

As the British approached the Sampit River, nine miles from Georgetown, Marion sent Horry's horsemen dashing ahead to throw the planks from the bridge. After destroying the bridge, Horry posted Lieutenant Scott and his riflemen about fifty yards beyond the river. But the Guards never slackened their pace. When they reached the Sampit, they formed in close column and plunged across. Frightened by the glittering English bayonets, Scott ordered his men to hold their fire. "Infamous poltroon," cried Horry as soon as he could reach the Lieutenant, "where is that *hetacombe* of robbers and murders due to the vengeance of your injured Country?"

While the advance guard of the British was forcing the Sampit, Marion fell upon the rear guard with fury. There was heavy firing. Colonel Watson rallied his men, but a sharpshooter killed his horse. Quickly mounting another, he ordered his artillery to open with grapeshot. When Marion's horsemen wheeled back from the cannon fire, Watson loaded his wounded into two wagons, left twenty dead upon the field, and plunged across the ford, the blood on the wagon floors tinging with red the dark waters of the Sampit. Late that evening he camped at the Trapier Plantation. He was very bitter. "They will not sleep and fight like gentlemen," he complained of Marion and his men, "but like savages are eternally firing and whooping around us by night, and by day waylaying and popping at us from behind every tree!"

CHAPTER XII

Raid of Colonel Doyle

GENERAL MARION and his victorious troops bivouacked beside the Sampit. They had scarcely spread their blankets upon the ground, however, when a messenger from Kingstree rode into camp. He brought alarming news. Colonel Welbore Ellis Doyle and the New York Volunteers had crossed Lynches River at Witherspoon's and were already floundering through the swamps toward Snow's Island. The Swamp Fox was surprised. He had not expected the enemy to attack his rear. With all of his energies bent on defeating Watson, he had neglected his scouting and knew nothing of Doyle's approach. He had also failed to leave guards at the ferries. Now he was a full day's march from the threatened action, and his men were exhausted from riding and fighting. He would have to wait until daybreak before starting his return.

On Snow's Island, in the meantime, Colonel Hugh Ervin had begun preparing for a desperate stand. He chose the best men from his small band of cripples, convalescents, and prisoner guards and posted them along Clark's Creek. He then set the rest dumping guns, ammunition, and other stores into the stream.

Colonel Doyle knew that his advantage was only momentary and he pressed rapidly forward. With his Tory guides he followed the trails of Marion's horsemen through the swamps and by mid-morning reached the boat landing on

Clark's Creek. By extending his regiment along the bank he outflanked Ervin's men and his marksmen began driving them from the boats. After a bloody skirmish in which they killed seven and dispersed the other defenders, the New York Volunteers began crossing to the island.

Cornet Merritt, still a prisoner at Goddard's, saw the hurrying and scurrying and destruction of military supplies. He realized that the King's troops were threatening the island fortress. When he heard the sound of firing, he thought that Watson had defeated Marion and was coming to rescue the British prisoners. Soon he learned the truth. Colonel Ervin came to Goddard's house and released him. The Colonel gave the enemy Cornet sidearms and placed him in charge of some twenty-five prisoners and some fifteen Americans too ill to flee. Ervin then abandoned Snow's Island.

"Marion's repository of stores and plunder on Snow's Island, was a few days since destroyed by a detachment of his Majesty's forces, under Lieut. Col. Doyle," *The Royal Gazette* of Charleston said on April 4, 1781. "Some days since, Mr. Meriott of the Queen's Rangers, made his escape from the rebels, and brought in with him, to Georgetown, 25 men; this event is the more fortunate, as he had been unjustifiably seized, in breach of a Flag of Truce, by Marion, under the pretext of retaliating the detention of Postell. . . ."

Colonel Doyle captured Snow's Island without losing a man. His exploit was brilliant, climaxing a tedious march in which he had blazed a trail from McCallum's Ferry to the Peedee Road. He had forever destroyed the usefulness of Marion's favorite rendezvous. But he realized that he was in an inextricable trap should the Swamp Fox suddenly appear. As soon as his men had set the torch to Goddard's house, barn, and bins, and to the shelters of the camp, he recrossed Clark's Creek and retreated as rapidly as he had come. That afternoon he recrossed Lynches River and encamped on the north side of Witherspoon's Ferry.

Francis Marion returned swiftly from the Sampit. In his

march through Williamsburg he passed near the homes of many of his followers. Here the magnificent corps, with which he had defeated and driven off the Buffs, began to disintegrate. Simple, undisciplined farmers, whose very existence depended upon their crops and cattle, his militiamen slipped off without leave or compunction, to spend a few hours with their families. When the Swamp Fox went into bivouac at Indiantown, he had only seventy men in his Brigade.

There was no time for dejection or recrimination. At daybreak he sent out his scouts. They returned to report that Doyle had sent his foragers to the Whig plantations south of Lynches River. Immediately Marion ordered Colonel Hugh Horry and the mounted infantry to drive them away. Finding them ransacking a plantation, Horry's men shot down nine and captured sixteen of the fleeing marauders. After the skirmish Captain McCottry and his riflemen pursued the enemy to Witherspoon's. There they caught the frantic rear guard scuttling the ferry boat. After frightening them from the sinking craft, the sharpshooters fanned out along the river's edge and began an intermittent fire into Doyle's camp. The balls from their long rifles carried well and, although Lynches River was flooded and wide, they toppled a private and an officer of the Volunteers.

Doyle replied vigorously. With an infantryman's trust in fire-power, he formed his men along the bank and they delivered a terrific volley. The sound echoed up and down the river and the smoke from the black powder settled upon the water, but the buckshot only cut the twigs from the trees which sheltered the Americans. Outgunned, the British struck their tents, mounted, and trotted off toward the Peedee.

While McCottry's rifles were routing Doyle, in his camp at Indiantown Francis Marion waited, silent and discouraged. He had been in the field day and night for three weeks. Seven months had passed since he took command of Major James' militia. Some of the volunteers were now dead. Many others had been wounded. The homes of nearly a hundred had been burned. He had just driven Watson from Williamsburg, it was true. But the Guardsman would certainly return, and Doyle would march to join him. Micajah Ganey, miraculously recovered from McDonald's bayoneting, was afield, again mustering his Tories and thirsting for revenge. And on the only day when such a feat was possible, the enemy had destroyed the little hoard of military supplies he had so carefully stored on Snow's Island.

Marion's men were also discouraged. The forces mounting against them seemed overwhelming. As they sat around their campfires, they began to talk as if certain ruin would overtake them. Finally Colonel Peter Horry said to his troops: "I am ashamed to hear you talk like this. We have often, before now, seen as heavy clouds hanging over us; and yet, with heaven's blessing on our arms, those clouds have been dispersed, and golden days restored. And who knows we may shortly see it so again?"

In spite of his fervor, Colonel Horry was disturbed. Soon he slipped away to confer with Marion. He found the Swamp Fox pacing to and fro before his campfire, his hands clasped behind his back and his head bowed in meditation. "General Marion," began Horry, "I am sorry to tell you that our men are now so few, especially since, according to report, we shall soon need so many."

"Why, that is the very thing I have been grieving at," Marion replied. "But it will signify nothing for us to stand here sighing and croaking. Pray go and order a muster of the men, that I may say a few words to them before they all run off and leave me."

Francis Marion was unshaved, unshorn, and haggard. His faded Continental uniform was dirty and tattered. Only the polished silver crescent on his old scorched leather cap retained any luster. But as he stood under the budding trees at Indiantown, he was the guerrilla chief supreme, who fights on beyond hope because his soul is imbued with the sacredness of his cause.

"It is not for words to express what I feel, when I look

around upon your diminished numbers," Marion began after
Horry had assembled the remnants of the brigade. "Yesterday I commanded 200 men——whom I gloried in; and who,
I fondly thought, would have followed me through any dangers for their country. And now, when their country most
needs their services, they are nearly all gone! And even those
of you who remain, are, if report be true, quite out of heart;
and talk that you and your families must be ruined if you
resist any longer! But, my friends, if we are to be ruined for
bravely resisting our tyrants, what will be done to us if we
tamely lie down and submit to them?"

He reminded them of the taxes demanded by the Royal
Government. He spoke of the outrages of the King's troops
and their Tory allies. Knowing that his words stirred bitter
memories, he pictured the desolation wrought by Wemyss
and Tarleton.

"Now my brave brethren in arms," he concluded, "is there
a man among you, who can bear the thought of living to
see his dear country and friends in so degraded and wretched
a state as this? If there be, then let that man leave me and
retire to his home——I ask not his aid. But, thanks to God,
I have now no fears about you: judging by your *looks,* I feel
that there is no such man among us. For my own part I look
upon such a state of things as a thousand times worse than
death. And God is my judge this day, that if I could die a
thousand deaths, most gladly would I die them all rather
than live to see my dear country in such a state of degrada-
tion and wretchedness."

As Marion spoke, his men began to cheer. With reviving
enthusiasm they shouted that they would fight beside him
until death. Inspired by the renewed courage of his men,
he cried: "Well, now, Colonel Doyle, look sharp, for you
shall presently feel the edge of our swords!"

Calling in his outposts and detachments, Marion passed
word for his men to prepare for marching. As soon as they
had fastened their blankets, coats, and bags to their saddles,
he broke camp. Avoiding Witherspoon's, where flooded

Lynches River was wide, deep, and swift, he led them upstream and struck the swamp behind the James Plantation.
Although the night was dark, he reined Ball into the water
and began splashing and plunging toward the opposite shore.

"As God was pleased to have it, none of us lost our lives,
though many did their great coats, blankets, and saddles, and
some few their guns," said Peter Horry. "As to myself, I must
needs say, I was never so near the other world in my life.
For, as we were borne along the stream in the dark, my horse
and I were carried under the limb of a tree hung with wild
vines, which soon caught me by the head like Absalom, and
there held me fast, dangling in the furious flood, while my
horse was swept from under me——I hallowed some time like
a lusty fellow, without getting any answers, which made me
begin to think my chance was bad."

While Horry dangled from the limb, his horse swam safely
across the river. But he lost the Colonel's saddle, and with it
his blankets and clothes. "But God be praised," continued
Horry, "for, as I was near giving out, a bold young fellow of
the company overheard me bawling, and having the advantage of a stout horse, dashed in and took me safely off."

In the dark others were cast up on ridges which the freshet
had turned into islands, and there they sat shivering until
dawn. Then they swam their horses on across the stream.
Safely ashore, they built fires and dried their clothes and
firearms. Comfortable again, they poured dry powder into
their guns, primed them anew, and set out in quest of Colonel Doyle.

All day they trailed him along the muddy River Road. In
the late afternoon they passed through Hopewell community. After dark they reached the home of a noted Whig
named Burch. The old man had seen Doyle. On the previous afternoon the New York Volunteers had camped on
his plantation. During the evening an express from Lord
Rawdon had raced into camp. Immediately Doyle had destroyed his heavy baggage and moved rapidly off toward
Camden.

Events had taken a mysterious turn. Something had disturbed the British. Doyle had retreated to Camden, sixty
miles to the west. Watson was still in Georgetown, seventy
miles down the Peedee. Quick to grasp a strategic advantage,
Marion decided that a favorable time had come to undertake
a long meditated project. Issuing a call for his militia to come
to him at Burch's, he waited until his Brigade was at full
strength. Then, crossing the Peedee at Mars Bluff, he encamped on the sand ridges of Wahee Neck, abreast of the
settlements of Ganey's Tories.

After his brush with Major Fraser, Sumter had rambled
on to the Waxhaws. Here Mary Sumter collapsed and could
ride no farther. Leaving her at the home of John Barnett,
he rode on to his camp. He found his troops mutinous and
out of control. They accused him of leading them on a wild
goose chase. They raised such a clamor against him for de-
ceiving them as to Lord Rawdon's strength that he was
obliged to enter into a long vindication of his conduct.

While still smarting from his failure, Sumter received a
letter from Governor Rutledge. On the point of leaving
Greene's army for a visit to the Congress in Philadelphia, the
Governor wished to leave his militia generals in harmony.
"I am persuaded of your utmost attention and that you will
pursue such measures as may be most serviceable to the
State," he wrote the senior General, "and I doubt not that
General Marion (to whom I have wrote) and General Pickens
(to whom I have spoke on the subject) will forward your
views to the utmost of their power."

With his command of all the militia of South Carolina
newly confirmed by the Chief Executive, Sumter immediately turned his attention to the only corps still in the field.
From his camp in the New Acquisition, on March 28, he
wrote a long letter to Marion. Although attributing his bad
temper to his old wound and confessing "I write in so much
pain as hardly to know my own meaning," the senior gave
the junior Brigadier a thorough upbraiding. "It was exceed-

ingly mortifying to me, after so much pains taken to be deprived of a conference with you," he began. "My unfortunate failing therein and withal finding contrary to my expectation, that you had neither men, or surplus of any kind, and the force I had with me but small and from many causes decreasing, rendered my retreat at once both necessary and difficult."

Instead of praising Marion for outmaneuvering and defeating the finest British regiment still in South Carolina, Sumter charged him with allowing his troops to plunder. "I find that the disorders are prevalent in your Brigade," he scolded, "which have for some time past been practised in the frontiers with such avidity as to threaten the state with inevitable ruin."

Sumter then sketched a hazy plan for raising "several Regiments of Light Dragoons upon the State establishment." Without suggesting means for purchasing dragoon horses, saddles, bridles, swords, pistols, or blankets, he wrote: "I therefore request that you would be pleased to have raised in your Brigade two Regiments agreeably thereto."

The Gamecock then ordered the Swamp Fox to be prepared to cooperate the next time he should come rambling down the Santee. Without knowing the conditions in Marion's Brigade or the strategic reasons for his position, he wrote peremptorily: "At present it is my desire that you should have a position higher upon Black River, which is very necessary to not only prevent the stock from being drove to Camden, but also to facilitate my plans and designs on the west side of the Wateree——The more speedy your movements are, the better they will answer."

As commander of the only American corps in the field in South Carolina, Francis Marion resented being told to step lively. Although Sumter had not spelled out his scheme for enlisting ten-months men on the state establishment, from rumor Marion knew the proposal for paying them with confiscated goods and forfeited lands, especially with slaves seized from the Loyalists. Knowing this to be simple plundering,

illegal and subversive of morality, he refused to have anything to do with the plan.

But this was no time to start bickering. Lieutenant Colonel John W. T. Watson was relentless. He did not tarry in
Georgetown. After resting the Buffs and renewing their
clothes and armor, he marched again in search of Marion.
Passing through lower Williamsburg, he crossed the Peedee
at Britton's Ferry. About 9 o'clock on the morning of April
7 he reached the home of Widow Elizabeth Jenkins. The
Buffs camped in the dry sand field, and during the day Watson used the Jenkins home for his headquarters. He was affable, and the widow was polite. She asked him if he had any
difficulty getting from the ferry to her place, as Marion's
men had torn up the bridges.

"No, madam, I never find any difficulty when on British
ground. Do you not believe, madam, the British will conquer
the Americans?"

"No, sir, I wish I were as sure of heaven as I am that the
Americans will gain their independence. And I think, sir,
you believe so, too."

Watson flushed angrily. "No, madam, I do not believe it,"
he replied. "How many sons have you among the rebels,
madam?"

"None, sir. The King has rebelled against us, and not we
against the King."

"Well, madam, how many sons have you with Marion?"

"I have three, sir," she replied, thinking tenderly of Francis, Samuel, and Britton. "I only wish they were three thousand!"

"Send for them. Send for them, madam," Watson pleaded.
"Let them take protection, marry wives, and settle their
plantations."

"Will you stay, sir, and protect them?"

"No, madam, indeed," he replied angrily. "It is enough
for me to pardon them."

"Pardon them, sir! They have not asked it yet."

Out-argued by the plucky widow, Watson cooled off and became affable again. He asked her to have a glass of wine with him. As he raised his glass, he cried: "Health to King George!"

Mrs. Jenkins drank the toast. She then slyly refilled the glasses. As he raised his, she cried: "Health to George Washington!"

Watson made a wry face, but being a gentleman he cheerfully toasted the American Commander in Chief. He then tried a gambit. "Well, madam, have you heard that General Marion has joined Lord Rawdon?"

"No, sir, indeed I have not," she retorted, knowing that John Jenkins had seen Marion the previous day.

"Well, madam, it is a matter of fact."

"Sir, I don't believe it."

"Why, madam, you might as well tell me I lie."

"I don't say you lie, sir," she said with a smile, "but I don't believe it."

By then Colonel Watson was so vexed with his unwilling hostess that he moved a mile across the sand fields and camped at John Rae's for the night.

When the redcoats had gone, which was just before night, James Jenkins, the youngest son of the widow, came out of hiding in the Back Swamp. He had spent the day with his cousin John Jenkins whom Colonel Peter Horry had scouting Watson's advance. Young Jenkins was enraged by the actions of the Buffs. "Upon my return home, I found that they had made sad havoc among the beeves, having killed no less than seven, which they skinned and left on the spot, because too poor for them," he wrote in his autobiography. "The garden was almost entirely destroyed. My mother had a considerable quantity of fine English peas, but they stood no chance before those hungry soldiers."

Next morning Colonel Watson marched away and on April 9 encamped on Catfish Creek, only a few miles from Marion in the Wahees. In anticipation of flogging the Tories,

Marion's militia had trooped in, and he had five hundred effectives in his Brigade. But with the Guards, Harrison's Provincials, and Ganey's Tories, Watson commanded nine hundred men, the most formidable British army still in the field in South Carolina.

The Swamp Fox now made one of his most serious decisions. He dared not throw his Brigade against Watson's superior force. During the campaign against the Buffs, his men had almost exhausted their powder and shot, and Colonel Ervin had thrown the reserve into Clark's Creek. While he had enough ammunition to harass the Tories, he did not have enough to fight the Guards.

Faced with almost certain defeat, Marion decided to retreat into North Carolina and draw Watson after him. Perhaps he could join the army under Greene. To prepare for the move, he called a conference of his field commanders. Colonels Peter Horry, Hugh Horry, John Ervin, and James Postell came in, and with them came Majors John James, John Baxter, and Alexander Swinton. Marion spoke earnestly. He pointed out the strength of the enemy and their own numbers. He noted their lack of powder. He then detailed the tragic consequences of a defeat. "If I should retreat into the upper parts of North Carolina, or if necessary to the mountains," he finally asked, "will you follow me?"

"Yes," they replied in firm, unanimous voice. Should he march to join Greene, they would follow him even to Virginia.

As Marion had anticipated, the decision was not popular with the Brigade. "General," Captain Gavin Witherspoon enquired soon after the conference, "had we not better fight Colonel Watson before any more Tories join him?"

"My friend," replied Marion, "I know that would be best, but we haven't the ammunition."

"Why, General, my powder horn is full," said Witherspoon, holding his horn up for inspection.

"Ah, my friend! You are an extraordinary soldier," answered Marion, "but as for the others, there are not two rounds to a man."

As Witherspoon walked toward his camp, he saw Ensign Baker Johnson, a Whig of great enterprise, dismounting from a lathered horse. "Gavin," cried the Ensign, who had just returned from a long scouting trip and was famished, "for God's sake give me something to eat."

"What news, Baker?" asked Witherspoon, as he set a pot of cold rice before the scout.

"Fine news," Johnson answered between bites. "Fine news. I saw a great number of Continental troops, horse and foot, crossing Drowning Creek."

"Come and tell the General," exclaimed the Captain.

"No!" retorted the Ensign. "I'm starving. If the General wants the news he must come to me."

Understanding the vagaries of scouts, Marion good-humoredly went to question Johnson. Great indeed were the tidings. Colonel Henry Lee and his Legion had returned to South Carolina. As the jubilant men crowded around to hear about the return of the Continentals, they heard the sound of a distant drum. A few minutes later Captains James Conyers and Edmond Irby rode into camp at the head of a detachment of Lee's magnificent dragoons.

"This will be handed you by Capt. Conyers, who will inform you what we have contemplated," began a letter from General Greene, dated at Deep River on April 4. "He is sent forward to collect provisions for the subsistence of the army, and I beg you will assist him in this necessary business. The army will march tomorrow, and I hope you will be prepared to support its operations with a considerable force."

After Marion had finished the letter, Conyers began briefing him on Greene's strategy. At Guilford Courthouse Lord Cornwallis had driven the American Army from the field, but his victory was Pyrrhic. Too weak to fight again after losing one-third of the British Army, he had begun retreating toward Wilmington. After the rear guard under Tarleton had broken down the bridge over Deep River, Greene had given up his pursuit and encamped at Ramsay's Mill. There the Commanding General of the Southern Department had begun planning a daring venture. On March 30 he had written Sumter, mentioning the retreat of Cornwallis, the expiration of the enlistments of the militia, and the difficulty of subsisting the army. "All these considerations have determined me to change my mind and push directly in South Carolina," he said. "I beg you will therefore give orders to Generals Pickens and Marion to collect all the militia they can to cooperate with us."

Light Horse Harry Lee, burning to distinguish himself, remembered the British posts along the Santee and the plans that he and Marion had made while resting at Cordes'. With great affection, he remembered the Swamp Fox for his courage, understanding, and humanity. When Greene decided to return to South Carolina, the intrepid Virginian requested to be sent back to the Low Country. Greene consented. And on April 4 Colonel Lee and his Legion, resplendent and vigorous, hurried off in the direction of the old rendezvous on Snow's Island.

News of the return of the Continentals caused panic in the British camp beside Catfish Creek. The powerful force that the Swamp Fox had feared to' attack disintegrated. When Ganey's Tories learned that Lee's dragoons were passing through their settlements along the Little Peedee, they began squandering. Colonel Watson was no less distressed. Deserted by the Loyalists, he was afraid of getting caught between Marion and Lee. With a Guardsman's fortitude he ordered a retreat. After the Buffs had burned their baggage, he dumped his two field pieces into Catfish and started back toward Britton's Neck at double time. With his hardened veterans moving like cavalry, he was soon beyond danger. Scarcely pausing, he crossed the Little Peedee at Potato Bed and the Waccamaw at Greene's and then pushed relentlessly down Waccamaw Neck. After crossing Winyah Bay in British boats, he sent his exhausted troops back into quarters in Georgetown.

CHAPTER XIII

Capture of Fort Watson

Francis Marion was elated by the dramatic reversal of fortune. The return of the Continentals explained the recent mysterious behavior of the British. Lord Rawdon had already received information that Cornwallis was retreating toward Wilmington. Expecting Greene to move against Camden, he had begun calling in his detachments. He had recalled Doyle from the Peedee with all possible haste. To scatter the Whig militia, he had sent Watson again through Williamsburg. And to augment the ranks of the veterans, Colonel Balfour had called out Ganey and his Tories.

Intuitively Marion knew the enemy's next move. Colonel Watson would try to reach the concentration in Camden. Again master of partisan strategy, the Swamp Fox decided to thwart him. Sending Lee directions to cross at Port's, where he would find flatboats, he led his Brigade back across the Peedee at Mars Bluff. Swiftly down the muddy River Road he marched, his horsemen ramping and their morale soaring. But not for long. As the Brigade jogged through Williamsburg, the men began peeling off like young homing pigeons leaving a flock. By the time Marion reached the bridge over the Black River, he had only eighty men to throw between Watson and Camden.

As Marion waited, Colonel Lee and his Legion reached the Black River on April 14. There was great rejoicing in both corps. Scarcely has there ever been a greater contrast in men than that between Marion and Lee. And yet there was complete harmony in their motives and actions. The semiliterate, ragged little Huguenot looked up to the stately Virginian with superb education, polished manners, and fierce courage. The cavalier revered the Carolina Brigadier for his unyielding patriotism and his defiance of adversity. Without quibble about rank, Henry Lee placed himself and his Legion under the command of General Marion.

The two had much to discuss, for glorious events had taken place since their separation at Cordes' Plantation. Marion recounted his struggle with Watson from the Wiboo to the Sampit. Lee told of his overtaking the army and retreating with it into Virginia, his dragoons in the rear guard constantly skirmishing with Tarleton's Green Horse. When Greene had turned back into North Carolina, he had served in the advance guard. He traced the movements in the Battle of Guilford Courthouse, a magnificent action which sent the British Army staggering to Wilmington for help and left Greene the master of the Carolinas.

Soon the commanders began planning their next campaign. Still disgruntled over his long tactical and epistolary contest with Colonel Watson, Marion was eager to march directly to Georgetown and pick a fight with the Buffs. Lee disagreed. He knew Greene's strategy for the recovery of South Carolina and argued that such a diversion would throw them too far east for effective cooperation in an attack on Camden. Marion yielded. They then decided to carry out the attack they were planning just before their separation.

At daybreak on April 16 Colonel Lee sent Major John Rudolph and his dragoons toward Georgetown to watch and report the movements of Watson. At the same time Marion started his Brigade and the infantry of the Legion marching rapidly toward Nelson's Ferry. That evening they entered the old field behind Wright's Bluff, erected their tents among the flowering haws, and laid siege to Fort Watson.

Next morning, when Lieutenant James McKay, Commandant of Fort Watson, saw the blended green uniforms of the legionnaires and the blue jeans of the militia, he began surveying his defenses. He had plenty of food. He had great stores of ammunition. The morale of his men was high. So he loaded his muskets——Colonel Watson had hauled off the two cannon——and answered his besiegers shot for shot.

General Marion soon realized that he would have to reduce the fort by strategem rather than by force. Observing that the defenders were drawing their supply of drinking water from Scott's Lake, he sent a detail of McCottry's riflemen to take position between the stockade and the water's edge. As the bluff was treeless and there was no other protection, the sharpshooters simply sat down out of range of the enemy's muskets and dared anyone to come for water. But McKay was equal to the challenge. Instead of succumbing to fright, he set his troops digging a well just inside the stockade. On April 18 they struck water.

Colonel Lee thought of a better plan. Learning that Greene was only a day's march from Camden, he wrote the General: "I beg you will send down a field piece; it can get to me in one day and a half. I will have horses to meet it, which will go off from me on hearing from you. All things are well here, and no possible danger can attend the sending the cannon. Five minutes will finish the business, and it can immediately return."

As Marion and Lee waited for the cannon, with the siege going well and only an occasional roar of a musket or crackle of a rifle to remind them of war, smallpox struck their camp. The militiamen, who had never been inoculated, began deserting, the healthy hoping to escape the dreaded plague and the ill to seek medical care and nursing. Samuel Jenkins came down with the disease, and Britton tenderly carried him home to Britton's Neck.

The Swamp Fox was a genius at open warfare. He excelled in hiding in a rendezvous and planning a sortie. He was at his best in swiftly advancing, attacking, and then rapidly re-

treating. But besieging a post and just waiting for the enemy
to surrender wore him out. As he sat before Fort Watson,
he began to droop. He took offense easily. As he watched his
militia dash into camp, spend a day or two, and then rush
off home again, he became indignant at their behavior. He
was infuriated by the flagrant conduct of Captain William
Clay Snipes.

During the fall campaigns, Captain Snipes, powerful, am-
bitious, but withal contentious, had distinguished himself
under Peter Horry. In the organization of Marion's Brigade
he had received no command. Disappointed, he rode up to
Camp Hicks and laid his grievance before Governor Rutledge. "Captain Snipes is desirous of raising men to the southward, westward of Santee, and requests to have command of
an independent company," Rutledge, who acted on insufficient information, wrote Marion. "I have no objections to
giving him a company . . . but I refer Capt. Snipes to you
for instructions."

Snipes did not wish to serve under Marion. Colonel William Harden, from near Beaufort, had begun recruiting a
regiment to harass the rear of the British. "Captain Snipes
has received an invitation from Col. Harden to join him on
the South of Charles Town with 150 men," General Huger,
acting for Greene, wrote Marion in endorsing the Governor's
orders. "Capt. Snipes has permission to proceed on the expedition."

Snipes returned from Camp Hicks flaunting his new authority. Irritated by the interference with his command, on
February 6 Marion wrote a protesting letter to Huger. His
express caught up with the retreating army at Halifax, Virginia, and General Greene took matters into his hands. "I
have seen your letter to Gen. Huger," he wrote Marion, "and
am surprised that Col. Baker or Capt. Snipes should pretend
that they had my directions for crossing the Santee."

In spite of Greene's disavowal, Snipes continued making
trouble. When Marion called for more men to help reduce
Fort Watson, Snipes tried to prevent their going. Colonel

Kolb, slow but conscientious, mustered his men; but Snipes appeared among them, told them wild and disrespectful stories about Marion, and then ordered them off to join Harden. "I am informed you are taking all the young men that I have ordered to join Gen'l Marion, with you to the southward," Kolb finally wrote Snipes. "I must now beg leave to inform you of Gen'l Marion's orders against such proceedings, which I have just received, forbidding any persons leaving his Brigade without his leave."

The militant Captain brushed aside the Colonel's memorandum with a discourteous retort: "I received yours, and this will inform you that I have instructions from Gen'l Sumter, who commands General Marion, to raise men where I can, and as to Gen'l Marion's orders, in this case it avails nothing."

Colonel Abel Kolb wrote Marion on April 18, enclosing his letter from Snipes. He also complained that Lieutenant Lyons, of his regiment, had been mustering the men in his company and sending them to Sumter. "I saw Lyons yesterday myself, I asked him about the men that he had raised, he said that he had sent them to Gen. Sumter and that he would send every other man of the Regiment that he could recruit to him," Kolb said. "He damned himself if he would serve any officer but whom he pleased; that he disregarded any orders that might be issued to the contrary."

The squabble in his militia distressed the sensitive little Brigadier. After reading Kolb's letter, on April 18 he wrote Sumter. He complained of the calumny of Snipes and of the insubordination of Lyons. He was indignant at Sumter's interference with his militia. He did not accept "Sumter's Law" of paying regular state troops with plunder. In his irritation he even threatened to appeal the entire matter to Governor Rutledge.

The Gamecock replied on April 30. He denied any interference in the militia east of the Santee. Concerning Captain Snipes, he said: "Whether he gave a cause of umbrage, I know not, he was acting by no particular direction of me. If he has transgressed, he is amenable, and may be, as an officer, punished with great propriety, notwithstanding there is neither executive or legislative body in the State." To Marion's charge that he had abused the laws of the country, Sumter replied: "If I have done it, I think myself accountable and shall no doubt be called upon by the gentleman to whom you say you shall represent the matter, and if he is unacquainted with my motives and the steps I have taken, should be happy to have his opinion upon the head. To his judgment and authority I pay the greatest respect." And speaking as the senior, Sumter concluded: "As to the powers by which I act, they ought not to be called in question by any man, until gentlemen whom it might concern, had used proper means to obtain information."

As Francis Marion continued to besiege Fort Watson, trying to remove the friction in his Brigade and growing more silent and morose, he received a poorly concealed reprimand from his oldest and most respected friend in the army. "I have this day received information from Lieut. Col. Balfour in Charles Town, that your troops have been guilty of many cruelties upon the people in the country," General William Moultrie wrote him on April 16. "As I know you are well acquainted with the customs of war, and that your disposition will not countenance such cruelties, especially as it cannot answer any good purpose, I am therefore to request the favour, you will give such orders as will prevent private animosities from taking revenge at this time by such unwarrantable practices, as can only serve to disgrace the generous and the brave."

Light Horse Harry Lee, his own enthusiasm soaring, began to worry about Marion's flagging spirits. The Virginian was thoroughly sympathetic with the Carolinian. He knew of the hardships that the Brigadier had suffered. He was aware of the neglect that Congress, Greene, and Rutledge had shown the spearhead of their hopes. With the understanding of an experienced strategist, he realized that after Greene's retreat into North Carolina the Swamp Fox had saved South Carolina from being overrun by the British.

Colonel Lee resolved to bring Marion's situation to the attention of General Greene. On April 20, the day after Greene had reached his objective and encamped the army to the eastward of Camden, Lee wrote him. "I wish you would write a long letter to General Marion," he said. "His services demand great acknowledgements, and I fear he thinks himself neglected."

But Nathanael Greene relied on his Continentals and held little respect for the local militia. "The conflict may continue for some time longer; and Generals Sumter and Marion, and many others, deserve great credit for their exertions and perseverance," he wrote Washington after his arrival at Camden, "but their endeavours rather seem to keep the contest alive, than lay any foundation for the recovery of these states." He did not share Lee's enthusiasm. "You frequently hear of great things from Generals Marion and Sumter," he wrote Governor Reed of Pennsylvania. These are "brave and good officers, but the people with them just come and go as they please."

While besieging Fort Watson, the Swamp Fox became involved in one of the bitter tragedies of the Revolution. Inspired by Marion's example, Colonel William Harden came out of retirement during the winter and began raising a regiment. He visited Marion, received commissions for his officers, and set about recruiting. But the Whigs along the Edisto River were reluctant to join him. They were influenced by the example of Lieutenant Colonel Isaac Hayne.

When Sir Henry Clinton invaded South Carolina, Colonel Hayne raised a troop of cavalry and was soon afterward appointed Commandant of the Colleton County Regiment. After the fall of Charleston, he quietly returned to his plantation on the Edisto under the protection of the Articles of Capitulation. When Sir Henry revoked all such paroles, Hayne signed a stipulation "to demean himself as a British subject so long as the country should be covered by the British army." On a visit to Charleston he showed this paper to General Patterson, and the General refused him permission to return home unless he signed a declaration of allegiance to the King of Great Britain.

As Colonel Hayne was very popular, wealthy, and able, the Partisans were eager to arouse him again to action. Marion sent him a commission in the militia, but he returned it. "You will receive a letter from Col. Hayne with the commission," Harden informed the Swamp Fox on April 7. "You will hear his reasons for not accepting it. This gentleman has kept many from joining me on his staying on too much formality."

In spite of Hayne's not taking command of a regiment, Colonel Harden organized a considerable force and began campaigning. On April 14 he struck a Tory muster field at Four Holes, capturing and paroling a captain and twenty-five men. The next evening his men surrounded the home of Captain Barton and captured him and six privates. After skirmishing, bushwhacking, and running, he took Colonels Fenwick and Letchmere. He then moved on to Pocotaligo and laid siege to Fort Balfour. After surrounding the fort, Colonel Harden sent in Captain Harden to demand surrender. Colonel Fletcher Kellsal refused. Harden sent the Captain back with a warning that, if he had to storm the fort, he would give no quarter. Kellsal asked for thirty minutes to deliberate. Harden gave him twenty. At the expiration, Kellsal, eight other officers, and eighty-two men came out and stacked their arms under the abatis.

Colonel Harden's rampage so frightened the Tories that Balfour ordered Major Thomas Fraser and his dragoons to drive him off. Upon their appearance, Harden vanished in the swamps below the Salkehatchie. "I am obliged to haul off southwardly to collect all the men I can in those parts," he reported to Marion on April 18. He was still displeased with the reluctance along the Edisto and he needed some blank commissions. "I beg you will send some immediately with your orders, it seems they wait for Col. Hayne's, and he says he can't without a Commission, and is sure, if he turns out, that at least two hundred will join him, if so, I am very sure that this part of the country may be held."

Marion sent the commissions. Isaac Hayne organized his regiment and in the late spring again took the field. But, as he well knew, he was campaigning with a halter about his neck.

As soon as Greene received Lee's request for a field piece, he sent forward Captain Ebenezer Finley and a six-pounder. To escort the gun crew to the Santee he also sent Major Pinketham Eaton and his infantry. The Major promptly got lost. After wandering for a day in the direction of the Black River, he realized that he was on the wrong road and turned back toward Camden.

During the delay in the arrival of Finley's cannon, Marion began to despair of reducing Fort Watson. He knew that he could not take the bastion by storm. His militiamen were getting restless, having seen two of their comrades killed and six wounded without having done any visible injury to the defenders. As he was considering abandoning the siege, Major Hezekiah Maham, an ingenious Continental officer from St. Stephen's who had recently joined the Brigade, suggested a way to overawe the fort without cannon. After considering the Major's suggestion, the Swamp Fox sent some of his horsemen to scour the neighboring plantations for axes. He then set the woodsmen felling pine saplings. He had others carry the slender poles and dump them in a pile just out of range of the British muskets. During the evening Maham and a squad of volunteers began chopping, lifting, and settling the logs into an oblong tower. At a point higher than the enemy's rampart the Major laid a floor. He then reinforced the front with a shield of timber. Before cockcrow Marion tolled off his men, and the crack shots from McCottry's Rifles climbed into the crow's-nest of the prototype of the famed Maham towers.

At daylight on April 23 Lieutenant McKay found himself
looking up to a tower filled with sharpshooters. The buckshot from his muskets could not penetrate the logs, but the
bullets from the long rifles whistled into the fort. Afraid to
rise above the breastworks to fire, for a time he and his men
crawled around behind their palisade. Through the cracks
he saw Ensign Baker Johnson and Robert Lee, a volunteer
with the Legion, pull down a section of the abatis—while
the riflemen in the tower sprayed the enclosure with bullets.
Helpless, he watched the two pioneers start tearing at the
logs of the stockade while back of them stood Captain Patrick Carnes and the Legion infantry, helmets down and bayonets fixed, ready to charge through the opening and storm
the fort. He raised the white flag.

Captain Carnes entered the fort for a parley. Marion and
Lee agreed to offer generous terms to men who had defended
themselves bravely for eight days. They agreed to allow the
officers to sign paroles, to wear their swords, to remove their
baggage, and to wait in Charleston for regular exchange.
They treated the regular and the Loyalist troops alike as
prisoners of war.

For the first time since the invasion of South Carolina,
American troops had toppled a British strong point. Continentals and militiamen, working in harmony, had set a
pattern for reducing the chain of enemy posts along the Santee. As senior officer, General Marion wrote the official report of the capture of Fort Watson. The burst of work in
erecting the tower had been a tonic for his depression, and
the surrender of McKay had again fired his ardor. "The
officers and men of the Legion and militia performed everything that could be expected," he wrote with great enthusiasm, "and Major Mayham of my Brigade had in a particular
manner a great share of this success, by his unwearied diligence in erecting a tower, which principally occasioned the
reduction of the fort."

He praised the spirit and address of Ensign Johnson and
Robert Lee. "I am particularly indebted to Lieut. Col. Lee

for his advice and indefatigable diligence in every part of this tedious operation, against as strong a little post as could well be made on the most advantageous spot that could be wished for." Like a sterling soldier he concluded his report: "I shall march to the High Hills at Captain Richardson's plantation, where I will await your further orders."

While the Swamp Fox was triumphantly encamped at Bloom Hill, Captain William Richardson's plantation, General Greene wrote him the long letter suggested by Lee. "Your favour of the 21st has just come to hand," he said and then turned his reply into a panegyric.

> When I consider how much you have done and suffered, and under what disadvantage you have maintained your ground, I am at a loss which to admire most, your courage and fortitude, or your address and management. Certain it is no man has a better claim to the public thanks, or is more generally admired than you are. History affords no instance wherein an officer has kept possession of a country under so many disadvantages as you have; surrounded on every side with a superior force; hunted from every quarter with veteran troops, you have found means to elude all their attempts, and to keep alive the expiring hopes of an oppressed Militia, when all succour seemed to be cut off. To fight the enemy bravely with a prospect of victory is nothing; but to fight with intrepedity under the constant impression of a defeat, and inspire irregular troops to do it, is a talent peculiar to yourself. Nothing will give me greater pleasure, than to do justice to your merit, and I shall miss no opportunity of declaring to Congress, the Commander-in-chief of the American Army, and to the world in general, the great sense I have of your merit and services.

Marion was in a highly strategic position at Bloom Hill. He could quickly join Greene at Camden or he could march against Watson in Georgetown. His men could stop all shipping on the Santee River and his patrols could sweep in both directions along the Santee Road. So he began campaigning vigorously. He pushed the prisoners across the Black River to the depot in the rear of Greene's army. He then dis-

patched Colonel John Ervin and eighty men to Rafting
Creek to prevent the Loyalists from driving cattle and hauling provisions to Rawdon's commissary. Ervin's raid through
the High Hills, along Rafting Creek, and around the headwaters of the Black River, quieted the Tories. Threatened
with fire and sword, none dared leave for Camden. The
British troops quickly felt the loss of supplies, ". . . for want
of which, occasioned by the long interruption of our com-
municative," Lord Rawdon advised Cornwallis, "they suffered serious distress."

Lord Rawdon realized that if the victorious troops of Marion and Lee should join those of Greene at Hobkirk's Hill,
the American Army before Camden would be greatly superior to that of the British. So he decided to fight. With unexpected suddenness he marched his corps of nine hundred
veterans from Logtown at nine o'clock on the morning of
April 25 and began forming them for attack under cover of
the thick woods along Pine Tree Creek. He gave the order
to advance and his troops started toward Greene's camp. In
his movement he achieved tactical surprise, one of the most
desired of all military advantages. Provisions had just arrived
and Greene was eating breakfast when his pickets fired the
alarm. Most of his men were cooking. But neither the Quaker
General nor his troops panicked. Quickly he formed his defense. Calmly he sent every battalion to its proper place in
a straight line across the hill. He ordered his artillery into
battery behind the infantry. He sent the baggage to security
in the rear. And then he waited.

When the British reached the foot of Hobkirk's Hill, the
American infantry stepped aside, unmasking their cannon.
The gunners raked the enemy with grapeshot. As Rawdon's
advance faltered, Greene assumed the offensive. He tried
desperately to pinch off the advancing front by throwing his
troops against both of the British flanks. But Rawdon's musketeers beat off the attacks. Then, when the British moved
in counterattack, the fighting became general, confused, and
bitter, with the Americans slowly giving ground. As Greene's

troops fell back, Rawdon's surged toward the cannon on the hill. Captain John Coffin and his dragoons led the charge, but the defenders drove them back from the guns. At that critical stage, as the infantry of the Volunteers of Ireland and the New York Volunteers moved steadily uphill, Colonel Washington led his dragoons around the left flank and got behind the British Army. Instead of charging into the rear of the advancing infantry, however, he frittered away his advantage by capturing and paroling about two hundred doctors, surgeons, quartermasters, wagon masters, and waiters.

Under the pressure of the steady advance, Greene pulled back his artillery. Next he started his ammunition wagons to safety. Carefully he collected his wounded, and then began retreating. Moving slowly and defiantly, and pausing frequently to gather his stragglers, he covered only four miles by late afternoon. That evening he went into bivouac on Saunders Creek.

Lord Rawdon also had enough. Gathering up his wounded and leaving Captain Coffin to hold the field, he withdrew to Logtown. But Colonel Washington was waiting. Concealing his dragoons behind a thicket, he sent a weak detachment to lure Coffin's horse into ambush. After cutting them to pieces, Washington took undisputed possession of Hobkirk's Hill.

"We were obliged to retire and give up the field," Greene wrote Marion, "though without material loss." Although driven from the field, Greene was not daunted. "We are now within five miles of Camden," he continued, "and shall closely invest it in a day or two again. That we may be able to operate with more certainty against the post, I should be glad you would move up immediately to our assistance, taking post on the north side of town." After reflection he added, "I should be glad you would move up within seven miles of Camden." Although at times tactless in his comments, Nathanael Greene was warmhearted and magnanimous. With cordiality he wrote: "I congratulate you on your success against Fort Watson."

CHAPTER XIV

Ruckus at Motte's

GENERAL MARION and his Brigade lay encamped under the fresh green oak and hickory trees at Bloom Hill. Spring had warmed the High Hills and his camp was pleasant. The surrounding plantations were peaceful, the laborers working and singing cheerily. The fields were green with oats, wheat, and early corn, and the springing pastures were alive with calves, lambs, and pigs, feeding and frolicking around their dams. For two days, as the Swamp Fox relaxed and rested his men, the war seemed remote, but on April 28 General Greene sent him further orders.

"In my last I desired you to move up within 7 miles of Camden," Greene wrote, "but Capt. Conyers thinks that with 50 men below, at a distance of 15 or 20 miles, all the supplies can be as effectually cut off as if you were at a less distance, and that if you cross the Santee you can take all the posts upon the Congaree, and those posts that lie between Camden and the River."

Unfortunately, in his rambling letter, after setting Marion and Lee the task of subduing Fort Motte, Belleville, and Fort Granby, the General touched a spot already growing tender. "Get all the good dragoon horses you can to mount our cavalry," he pleaded. "This is a great object, and I beg you pay particular attention to it."

Upon Greene's suggestion that he move back fifteen or

twenty miles, Marion broke camp and marched from the High Hills to the Black River and bivouacked near Salem. "I am with General Marion, who has moved to this place, thirty miles from you, in consequence of your orders," Lee reported that evening. "I have my hopes that you will order me and Major Eaton to pass Santee, and to pursue the conquest of every post and detachment in that country."

The Partisans had scarcely camped at Salem when messengers raced in with tales of outrage and terror. The Tories had risen. As soon as Marion had recrossed the Peedee at Mars Bluff and Lee had ridden on to Port's Ferry, some of Ganey's more resolute militia had reassembled at their rendezvous on Drowning Creek. Colonel Abel Kolb, fearful of their marauding, had resolved to disperse them. Marching swiftly with the militia companies of Captains James Gillespie and Josiah Cantey, he surprised and routed them.

Embittered by Kolb's scourging, as soon as the Colonel and his militia withdrew from their settlements, the Loyalists assembled again. Kolb now determined to crush them. With the militia of Major Lemuel Benson and Captain Joseph Dabbs, he started again for the Little Peedee. At Hulin's Mill he surprised John Deer and Osburn McLean, among the most notorious of Ganey's followers. As the two bounded up and started running toward Catfish, Whig marksmen killed Deer and severely wounded McLean. Kolb's men then captured and hanged Caleb Williams, a desperate ruffian. Satisfied that he had shown the Tories a salutory example of Whig justice, the Colonel returned to his home on the Peedee.

But his killings only infuriated the Loyalists. They decided to retaliate and Captain Joseph Jones issued a call for volunteers. On April 28 some fifty assembled at Maidendown Bay. That afternoon they rode off toward the Peedee. Late that night they surrounded Kolb's home.

As the Tories closed in, Abel Kolb realized that he was in a fight to the death. In the barbaric civil war in eastern Carolina quarter was seldom asked or given. So he determined to exact the highest possible toll for his life. He handed muskets to the two Evans brothers, who were his guests for the night, and the three drove off the attackers with gunfire. But Captain Jones rallied his men and returned. This time he threatened to burn Kolb's house. Although the Colonel knew that he could not trust his enemies, in order to save his wife and children from the flames, he decided to surrender. He raised his hands and stepped through the door, but a violent Tory named Mike Goings shot him down as he crossed over the threshold. The Tories shot the Evanses and then began plundering the Kolb home. After seizing everything of value, they set a torch to the simple frame house. As the fire swelled and crackled and the Kolb family wept, John Jones, the Captain's brother, caught the Colonel's riding horse and swung a feather mattress across the saddle. Then, like triumphant Bedouins, their horses loaded with spoils, the brothers and their followers set off toward Catfish Creek.

Greatly distressed by the murder of Abel Kolb, Marion sent Colonel John Ervin and his regiment to punish Jones and his marauding thieves. He also began preparing his Brigade to return to Wahee Neck to stop malevolence and reprisal. Again he was frustrated.

After the return of General Greene to South Carolina, Brigadier General Marion and his Brigade became a part of the American Army. Instead of running, dodging, and hiding, to attack when least expected, they now moved only when ordered to move and spent the interval waiting for further orders. Under these conditions the Brigade began to wither. South Carolina law provided that the militia serve only thirty days when called up. Many in the Brigade had already served sixty and at Salem they were too near to resist the temptation to go home to look after their families, cattle, and crops. So they began deserting.

Unfortunately, at this critical time, Greene was conducting a secret correspondence with Colonel Lee. In his eager way

Light Horse Harry reported that Marion could spare sixty
horses.

"You would promote the Service greatly if you could furnish us with sixty or eighty good dragoon horses," Greene
immediately wrote Marion, pressing the nettling question
which the Swamp Fox had ignored. But he was affable and
concluded cordially: "I am sorry for Colonel Kolb's death,
and the necessity there is for detaching a part of your regiment."

"Keep a good lookout for Tarleton," Greene cautioned
Marion on May 1. "I think it is probable he is on the Georgetown route." The General, however, was only guessing. From
his spies he had learned that on April 25 the Royal Navy
had ferried the British Army across the Cape Fear River and
that, with Tarleton's Green Horse leading his van, Lord
Cornwallis had marched from Wilmington. He could not
learn the direction of his march, but Cornwallis would probably return to his base in South Carolina. In his uncertainty
Greene continued: "Should Tarleton get into Camden, Lieutenant Colonel Lee with his force must join us immediately."

General Greene was worried. When he left Lord Cornwallis retreating toward Wilmington, he had evolved a broad
strategy for the recovery of South Carolina. He ordered General Sumter to move into the country between the Wateree
and the Broad Rivers, there to collect food and forage and
to pin down the enemy. He sent Colonel Lee to join General
Marion in knocking over the string of posts from Georgetown to Fort Granby. And he marched his army to drive
Lord Rawdon out of Camden. After that he could force
Colonel Cruger, at the end of a dead supply line, to abandon
Ninety-Six.

But Greene's army had not been strong enough for the enterprise. He had failed to drive Lord Rawdon from Camden;
instead, he had been driven back to Rugeley's Mills. Still
uncertain of the direction taken by Cornwallis and fearful
of getting caught between Tarleton and Rawdon, he aban-

doned his camp at Rugeley's. After crossing the Wateree above Camden Ferry, he settled in a strong position behind Twenty-five Mile Creek.

Greene's fears were groundless. After resting for a couple of weeks at Wilmington, Lord Cornwallis had held a council of war. With his field officers he threshed out the question of retreating to Charleston or of advancing to Richmond. A return to South Carolina would be an admission of defeat and would mean a repetition of the last campaign. On the other hand, Major General William Phillips already had a sizeable corps on the Chesapeake. There was a shorter communication line with New York. The climate of Virginia was more equable and there was less malaria. And so Cornwallis set out on the desolate road to Petersburg. He was abandoning the Carolinas forever.

The war in South Carolina now became a contest between Greene, Sumter, and Marion; and Balfour, Rawdon, and Cruger. Lieutenant Colonel Nisbet Balfour, senior to Lord Rawdon in the regular army, became British Commander in Chief. Although poorly educated and somewhat inept, he was conscientious and hard-working. Knowing that Rawdon's force was inferior to that of Greene, he began mustering reinforcements. He ordered Major Archibald McArthur, now exchanged after having been captured at Cowpens, to collect all replacements still in Charleston. The Major gathered together three hundred infantrymen and eighty dragoons and moved up to Moncks Corner. Colonel John Watson, having been held in Georgetown to aid in a possible retreat of Cornwallis, rushed across the Santee and joined him. With McArthur's troops screening his advance, Watson started hiking toward Camden, Harrison's Provincials scouting and riding patrol and the veteran Guardsmen keeping up with the cavalry.

Marion knew that Watson was on his march to Camden. From Major Rudolph and his dragoons he had learned that Watson was apparently determined to cut his way through to Rawdon. How he longed to throw his Brigade and Lee's

Continentals in front of the Buffs and renew their struggle. But he was waiting for orders. On May 2, however, Major Eaton with his infantry and Captain Finley with his artillery reached the Black River. Eaton brought orders for both Marion and Lee to cross the Santee.

"Major Eaton's not coming up sooner has made me lose a great deal of precious time," Marion complained to Greene on May 3. "I shall cross Santee at Wright's Bluff tomorrow." Late in the afternoon of May 4 Marion arrived at the Bluff. During the night Partisans ferried his troops across Scott's Lake. At daybreak he struck the main highway——but too late!

"Yesterday evening agreeable to the Intelligence sent to you I was informed that Col. Watson was crossing Santee at Buckenhams ferry," General Sumter, who was scouting Orangebury with his horsemen, wrote Greene on May 6. The Colonel was already marching through the High Hills toward Camden "where he may perhaps arrive by tomorrow Noon——I am not well informed of his strength, his men much fatigued & hungry."

General Marion was frustrated, angered, and shaken. Because of the delay in Greene's orders, Colonel Watson had evaded him. Had he been a free agent, this would not have happened. Colonel Lee was more philosophic. "Mortified with the result of their unceasing exertions, the deranging information was immediately forwarded to General Greene," he said, "and the disappointed commandants moved upon Fort Motte."

Fort Motte, erected around the spacious mansion of Mrs. Rebecca Motte on Mount Joseph Plantation, sat on a hill below McCord's Ferry over the Congaree River. To the natural strength of the dwelling, British engineers had added fosse, earthwork, and abatis and strong palisades. Inside Balfour had stationed Lieutenant Donald McPherson with some 140 men, mostly British and Hessians. And because it could be reduced only by siege or cannon fire, he used it as the principal depot for the convoys moving supplies up from Charleston.

Just as Marion and Lee began reconnoitering Fort Motte, Marion received another letter from Greene. The General wrote the little Brigadier:

> Several times I have written you respecting dragoon horses. We are in the utmost distress for the want of a number. I beg you will furnish us with all you can. I am told the militia claim all they take from the Tories; and many of the best horses are collected from the inhabitants upon this principle. I cannot think this practice warranted either in justice or policy. If the object of the people is plunder altogether, government can receive but little benefit from them. The horses would be of the highest importance to the public in the regular service."

The arrival of Greene's letter was extremely inopportune. The Brigadier was already bitter because the militia had deserted him just when the British line had begun to totter. He was mortified at being outmaneuvered by Watson. He resented interference in the affairs of his Brigade. The Tories, it was true, owned many blooded horses. His militia, serving without pay and furnishing their own means of campaigning, helped themselves to these horses. Greene's sequestering them for public service would bring dismay and resentment. To save what they considered legitimate property, the militiamen would slip bridles and saddles upon their chargers and ride them away to safety. Marion replied from Motte's on May 6:

> Yours of the 4th instant I received and am sorry to acquaint you that I brought here but one hundred and fifty men, the rest have dropped away wearied with duty, and I believe in not seeing greater support. I acknowledge that you have repeatedly mentioned the want of dragoon horses, and wish that it had been in my power to furnish them, but it is not, and never has been. The few horses which has been taken from Tories has been kept for the service, and never for private property; but if you think it best for the service to dismount

the militia now with me, I will direct Colonel Lee and Captain Conyers to do so, but am certain we shall never get their service in future. This would not give me any uneasiness, as I have some time determined to relinquish my command in the militia as soon as you arrived in it and I want to do it as soon as this post is either taken or abandoned. I shall assist in reducing the post here, and when Colonel Lee returns to you I shall take that opportunity in waiting on you, when I hope to get permission to go to Philadelphia.

After sending his threat of resignation to Greene by express, Marion turned back to the siege. Colonel Lee had posted his Continentals to the north of Mount Joseph and around an old log cabin in which Mrs. Motte was then living. Marion had posted his Brigade at the foot of the hill east of the fort. Because he had only one hundred and fifty militiamen and Lee had three hundred regulars, he gave the honor of subduing the post to the Virginian. After besieging the fort for several days, Colonel Lee decided to take it by storm. He sent Finley to Marion's quarter to emplace his six-pounder, so that he could rake the northern face of the enemy's parapet. He then began formal sap. Starting his trench in the valley about four hundred yards from the enemy's earthwork, he kept his soldiers digging in four-hour shifts. By May 10 the trenches were so far advanced that he decided to summon the British Commander. Lieutenant McPherson returned a polite answer, but continued to defend his post.

While the blockading, digging, and sniping continued, Major Edmund Hyrne arrived with dispatches from General Greene. The Major had a long talk with Marion, explaining the General's preoccupation with the subject of dragoon horses. Hyrne's explanation mollified the ragged Brigadier. But it did not remove the principal cause of his desire to resign. He had lost confidence in his men. His militia was cutting such a sorry figure in operating beside Lee's disciplined Continentals.

"I assure you I am very serious in my intention of relinquishing my command," General Marion wrote Greene after his chat with Major Hyrne, "not that I wish to shrink from fatigue or trouble for any private interest, but because I found little is to be done with such men as I have, who leave me very often at the very point of executing a plan; and their late infamous behavior in quitting me at a time which required their service, must confirm me in my former intention. If I cannot act in the militia, I cannot see any service I can be to remain in the State; and I hope by going to the northward to fall in with some employ where I may have an opportunity of serving the United States in some way that I cannot be in this country."

While the discouraged Brigadier was penning his threats of resigning, Colonel Watson was hiking northward. He had scarcely paused at Buchanan's Ferry. With McArthur still below Nelson's furnishing intelligence, he knew the exact position of Marion and Lee. Having put a wide river between them and his tired Guards, he now slackened his pace. Early on the morning of May 7 he led his weary Buffs triumphantly into Logtown.

General Greene wrote Marion on May 7 that he considered Watson's having reached Camden "an unfortunate circumstance, as the enemy will begin to be impudent and to show themselves without their works, which they have never ventured upon since the morning of the 25th." Their concentration while his force was divided put matters on an unmilitary footing. Greene retreated five miles up river and took a stronger position behind Sawncy's Creek.

Rawdon moved as anticipated. As soon as the Buffs had rested, he crossed the Wateree at Camden Ferry and bore westward to turn Greene's flank. But the Quaker General was vigilant. Leaving his light infantry and horse pickets at Sawney's, during the night he pulled back another four miles and took a still stronger position behind Colonel's Creek.

Early on the morning of May 8 Lord Rawdon advanced along the main road to Sawney's. Mistaking Greene's light troops for the American Army, he drew up his troops for battle. "Having driven in his pickets, I examined every point of his situation; I found it everywhere to be so strong that I could not hope to force it without suffering such loss as must have crippled my force for any future enterprise," he reported to Cornwallis. "I therefore returned to Camden."

As soon as Rawdon had retreated across the Wateree, Greene began putting his own house in order. Realizing the blunder in his imperious letter to Marion, he tried to placate the Brigadier. "I am sorry the militia are deserting you because there is not greater support," he wrote from Colonel's Creek on May 9. "If they were influenced by proper principles, and were impressed with a love of liberty, and a dread of slavery, they would not shrink at difficulties. . . . I shall always be happy to see you at head-quarters, but cannot think you seriously mean to solicit leave to go to Philadelphia. It is true your task has been disagreeable, but not more so than others."

Nathanael Greene was intelligent, and he had the ethics of a Quaker. "My reasons for writing so pressing respecting the dragoons was from the distress we were in," he declared. "It is not my wish to take the horses from the militia, if it will injure the public service. The effects and consequences you can better judge of than I can. You have rendered important service to the public with the militia under your command, and done great honor to yourself; and I would not wish to render your situation less agreeable with them. . . ."

That evening Greene sent for Colonel William Davie earlier than usual. He was bending over a map when his aide entered. "You see we must again resume the partisan war," he began. "Rawdon has now a decided superiority of force; he has pushed us to a sufficient distance to leave him free to act on any object within his reach. He will strike at Lee and Marion."

After complaining that Congress had lost sight of the Southern states and was supplying neither men nor matériel,

Greene said dejectedly: "We will dispute every inch of ground in the best manner we can, but Rawdon will push me back to the mountains. Lord Cornwallis will establish a chain of posts along James River, and the southern states thus cut off will die like the tail of a snake."

Lord Rawdon thought his prospects even worse. "Camden had always been reprobated by me as a station," he wrote Colonel Lee in after years; "not merely from the extraordinary disadvantages which attended it, as an individual position; but from its being on the wrong side of the river and covering nothing; whilst it was constantly liable to have its communication with the interior district cut off." For these reasons Rawdon issued an order for his troops and the Loyalist militia to prepare to retreat.

Across the Wateree the Americans were also working zealously. "I employed the whole night in writing until an orderly sergeant summoned me to headquarters about daylight," said Colonel Davie. "On entering the General's tent I soon perceived some important change had taken place."

"I have sent for you," said Greene, his countenance radiant, "to inform you that Lord Rawdon is preparing to evacuate Camden——that place was the key of the enemy's line of posts, they will now all fall or be evacuated——all will now go well. Burn your letters. I shall march immediately to the Congarees."

During the day Rawdon destroyed much of Camden. He released the prisoners and fired the jail. He burned the mills and many private dwellings. Then, aften setting the torch to all remaining supplies, he collected his sick——except thirty too ill to travel, for whose exchange he left an equal number of captured Continentals——and set his army retreating down the road toward Charleston.

The war of posts was rising to a climax. General Sumter was again besieging Fort Granby. On May 4 Greene sent him a six-pounder. Leaving Colonel Thomas Taylor to watch Major Andrew Maxwell, Sumter marched off to strike the

British post at Orangeburg. The roar of his field piece brought the garrison quickly to terms and on May 11 they surrendered. Learning that the Tories had been ordered to drive cattle to the line of Rawdon's retreat, the Gamecock and his horsemen began sweeping the country as far down as Wassamassaw.

Marion was still pressing his siege of Fort Motte. But on the night of May 11 McPherson's beleaguered troops gave a shout of triumph. They could see Rawdon's campfires twinkling in the High Hills. Realizing that the British would cross at Nelson's and reach Motte's within forty-eight hours, the Swamp Fox undertook a desperate stratagem. He sent Colonel Lee to ask Rebecca Motte's consent to his burning her home.

"If it were a palace," she told Lee, "it should go." Courageously she turned to a closet and brought out a curiously wrought bow and a quiver of fire arrows, a gift from the captain of an East Indiaman. Handing them to Lee, she said quietly: "This will serve your purpose."

As he prepared assault with flames, Light Horse Harry sent Dr. Mathew Irvine, surgeon to the Legion, to warn McPherson. But the Lieutenant was resolute. Politely he refused the summons. And so, after waiting until noon when the roof had become hot and dry, Lee ordered a marksman to begin shooting the fire arrows. As they struck, the flaming material fell upon the shingles. Not to be outdone by the Continentals, Nathan Savage, whose home Wemyss had burned, repaid his debt to Lucifer. Rolling a ball of tar and sulphur, he ignited it and threw it on the roof from a sling. Soon the housetop was blazing in several places. As the flames began to crackle, McPherson sent a detail aloft to rip off the burning shingles. Captain Finley raked them with grape. Faced with a fiery death, with his men already jumping from the house into the fosse, McPherson hurriedly raised a white flag.

As soon as the British cast down their arms, Marion sent stalwarts to douse the flames. He treated the prisoners with kindness. But because of their considerable losses the Americans held deep resentment against Lieutenant McPherson. During the parley the commanders charged him with prolonging his resistance, ignoring their summons, and wasting their time. The Lieutenant answered that he was ready to face the consequence of doing his duty. Knowing that they would have done the same thing, Marion and Lee offered him honorable terms. But during the prolonged siege friction between the Continentals and the militia had become so strong that, when the British marched out, Colonel Lee received the surrender of the troops of the regular army and General Marion only those of the Loyalist militia.

Immediately after the surrender, Rebecca Motte invited both the American and the British officers to dine with her. In order to accommodate so many guests, she set her table under an arbor in front of her cabin. "For my life I could not keep my eyes from her," said Peter Horry in praising her hospitality. "To think what an irreparable injury these officers had done her! And yet, to see her, regardless of her own appetite, selecting the choicest pieces of the dish, and helping them with the endearing air of a sister, appeared to me one of the loveliest spectacles I had ever beheld. It produced the happiest effect on us all. Catching her amiable spirit, we seemed to have entirely forgotten our past animosities, and Britons and Americans mingled together, in smiles and cheerful chat, like brothers."

During the dinner General Marion was in exceedingly high spirits. But as he mingled and chatted, he saw a British soldier run up and whisper something to McPherson. Greatly agitated, the Lieutenant relayed it to Marion. The little Brigadier sprang up, grabbed his sword, and ran downhill toward his camp. On turning the corner of the garden, he saw a grisly scene. Two men were lying dead on the ground and a notorious Tory named Levi Smith was swinging by the neck from the beam of the garden gate.

"Cut him down! Cut him down!" yelled Marion. "In the name of God, what are you doing?"

"Only hanging a few Tories, sir," replied Cornet William Harrison of Colonel Lee's dragoons.

Francis Marion hated cruelty. Wanton murder had no place in his code. He would tolerate no prisoner killing. Too well he understood the emotions of the frail, the weak, the helpless. Now, as he confronted Lee's powerful, well-fed, splendidly uniformed dragoons, he seemed a ragged urchin surrounded by a gang of bullies. Overcome by a sense of rivalry, comparison, and defeat, he felt the fullest measure of frustration. His dark, unhandsome face reflecting his rage, he shouted at Cornet Harrison: "I'll let you know, damn you, that I command here and not Colonel Lee!"

CHAPTER XV

Partisan Generals

As soon as Lord Rawdon had evacuated Camden, General Greene sent a detachment to occupy the village. He ordered the army to follow him and then rode down the west side of the Wateree. After bivouacking at McCord's Ferry, he crossed the Congaree to visit Marion and Lee. After an introduction, the General and the Brigadier sat down for a long conference. As they sat chatting, increasingly admiring each other, Greene outlined his strategy for the recovery of South Carolina. Finally Marion, warmed and cheered by the meeting, firmly won by the magnetism of Greene and with all thought of resignation vanished, bade him good-by. Then, calling his militia, he slipped off down the Santee.

General Greene also conferred with Henry Lee and ordered him to march at once to Fort Granby. Light Horse Harry did so and reached Granby before daybreak on May 14. He erected a battery to the west of the fort, and when the fog lifted Captain Finley was ready to open a bombardment with his six-pounder. But his high-handed behavior offended the militia under Colonel Taylor. "I hope it may not be disagreeable to recall Colonel Lee, as his services cannot be wanted in that place; and as to his taking command, as at the post at Motte, I cannot believe it would be your wish," Sumter wrote Greene from Orangeburg.

Instead of continuing the formal siege, Lee decided to

negotiate a surrender. Before noon on May 15 he sent Captain Joseph Eggleston to treat with Major Maxwell. During the conference there was an argument over the retention of horses and other personal property, and twice Eggleston returned to Lee for further instructions. Meanwhile an express arrived with the intelligence that Rawdon had crossed the Santee and was marching toward Granby. To hasten capitulation, Lee agreed to the amendments. Maxwell, with 340 officers and men, two pieces of artillery, and a vast quantity of baggage, marched out of the fort.

Greene, who had just reached Ancrum's Plantation across the Congaree from Granby, rushed across the river to join Lee. He ordered the valiant cavalier to march that afternoon to join Brigadier General Andrew Pickens in his siege of Augusta. When Sumter reached Granby next day and learned that Andrew Maxwell had been allowed to carry off all his plunder, he became furious. He bundled up his commission as Brigadier General, wrote a letter of resignation, and sent both to Greene.

That two Brigadiers should try to resign in the hour of victory shocked the General. He became conciliatory. On May 17 he wrote Sumter: "I take the liberty to return you your commission which you forwarded me yesterday for my acceptance & to inform you that I cannot think of accepting it & to beg you to continue your command."

The British Army began crossing the Santee during the night of May 13, and so diligent were the ferrymen that by next evening troops and baggage were on the southern bank. Rawdon immediately marched to the relief of Fort Granby. By the morning of May 15 he had reached the fork from which the roads led to McCord's Ferry and to Fort Granby. But Sumter's horsemen had so terrified the Loyalists that none would come near the British Army and Rawdon could get no reliable intelligence. Learning that there was an army corps at Orangeburg, which he mistook for Greene's, he turned back and hurried his troops to Eutaw Springs. From there he moved leisurely down to Moncks Corner.

The American Army, however, was marching in the opposite direction. On May 18 General Greene started toward Ninety-Six. But he was afraid that Lord Rawdon might turn back, cut his lines, and fall upon his rear. So he instructed Sumter to recall Marion from the Low Country at the first signs of the enemy's advance.

By that time the Swamp Fox had trailed Rawdon down into St. Stephen's. Among Huguenot friends and relatives, in the swamps where he and Gabriel had fished and hunted years before, he found another lair. On an island of the Peyre Plantation, surrounded by creeks and morasses, he pitched his new camp. His troops again built shelters, thatching them with canes. But there was a vast difference between his new position and that on Snow's Island. Here he was no longer an independent Partisan, riding and fighting as he chose, but a Brigadier General commanding an advanced militia unit of the American Army.

With a sense of greater responsibility he began patroling, seeking intelligence, and awing the Tories. To Major Maham he assigned the special task of watching Lord Rawdon. On May 19 he relayed the latest intelligence to Greene. Rawdon still lay at Moncks Corner. Georgetown had a garrison of only eighty British and Tory troops. With the zeal that had characterized him while on Snow's Island, he wrote: "I beg leave to go and reduce that place."

Marion knew that the capture of Georgetown would unhinge the whole British line. With the ardor of one chafing against delay, he again pleaded: "I wish to hear from you as quick as possible that the garrison in Georgetown may not slip through my hands."

Next day Marion renewed his plea. Rawdon was still at Moncks Corner and there was no need to join Sumter. He said that he had allowed his militia to go home for a few days, but that soon "I shall be stronger than I have ever been." The garrison was still in Georgetown. "Should be glad to have liberty of going against it, but will wait your orders."

From Peyre's on May 22 he again wrote Greene. "The militia expected has not yet come in & I have been oblige to let the men I had go home, but expect in a few days to be strong." He planned to lie close to the enemy and harass them "if you do not think it proper for me to go to Georgetown."

Francis Marion could not stand and beg. He had campaigned independently too long. He knew that Georgetown could be easily taken, but neither Greene nor Sumter seemed interested in its capture. Tired of their dilly-dallying, he crossed the Santee and bivouacked at Cantey's Plantation. From there he issued a call to the militia. They came in quickly, their spirits raised by the fall of the British posts. With his Brigade at full strength, on May 27 the Swamp Fox started toward Winyah Bay.

"In my last I acquainted you of my intention of marching to this place," Marion wrote Greene from Georgetown on May 29. "Yesterday I arrived and immediately began to open intrenchments, but the enemy thought proper to slip on board their vessels at 9 o'clock at night, and fell down towards the Bar, they had a galley, two gun boats and an armed schooner, I immediately took possession of the redoubt and town; in the first three nine pounders and a carronade, their trunnions being knocked off and spiked, their baggage all carried off.

"I shall only stay to level the works when I will immediately cross Santee river, take post near Moncks Corner and wait your orders."

While Marion had been writing excitedly about the prospects of capturing Georgetown, Greene had been marching steadily toward Ninety-Six. On May 22 he reached the village and immediately invested the fort. Too busy to worry about his Partisans, he waited four days before replying to Marion's first request. He then wrote Sumter, saying that Marion might have permission to go under two conditions:

that Rawdon was making no preparation to advance toward Ninety-Six; and that going to Georgetown would not expose Sumter. While Greene's orders were working down the chain of command, the Swamp Fox was on the alert in Georgetown. On June 5 he reported to Greene that the ships bearing the garrison were still lying inside the bar. His men had finished leveling the works, and he planned to leave a small guard in the village and march to join Major Maham over the Santee.

That afternoon Marion received a small piece of paper with a surprising message: "Just now received intelligence of the enemy has received reinforcements of near two thousand Men in Charlestown. This information may be depended upon from good authority which is from two officers from the first who says they saw ten of the transports go up at once the night and after night saw seven more and likewise Ninety-Six is fallen."

The report, originating among the officers of the First Regiment still held as prisoners of war on Sullivan's Island, came from Alex McGregor, a trusted spy. It gave the Americans their first hint of the arrival, on June 2, of Lieutenant Colonel Pasten Gould and two thousand regulars from Cork. The British were assembling their forces to re-establish their hold upon South Carolina. As the eyes and ears of the American forces, Marion's first duty was to warn the others. Calling his swiftest courier, he dispatched McGregor's letter to Sumter and asked him to relay it to Greene.

Whenever General Marion was near Murry's Ferry, he camped at the plantation of John Cantey, brother-in-law of General Sumter. Through Cantey the Brigadiers had a neutral channel of communication, but they did not use it. Their relationship was too unsatisfactory. Both were zealous patriots. Both had begun their careers in the militia and were veterans of the Cherokee War. They had been active in the resistance movements and had been members of the first Provincial Congress. In all of the subsequent struggle each had devoted himself valiantly to the cause of freedom. In contrast with the little Huguenot, Sumter was large, athletic, and powerful. He was better educated and far better read. He had a bolder imagination and often made great plans, even when he did not have the means to carry them out. Lionhearted, inured to suffering, he was imperious when balked. He did not like Marion's going over his head to Greene.

"Soon after your Departure from this, I received a letter from Genl. Marion wherein he expressed a desire of going against Georgetown & said he had wrote to you upon that head," Sumter wrote Greene on June 7. "Upon which I mentioned that he would consequently follow your Direction, until which I Requested that he would Cover the Country, & prevent the Enemy from Ravging it——he however proceeded against Georgetown."

After leaving Granby, Light Horse Harry Lee forced his march and reached Augusta on the third day. He was already acquainted with Andrew Pickens, having campaigned with the Brigadier against Tarleton during Greene's retreat across North Carolina. With Continentals to bolster the militia, the two fell with zest upon Fort Grierson and Fort Cornwallis. On May 23 their forces dislodged Colonel Grierson, capturing or killing his entire command. Immediately they concentrated upon Fort Cornwallis, garrisoned by Lieutenant Colonel Thomas Brown and the Tories who had so courageously defended Spring Hill redoubt in the Battle of Savannah. After a week of bombardment, sally, and skirmish, Colonel Lee began constructing a Maham tower. On June 5 Brown raised a white flag.

In the meantime Greene was vigorously pushing his siege of Ninety-Six. His troops were deeply entrenched and making a formal approach to the works. Not needing the dragoons for his operations, he sent Colonel Washington to join Sumter on the Congaree. But the General was disturbed by the arrival of Colonel Gould. "After you have dismantled the enemy's works, you will collect your force, take the position mentioned, and act in conjunction with Genl. Sumter," he wrote Marion. To Sumter, however, he wrote as to a senior. "Collect all the force you can and give positive orders to Genl. Marion's force to join if the enemy attempt to penetrate the Country."

Sumter immediately wrote Marion: "You will be pleased to disencumber yourself of all heavy baggage, and march with all possible expedition towards 96, so as for our whole force to act together as requisite." But the Gamecock then complained to Greene that Marion "is at Murries ferry on the North side of Santee, is not moving up, as he has but few men, thinks to gather some more. . . . I have given him positive orders to march with what he has & collect what he can by the way."

Lord Rawdon, who had just thrown off malaria, returned to the command of the corps at Moncks Corner. On June 7 he marched off slowly on the road toward Orangeburg. When Sumter heard of the advance, he ordered Marion to call out his brigade and take position in the High Hills. But he did not understand the temper of Marion's militia. They would fight only when they chose and then only around home. They refused to turn out. "Genl. Marion has crossed Santee & is moving up," he wrote Greene on June 16, "but at a great distance and but weak."

The siege of Ninety-Six was not going well. After toil and bloodshed, General Greene finished his second parallel on June 3. As he prepared to advance by sap and mine, he summoned the garrison. "I am honored with your letter," Cruger replied with sugary courtesy, but "a compliance with which my duty to my Sovereign renders inadmissable at present."

With Cruger's defiance ringing in his ears, Greene ran the gamut of his stratagems. Recalling the methods used successfully by Marion at Forts Watson and Motte, he began building a Maham tower. When he filled it with sharpshooters, Cruger piled sandbags around his cannon. He fired arrows carrying streamers of flaming material. Cruger merely knocked the shingles off the houses. After Light Horse Harry

Lee marched in from Augusta, Greene sent the infantry of the Legion against the stockade which guarded the enemy's water supply. On June 12 they routed the defenders and cut off the water. But Cruger sent naked slaves crawling through the dark to fill their pails at a nearby creek.

Late one afternoon, after the Americans had begun to despair of capturing Ninety-Six, an old farmer came riding slowly along their lines, chatting with the idle soldiers while his horse nibbled the grass beside the road. Suddenly he clapped spurs to his horse and dashed toward the fort. As he raced through the opened gate, there was a shout of triumph. He had brought word of the rapid approach of Lord Rawdon.

"I cannot persuade myself that the enemy mean to pay a visit to the place," Greene had written Sumter. Now he changed his opinion. On June 18 he made a frantic effort to storm the works. Next day he admitted defeat, abandoned his siege, and retreated across the Bush River.

Soon afterward Lord Rawdon marched into Ninety-Six. So rapidly had he come up from Orangeburg that his route was marked by a score of sunstruck Britons. Nor did he tarry. After a gesture of pursuing Greene, he left Colonel Welbore Ellis Doyle to help Cruger bring down the Loyalists, wheeled around, and began retracing his march.

Greene was greatly disappointed in his campaign, irritated by the militia, and exasperated with the militia Generals. "It is next to impossible to draw the militia of the Country from the different parts of the State," he confided to Lee. "Marion is below, Pickens I can get no account of, and Sumter wants to make a tour to Monk's Corner, and all I can say to either is insufficient to induce them to join us."

After camping at Sandy River, on June 25 Greene wrote a long letter to General Marion. "It was my wish to have fought Lord Rawdon before he got to Ninety-Six, and could I have collected your force and that of Gen. Sumter and Pickens, I would have done it," he said. "General Sumter is preparing for a manoeuvre down in the lower part of the state, and he will require your aid to bring it into effect. You will therefore call out all the force you can, and cooperate with him in any manner he may direct."

Although Marion feared Sumter's grand schemes, he tried to obey his senior. He called out his Brigade, but his summons went unheeded. The fighting was only a distant rumble, crops were growing, and his militia had no desire to fight under Sumter. The Gamecock would be as reckless with their lives as he had been with his own. But Sumter had no patience with their reluctance. The failure of the junior Brigadier irritated him and he reported to Greene: "By the Inclosed from Genl. Marion you will find no assistance is to be expected from him, at least not soon."

In the meantime Colonel William Washington, patroling the roads south of the Congaree, ran down an express with dispatches for Lord Rawdon. He learned that Lieutenant Colonel John Watson, battered and baffled by his six-months campaign against the Swamp Fox, had retired as Commandant of the 3rd Guards and was on his way back to England. Lieutenant Colonel Alexander Stewart had taken command of the Guards. Fresh and vigorous, Colonel Stewart was already moving up with supplies for the suffering troops of Rawdon. Sending this intelligence to Marion, Washington urged him to bring his Brigade to the Congaree to help prevent a junction of the British forces. Marion had four hundred horsemen from his four regiments and with these he came rapidly up from Nelson's Ferry.

General Greene, leaving the army to follow, rushed down to Ancrum's Plantation with only an escort of cavalry. Hoping to head off Stewart, he sent Marion down toward Moncks Corner. The Swamp Fox moved rapidly. Swinging to the east, on July 6 he passed around Lord Rawdon, whose troops were exhausted, sick, and mutinous. "Their troops are so fatigued they cannot possibly move," he informed Greene next morning. "Three regiments were going to lay down their arms, and it is believed they will today, if they are ordered to march. They have no idea of any force being near them."

At one o'clock, on the morning of July 8, Marion quietly broke camp and began moving stealthily down the broad highway between Orangeburg and Moncks Corner. He was eager as he and his horsemen plunged through the darkness, their vedettes expecting to meet the enemy at each bend in the way. But Stewart was astute. A better Partisan than Watson had been, he chose a less traveled road. In the early hours the two corps passed each other. At daylight Marion learned his mistake and sent Colonel Peter Horry back in pursuit of the Guards. Horry overtook the supply train and cut off several wagons. But in spite of Horry's efforts, Stewart joined Rawdon in Orangeburg.

The arrival of Stewart gave Rawdon a sizeable army. To counter it, General Greene ordered in all his detachments of Continentals. He also called for Sumter and Marion to bring their brigades to the Congaree. All came in quickly. At Ancrum's Plantation, for the first time during his campaigning in South Carolina, Greene had Sumter, Marion, Washington, and Lee under his immediate command. With his Brigadiers beside him, he began moving forward. On July 10, he took a position on the north side of Turkey Hill, four miles above Orangeburg. For two days his troops lay in array, offering insults to the British. But Lord Rawdon declined battle. On the afternoon of July 12, in company with Sumter, Marion, and his other field officers, Greene rode out with his cavalry and carefully reconnoitered the British. He found Rawdon well posted, on favorable ground, with his men in and around the brick courthouse and jail. Contented that he had offered battle and that the enemy had refused, Greene slowly turned his army around and retreated across the Santee. Moving on to the wooded ridges around Bloom Hill, he established a camp of repose in the cool and pleasant High Hills of Santee.

Ever since his rambling excursion to Wassamassaw, Gen-

eral Sumter had cherished an ambition to subdue the post
at Moncks Corner. Receiving Greene's permission to employ
Marion and Lee, during the evening of July 12 he sent them
off, their horsemen moving along every road leading to the
Low Country. The infantry he brought along the highway
west of the Santee, passing Nelson's and Murry's and leaving
boats ready in case of retreat. Learning that Colonel Cruger
had reached Orangeburg with his troops, Greene admonished
the Gamecock: "There is no time to be lost; push your operations night and day." He then added: "Keep Colonel Lee
and General Marion advised of all matters from above, and
tell Colonel Lee to thunder even at the gates of Charleston."

Sumter deployed his small force on a characteristic grand
scale. By-passing Lieutenant Colonel John Coates and the
19th Regiment at Moncks Corner, the Gamecock attempted
to cut them off from all possible relief, surround them, and
then destroy them. But, at the approach of the Americans,
Colonel Coates evacuated Moncks Corner. Crossing the
Cooper River, he drew up his troops around the parish
church of St. Stephen's, known locally as Biggin Church.
With brick walls three feet thick, Biggin was all but impregnable and there the 19th Regiment lay in security.
Alarmed at the sweeping movements of Sumter's force,
Coates decided to withdraw to a position nearer Charleston.
About three o'clock on the morning of July 17 he set fire to
the church and proceeded down the Cooper River.

After crossing Fair Forest Swamp, the Colonel ordered his
men to destroy Wadboo Bridge. At the forks he sent his cavalry toward Bonneau's Ferry. His infantry he led down the
road toward Quinby Bridge. For eighteen miles they trudged
along under a broiling July sun, pursued and harassed by
the American cavalry. Reaching Quinby Creek in early afternoon, they crossed and were throwing planks off the bridge
when Lee and Hampton charged them. After a hot skirmish,
Coates marched on and took a strong position on the plantation of Captain Thomas Shubrick.

Lee turned up Quinby Creek and waited for Marion.

After the Swamp Fox arrived, they forded the creek and re-connoitered Shubrick's Plantation. They found the 19th Reg-iment drawn up in front of the mansion in the conventional British square, its front covered by a howitzer. Around them in the messuage were cribs, barns, and slave quarters, flanked by rail fences. The position was formidable. Both Marion and Lee decided against attacking.

About five o'clock Sumter arrived with his infantry, but without Singleton's six-pounder. In spite of Marion's pro-tests, the Gamecock gave orders to engage immediately. In a trice he was all sweat and fury. To the far right he sent Horry's cavalry. He posted his own troops immediately to his right. They dashed to the cabins, entered, and began pot-ting away in safety. To his immediate left he sent Colonel Thomas Taylor and his veterans. Taylor's regiment charged across the open field to the fence, but Captain Scerrit drove them back with the bayonet. Seeing Taylor retreating, Mar-ion's Brigade, which had been posted on the far left, rushed to the fence, took cover in the jams, and opened a galling fire.

Early in the fight Lieutenant Colonel John Baxter, dis-tinguished by his large size and full uniform, was struck by a shot. "I am wounded, Colonel," he shouted to Peter Horry.

"Think no more of it, Baxter, but hold your place," re-plied the veteran of the Second Regiment.

"But I can't stand, Colonel. I am wounded a second time."

"Then lie down, Baxter, but quit not your post."

"Colonel, they've shot me again. If I remain here any longer, I shall be shot to pieces."

"Be it so, Baxter, but stir not," replied Horry.

Colonel Baxter heroically maintained his position. Around him fifty militiamen of Marion's Brigade lay dead or wounded. After the survivors exhausted their ammunition, Marion drew them off in good order.

Stunned and grief-stricken, Francis Marion left the field in silence. But he now knew that he had been right in his ap-praisal of Thomas Sumter. His dead and wounded justified his former reluctance, foot-dragging, and refusal to fight under a man whose courage exceeded his judgment. He resolved never again to fight under the command of the Gamecock.

Colonel Taylor was more forthright. He walked up to Sumter and said: "Sir, I don't know why you sent me forward on a forlorn hope, promising to sustain me, and failed to do so, unless you designed to sacrifice me. I will never more serve under you!"

In their wrath and grief Marion's and Lee's men attended the wounded as best they could, slung their dead comrades across the pommels of their saddles, and rode away from the scene of carnage. For fifteen miles they retreated before halting for a bivouac. Inflamed with resentment, because Sumter's men had remained unexposed in the cabins, during the night all but a hundred of Marion's militia deserted. Next morning Colonel Lee buried his dead in a common grave. Then without a word to General Sumter, who still commanded the corps, he headed for Greene's camp in the High Hills. Marion also crossed the Santee and encamped at Cordes' Plantation.

John Jenkins hurried on to Britton's Neck to tell Widow Jenkins of the death of her son Francis. "When Cousin John returned and brought the news, it was like a dagger to my heart," wrote James Jenkins. "And having heard that Sumter *would* go into battle, whether or not, live or die, I thought then I could never forgive him. I was also informed that Marion was opposed to risk his men under circumstances so forbidding; and, from what I have heard of his character, I am disposed to believe it. He loved his men, and would not expose them where there was no hope."

In his first report of the Battle of Quinby, Sumter did not mention Francis Marion. In his second he said merely: "Genl. Marion's Brigade diminished fast from the time I left you. When we overtook the enemy he had scarcely 100 left." In his fifth letter he finally wrote Greene: "Genl. Marion was upon the left and suffered considerably by supposing the enemy could not fire upon his men—when moving up in a certain direction—he soon found his mistake—but had his men brought off—& behaved well upon every occasion."

Before then, however, in spite of Sumter's neglect, the Swamp Fox had received his own encomium. "The gallantry and good conduct of your men reflects the highest honor upon your Brigade," said Greene, relaying the flattering reports of Colonel Lee. "I only lament that men who spilt their blood in such noble exertions to serve their country could not have met with more deserved success."

In the affair at Quinby, Sumter's men captured a paymaster's trunk with 720 guineas in gold. These the Gamecock divided among his own men. But his ten-months troops began demanding their pay and so he turned to plundering. On July 25 he ordered Captain William Ransom Davis to Georgetown to seize the slaves, horses, indigo, salt, and medical supplies of the Tories. Captain Davis' robbing the Loyalists brought the matter of plundering to a head. The British made a terrible retaliation. On August 2 Captain Manson brought up from the bar the galley he had used to awe the Whigs. After bombarding Georgetown long enough to frighten everyone from the streets, he sent his sailors ashore to fire the stores and warehouses. He also set fire to forty-two houses. As these burned, he shelled the streets to prevent fire fighters from extinguishing the flames. When the fires had burned out, the plight of the victims was distressing. Marion rushed them all possible aid.

"I am very sorry for the affair at Georgetown," Governor John Rutledge, who on August 1 had returned to Greene's headquarters after his visit to Philadelphia, wrote Marion. "The orders you have given respecting the inhabitants who have suffered by the destruction of Georgetown are very proper."

With all of South Carolina, except a narrow district around Charleston, recovered from the British, Governor

Rutledge had come to restore civil government. Confronted with many problems, he recognized as worst of all the vicious round of reprisals and retaliations visited upon each other by the Whigs and the Tories. Much of the hatred was the result of plundering. As his first official act, Rutledge issued a proclamation outlawing the practice.

The proclamation struck down the proud Gamecock. In discrediting the system by which General Sumter had raised troops on the state establishment, it discredited him. Exhausted from campaigning and tortured by his old wound, distrusted by his men and disliked by his fellow officers, General Sumter relinquished the command of his Brigade. In his actions he had been the boldest and yet the most reckless of the Carolina Partisans. Rutledge gave the command of Sumter's Brigade to Lieutenant Colonel William Henderson. "On my arrival to take command of them I found them the most discontented set of men I ever saw, both men and officers," Henderson reported to the Governor. Perhaps Light Horse Harry Lee, bitter and sarcastic, was correct when he wrote Greene: "General Sumter is become almost universally odious."

Upon the retirement of Sumter to North Carolina, Francis Marion became the senior Brigadier General of Militia in South Carolina. His power and influence soon became anomalous. General Greene admired and trusted him. To Governor Rutledge he was still a hero of the glorious defense of Fort Moultrie. In the state of martial government existing in the wake of the British withdrawals, Rutledge needed trusted lieutenants to help administer the laws. And so, in his lair on Peyre's Plantation, the Swamp Fox became virtually the vice-gerent of eastern South Carolina.

CHAPTER XVI

Battle of Eutaw Springs

FRANCIS MARION was assiduous in his efforts to help restore order and government. He and his staff were busier than they had been in the romantic days of Snow's Island. The responsibilities of helping administer civil government were more taxing than those in simply commanding a brigade of militia under Greene. He was called upon for all kinds of advice and services. "You will appoint justices of the peace in every district immediately, "Rutledge notified him. The Governor had appointed Captain William Richardson of Bloom Hill to collect indigo and specie to finance military operations and civil government in South Carolina. "I request that you give him every assistance in your power." Who was the best man for sheriff of Camden District? "I wish you would recommend proper persons who will undertake the office of ordinary for George Town, Cheraws and Charles Town Districts."

Could he use thirty or thirty-five guineas in hard money to pay for military intelligence? Could he forward the enclosed papers to Colonel Horry? Could he get a printing press, neats-foot oil, and lampblack? He must collect salt and keep it hidden at the homes of different Whigs.

Rutledge hated the Loyalists as a cowardly, robbing, killing banditti. His first thought upon returning to South Carolina was to extirpate them. He sent Marion order after order to harass them. He must gather the wives and families of all the Tories now with the British from "the district of your Brigade" and send them into the British lines around Charleston. Could he supply an alphabetic list of the names of all Tories owning property? "I therefore desire that you immediately have this Mr. W. taken and sent up to me with an appropriate guard," the Governor wrote him on September 2, in a vicious mood, "and that you will make the necessary inquiries, and having discovered what property he has with him or which he may come at, take the whole of it; let it consist of what it may——money, goods, negroes, boats, or any other article whatever."

From his headquarters in Camden Governor Rutledge wrote the Swamp Fox: "I request that you will send immediately to Col. Harden, and get a full and authentic account of the execution of Col. Hayne." The Governor was extremely agitated. Colonel Isaac Hayne, after receiving the commissions for his officers from Marion in April, had recruited and mustered his regiment. In May he had begun partisan warfare. A man of great boldness, he soon acted rashly. On June 5 he led a small squadron of horsemen to the suburbs of Charleston and captured Brigadier General Andrew Williamson, a distinguished Whig who had defected to the British.

Such temerity angered Balfour. Calling in Major Thomas Fraser, the Colonel dispatched him and ninety dragoons beyond the Edisto.

Fraser captured Colonel Isaac Hayne in uniform, bearing arms, and in command of American troops. Colonel Balfour decided to make an example of him. For three weeks he held him in the Provost under the Exchange Building. Then he ordered Hayne brought before a court of field officers on July 27 "in order to determine under what point of view you ought to be considered." Major Andrew McKenzie, a Loyalist, presided, and the prisoner appeared without counsel. The court met again the next evening. They properly identified Hayne, confirmed the circumstances of his capture, and then turned their findings over to the two senior officers. And Balfour and Rawdon "in consequence of the most express directions of Lord Cornwallis to us, that all those who should be found in arms, after being at their own request received as subjects" of Britain, ordered that Colonel Hayne be hanged.

Upon the advice of John Colcock, an eminent Charleston lawyer, Colonel Hayne protested the inadequacy of his trial. "I have to inform you that your execution is not ordered in consequence of any sentence from a court of enquiry," said Major Charles Fraser, "but by virtue of the authority with which the Commander in Chief in South Carolina and the commanding officer in Charleston are invested. And their resolves upon the subject are unchangeable."

"You see by Col. Harden's letter that the enemy have hanged Col. Hayne," Greene wrote Marion on August 10. The General knew only too well the anguish, hatred, and terror that would follow that announcement, for the Brigadier had been responsible for bringing Hayne again into the field. He also knew that since the Tories had been prominent in capturing and condemning the Colonel, Marion would cut a trail through their ranks like that of a Mohawk. "Don't take any measure in the matter towards retaliation," Greene wrote him, "for I don't intend to retaliate on the Tory officers, but the British."

While Greene continued to lie in the benign High Hills preparing his forces for a blow at Stewart, Marion lay at Peyre's Plantation. In late August Colonel Harden sent him a plea for help. The execution of Hayne had caused terror among the Whigs and the militia had begun to drop off. Tories, once quiescent, were now gathered in bands totaling four or five hundred and were ravaging the country below Charleston. To encourage them Balfour had sent Fraser and his dragoons into the territory south of the Edisto.

Burning to avenge Colonel Hayne's murder, Marion wished nothing better than a blow at Major Fraser. "If it is practical I wish you to give support to Col. Harden," Greene had written him. "You know the Colonel's force, your own and the enemy's, and will do as you think proper."

With two hundred men picked from his Brigade, Marion marched southward. By stealth, with long circuitous sweeps at night, he moved so skilfully that the British did not suspect that he had left Peyre's. After covering about a hundred miles and crossing the Edisto, on August 13 he joined Colonel Harden. Learning that Fraser and his dragoons were on their return to the Edisto, Marion decided to waylay them on the causeway leading to Parker's Ferry. After concealing his men in the swamp, he sent a detachment on the swiftest horses to lure them into ambush.

Major Fraser saw Marion's decoy and set out in pursuit. Along the causeway his dragoons thundered. When they came parallel to the ambuscade, Marion gave the signal, and from a distance of fifty yards his men opened fire with buckshot. The entire line of dragoons reeled, men falling, horses screaming and rearing. Courageously Fraser rallied his horsemen, wheeled back, and tried to charge into the swamp. The confusion and delay gave Marion's men time to reload and deliver a second volley. Fraser now turned back from the ferry and in retreating again came parallel to the ambush. After the third volley he fled, leaving the causeway choked with dead and dying men and horses.

Seeing a large body of infantry charging toward the sound of the fighting and being too low on ammunition for a pitched battle, Marion slipped away through the swamp. Next morning he sent Captain Melton and a detachment to reconnoiter. They found that the British had buried their dead, but that twenty-seven horses still lay on the causeway. As Marion's sharpshooters aimed at the men and only accidentally killed their horses, the Swamp Fox decided that Fraser had paid a hundred dragoons on the score for Isaac Hayne.

For more than a month General Greene and the American Army remained in his camp in the High Hills. Colonel Stewart and the British Army remained encamped in the hills west of the confluence of the Congaree and the Wateree. As they lay watching each other, Greene received heartening news from the North. General Washington was planning a combined American-French move against Lord Cornwallis. He had already sent LaFayette, Von Steuben, and Wayne and their troops into Virginia. Count Rochambeau had a powerful army and fleet at Newport and Admiral De Grasse was bringing a still more powerful fleet and army from the West Indies. The Commander in Chief suggested that Greene resume offensive operations in order to prevent any British reinforcements from leaving South Carolina.

On August 22 Greene called in all his detachments except those under Harden and Marion. Breaking camp, he marched toward Camden, looking for a place to cross the flooded Wateree. On the 28th he reached Howell's Ferry on the Congaree, from which he turned downward to advance upon Colonel Stewart. But instead of waiting to fight, Stewart hastily retreated thirty miles down the Santee and took a strong position around Eutaw Springs.

Greene marched leisurely on to Motte's, sending out Lee's Legion and Pickens and his militia to watch the enemy. On September 4 he ordered Marion, again safely encamped at Peyre's, to move up the Santee. The little Brigadier moved with startling swiftness. Passing Stewart undetected, on the afternoon of the 5th he was encamped and waiting for Greene at the plantation of Henry Laurens, seventeen miles above Eutaw.

At the Laurens Plantation Greene paused for a day, resting his troops and formulating his battle plans. For maneuverability he divided his force into four columns. From his light and mounted troops he organized an advance guard and a rear guard. In accordance with contemporary American tactics, he then separated his Continentals from his militia. He gave the command of the regulars to General Jethro

Sumner. The command of the militia he gave to General Francis Marion.

After organizing his army for attack, Greene moved down Congaree Road to Burdell's Tavern, only seven miles from the enemy. At four o'clock next morning, September 8, he marched from Burdell's, his army in four columns, each detailed to its place at Eutaw. Colonel Henderson led the advance with his South Carolina State troops and Lee's Legion. Marion came next with the militia of North and South Carolina. Sumner followed with the Continentals. And Colonel Washington brought up the rear with the cavalry.

Greene's advance took Colonel Stewart by surprise. Believing himself secure, with Greene above and Marion below him, that morning the Colonel had sent out a rooting party of one hundred men to dig sweet potatoes. He could scarcely believe two American deserters who came to warn him of the danger. But he sent Major John Coffin with a detachment of horse and foot to reconnoiter. Coffin met the American advance four miles above Eutaw Springs. Still believing it to be only a detachment, he hurled his small force upon the column. The rooting party came to his aid. But Henderson beat off the assault and Coffin's straggling horsemen galloped back to Eutaw, turning all they met into panic.

Stewart immediately pushed a detachment of infantry a mile forward, with orders to stop the Americans. "As we thought this was the van of the enemy, our first line was ordered to form, and the Legion and State troops to take post on our flanks," Greene said in his report to Congress. In this deployment Marion sent General Pickens and his Brigade of South Carolina militia to the extreme left. In the center he posted Colonel Malmedy and the militia of North Carolina. And from his own Brigade he formed the right wing. Colonel Henderson covered the left wing and Colonel Lee the right.

In the time gained Stewart formed his troops in one line across the Congaree Road. On his extreme right he posted

Major John Majoribanks and a flank battalion behind a thicket a hundred paces in front of Eutaw Creek. In the center he posted the 3rd Guards and Cruger's Loyalists, both under the command of Colonel Cruger. On his left he posted the 63rd and 64th Regiments, their flank in air, but supported by Major Coffin and the cavalry. And he posted Major Sheridan and sharpshooters from the New York Volunteers in the exceedingly strong brick house of Patrick Roche which stood in the field west of the springs.

At the signal Marion's line began advancing, the militia driving the skirmishing parties back through the woods and then falling upon the British line. The men in buckskin attacked with impetuosity. Both the British and the Continentals were astonished to see these militiamen, steady, unfaltering, advancing like veterans into the enemy's hottest fire. "The fire redoubled; our officers behaved with the greatest bravery, and the militia gained much honor by their firmness," Greene reported to Congress. To Von Steuben he wrote that "such conduct would have graced the veterans of the Great King of Prussia."

Marion's militia fired seventeen rounds. Then with ammunition exhausted, they retired in good order, leaving the fighting to Sumner's advancing Continentals. "My Brigade behaved well," the Swamp Fox wrote Colonel Peter Horry. His months of toil, privation, and disappointment had been rewarded. At the peak of his career, in his greatest battle, commanding the largest contingent of troops in his life, he had seen the men he had trained fight like professionals. His coolness and bravery had animated them. "That distrust of their own immediate commanders which militia are too apt to be affected with," Governor Rutledge wrote the South Carolina delegates in Congress, "never produced an emotion where Marion and Pickens commanded."

The Continentals moved forward with spirit. As the Americans advanced, the left of the British line fell back in disorder and Colonel Lee, wheeling his infantry upon them, increased their confusion. In the center Cruger's line held,

British regulars meeting Continentals in hand-to-hand fighting, bayonets meeting bayonets, and swords clashing on
swords. But the confusion on the British left soon affected
the center and, when the Marylanders delivered a terrific
fire, the whole line, save Majoribanks' flankers, sagged, faltered, and began retreating. Stewart rallied and reformed
his line in the field in front of Roche's house.

At that critical moment Greene ordered Washington to
turn Majoribanks' right flank. He charged but, foiled by the
deep thicket, turned to the left. This brought him and his
cavalry under a deadly fire. A marksman killed Washington's
horse which fell on him, pinning him down until the British
captured him.

By then the British line had again begun retreating. Back
through Roche's field they went, passing through their camp
and continuing beyond it. But this saved them. In their
tents lay abundant food and drink. The hungry, thirsty Continentals stopped to pilfer. As they feasted, their line fell into
confusion. Their officers lost control and Greene ordered a
retreat. From the brick house Sheridan's marksmen sprayed
the surging mob with death. Coffin hurled his cavalry upon
them, but Colonel Wade Hampton drove him back in vicious fighting. Majoribanks opened with a destructive fire
and drove off Hampton. Receiving reinforcements, he
charged the retreating Americans and drove them from
Roche's field.

Greene rallied his troops at the edge of Roche's woods,
halted long enough to collect his wounded, and then started
toward Burdell's Tavern. The day was hot, the field was
dusty, and his men were almost dying of thirst. Four or five
miles up the Congaree Road lay a pond through which the
cavalry had passed two or three times during the day. It was
now a filthy puddle, but into it the men threw themselves
headlong, over the shoulders of each other and, as James
said, drank "with an avidity which seemed insatiable."

Stewart claimed a victory, but his army was shattered.
Fearing a second attack, he sent McArthur orders to bring

his dragoons up from Fair Lawn. He burned his stores. And then, leaving many of his dead unburied and seventy wounded under a flag, he set his troops retreating toward Moncks Corner. Learning of the enemy's retreat, Greene called upon Marion and Lee for another heroic enterprise. He sent them and their exhausted troops to cut in between the two British forces. Although they moved rapidly during the night, they failed to prevent a junction between Stewart and McArthur.

From Burdell's Tavern Greene moved slowly back up the Santee, crossed over, and again went into camp in the High Hills. Although badly crippled, the British followed Greene up the Santee and encamped near Nelson's Ferry. Marion, too, crossed the Santee. After encamping on familiar ground at the Cantey Plantation, he dismissed the men who had behaved so gallantly. That evening Samuel Jenkins started for Britton's Neck to tell the widow that Cousin John would sleep forever beside the murmuring Springs of Eutaw.

CHAPTER XVII

Breaking of Friendships

SOON AFTER the Battle of Eutaw Springs General Marion dismissed his militia and, with only his staff, settled down at the Cantey Plantation. He was very busy. Besides attending to the affairs of his Brigade, he was diligently carrying out instructions from both Governor Rutledge and General Greene. With the British driven from all of South Carolina, except a small district around Charleston, Rutledge was trying to establish domestic peace. He issued a proclamation that all Tories, except those who had signed congratulatory addresses to Clinton and Cornwallis or who held commissions from the British Government, could have "a free pardon and permission for their wives and families to return and re-occupy their possessions, on condition that such men appearing at our headquarters, or before a Brigade or the Colonel of any Regiment, and there subscribing an engagement to serve the State faithfully as militia men for six months."

While Marion was accepting the surrender and allegiance of the Loyalists in the name of the Governor, he was also working with General Greene. During the summer Greene had decided that he needed more dragoons, something better than militia horsemen. After consulting Marion, he ordered Colonel Peter Horry and Lieutenant Colonel Hezekiah Maham each to recruit a temporary regiment of horse, the two ultimately to be placed upon either State or Continental establishment. Maham began recruiting below the Santee and soon had a respectable body of men. Horry moved up to Indiantown and began recruiting in the country along the Peedee.

Greene informed Marion of "the most flattering advices from the northward." Count De Grasse had arrived in the Chesapeake with twenty-eight French ships of the line, a number of frigates, and six thousand troops. "Gen. Washington has also arrived in Virginia to take command of the Army." With such pressure upon him, Lord Cornwallis would undoubtedly abandon Virginia and retreat down the coast to Charleston. Greene had sent Colonel Lee to confer with Washington about sending reinforcements to South Carolina.

Colonel Horry's recruiting was going badly. His officers, believing themselves already Continentals, had begun acting with a high hand. "I am informed that you or some of your officers have ordered a tar-kiln of Brockington's to be set on fire to make coals for your workmen, if it is done, those that ordered it shall pay the value of it," Marion wrote Horry, with a degree of heat unusual in dealing with an old and trusted comrade.

Governor Rutledge also wrote a sharp letter to Colonel Horry. He had heard that Horry's officers "have behaved very much amiss" in taking plowhorses, breeding mares, and yearlings to mount his dragoons. He ordered the Colonel to restore such horses to their owners immediately. The Governor sent his letter via Marion, saying pointedly: "I think Col. Horry's conduct very extraordinary. He is not yet a Continental officer and his Regiment is not yet on the Continental establishment."

But General Marion's troubles with Horry were nothing compared to those with Colonel Maham. Thinking himself a Continental, Maham refused to obey any orders except those from Greene. A showdown came when he impressed a horse belonging to one John Oliver and refused to return him

when Marion ordered him to do so. "To convince you," the
Brigadier wrote him, "I have sent the Governor's orders to
me, as I wish not to have any difference with a man whom
I have long had the greatest regard for, but in the meantime,
if you do not return Mr. Oliver that horse, which I now re-
peat the order to do, without any further hesitation, I shall
and will try the matter in a general court martial. . . . I think
it high time that you and I should know whether I have the
power to command you or not."

Francis Marion had never before threatened to court-
martial an old friend.

Greene sensed a change and on October 23 wrote Horry:
"You will please put yourself and corps under command of
General Marion, and follow his orders." Greene then advised
Marion to send for his old friend and "talk the matter fully
over with him." Marion obeyed and wrote Horry: "I wish
to see you as soon as possible."

In his camp at Indiantown next day Colonel Horry received three letters from the Governor. So distressed was he
that instead of riding down to Cantey's Plantation to confer
with Marion, he wrote a long letter to Rutledge. Point by
point he refuted Marion's charges. Neither he nor any of
his officers had ever threatened to fire Captain John Brockington's tar kiln. "Thus you see how tales run to the General," he wrote bitterly, "and how ready and willing he is
to believe them." He then demanded that, if his conduct
were so offensive, he be brought before a court of enquiry
or "be tried by a court martial."

"I used to submit to General Marion's orders with pleasure," the Colonel then wrote General Greene, "but at present I assure you it is disagreeable to me and all my officers
that have experienced his late usage."

With two of their most distinguished officers facing court-
martial, Rutledge and Greene had to effect a reconciliation.
"I am exceedingly sorry for the misunderstanding which
seems to have taken place between Gen. Marion and you,"
Rutledge told Horry in trying to smooth over the affair.

Greene, however, lectured the Colonel as if he were a school-boy. "Nothing gives me more pain than to find disputes and disagreements beginning among officers high in rank," he said. He was hopeful that patriotism and good sense would end the row. "Gen. Marion cannot wish to injure you after knowing how much you have done and suffered for the cause," he advised Horry. "The General is a good man; few of us are without faults; let his virtues veil his if he has any."

Marion still lay at Cantey's, but he had again called out his Brigade and waited only for Horry to come down with his dragoons before crossing the Santee. "My order from Gen. Greene is to take post on the left of the enemy, and I think to take post at or near Huger's Bridge, in St. Thomas," Marion wrote Horry on November 9. "My post will be active, and make no doubt the enemy's Horse will try to remove me, which is the reason I am anxious to get as many Cavalry as will be a match for them, you will find me there or about that quarter, and shall be happy to see you." Francis Marion had suffered during the wrangling and bickering. "If I find fault with officers for anything I am made to believe they have done wrong, I cannot be angry with any one, but the very action itself," he wrote Horry with great manliness, "and I assure you, I am not capable of anger with individuals, when I am acting in a public capacity, but for public errors against the good of my country."

Light Horse Harry Lee returned from Yorktown bearing Washington's official dispatches on the surrender of Cornwallis. And with him came a letter from Charles Thompson, secretary to Congress, containing an extract from the minutes of Congress for October 29: "*Resolved,* That the thanks of the United States, in Congress assembled, be presented to Brigadier General Marion, of the South Carolina Militia, for his wise, gallant, and decided conduct, in defending the liberties of his country, and particularly for his prudent and intrepid attack on a body of British troops, on the 13th day of August last, and for the distinguished part he took in the battle of the 8th of September."

Proud of congressional approval of his actions at Parker's Ferry and Eutaw Springs, Francis Marion wished the men who had shared his toil and danger to share his reward. On the evening of November 10 he gave a ball for their ladies at the home of John Cantey. In came the couples in subdued gaiety. But the Swamp Fox was tired, silent, meditative. "The General's heart was not very susceptible of the gentler emotions," observed William James; "he had his friends, and was kind to his inferiors, but his mind was principally absorbed by the love of country; and as the capture of Lord Cornwallis was intimately connected with this passion there is no doubt he felt joy on the occasion. But if he did feel joy upon a few occasions, certain it is that watchful anxiety was the daily inmate of his breast."

South Carolina was almost free of British troops and the people were restless under a government of martial law administered by Brigadier Generals of Militia. As every sign at home and advice from abroad indicated that the British Government was preparing to end the long struggle, Governor Rutledge decided that the time had come to re-establish civil government. To that end he prepared writs of election to the General Assembly.

He sent these to his militia generals, asking them to set up and supervise the election. In accordance with the Governor's instructions, Marion chose three reliable men in each parish of his militia district, inserted their names in the writs, and then forwarded the documents by trusted militiamen. The election went smoothly. As was expected, the electors chose the same men who had led them in war to lead them in peace. The voters in St. John's, Berkley, elected General Francis Marion to the Senate.

To show the weakness of the British to the world, Governor Rutledge decided to hold the first meeting of the General Assembly at Jacksonboro, a village only thirty-two miles from Charleston but safe in the rear of Greene's army encamped at the Round O. "I purpose setting out for Gen.

Greene's camp on the first of next month," he wrote Marion on December 15, "and request that you will send me an escort of 25 men, and a proper officer from Maham's corps; let them be here the day before, and well mounted, as I shall travel pretty expeditiously."

When Marion received the Governor's letter, he and his horsemen were moving restlessly about in St. Thomas' Parish. In the week before Christmas, however, he made a sweep around Moncks Corner and penetrated as far as Dorchester. The country was quiet, and the enemy was nowhere near Jacksonboro. On December 31 Greene relayed the Governor's proclamation for the Senators and Representatives to meet on January 8 to Marion, "for you to distribute agreeably to the Governor's orders." He then set a more important task for the Brigadier. "Your Assembly is to sit in Jacksonborough, and you must take measures for covering that part of the country with your own force, as it will not be in my power to detach for that purpose."

Marion and his troops encamped at Strawberry on the Cooper River. "You will take command of my Brigade until I return," the Swamp Fox wrote Colonel Peter Horry on January 10. After telling his senior officer to move toward the Santee, when he had exhausted the forage around Strawberry, he provided for the protection of the General Assembly. "Col. Maham's corps will be ordered to Mepkin to remain there until my further orders."

Without foreseeing it, Francis Marion had invoked trouble. As soon as he left for his seat in the Senate, the old row between Horry and Maham flared up anew. Proud and bad-tempered, Maham refused to obey orders from Horry. "I cannot imagine upon what principles Lt. Col. Maham presumes to dispute rank with Lt. Col. Horry." Greene wrote Marion on January 16, reviewing Horry's long service in the militia and the Continentals. "On this ground I think Col. Horry has clearly the right of out ranking Col. Maham."

Marion tried to quiet the disorder. He told Horry to order Maham to come to his aid if the British should sally from

Charleston, "and wish he may not be called on for no other purpose." With lack of tact Horry immediately called upon Maham "to make me a return of the strength of your Legion, that I may know what support I can have in case of need."

Instead of complying, Maham wrote an insulting reply. "I had my Regiment three months in the field on duty before you had yours," he taunted; "As I cannot think of being commanded by an officer of the same rank, I think it proper not to make you a return of my Regiment, and shall not obey any order that you may be pleased to send."

The quarrel between Horry and Maham was symbolic. After compaigning for eighteen months without relief, many of the officers were worn out and quarrelsome. As General Greene hovered around Charleston, keeping pressure on the enemy, the morale of his troops sagged. Both Continentals and militiamen resigned or deserted. They all wanted to go home. On January 26 Lieutenant Colonel Henry Lee asked Greene for indefinite leave that he might return to Virginia.

Nathanael Greene was not surprised. "I have beheld with extreme anxiety, for some time, a growing discontent in your mind; and have not been without my apprehensions that your complaints originated more in mental anxiety, than the ruin of your constitution," he replied. Greene knew that Lee was disappointed because Congress had not promoted him to the rank of Brigadier General. The cavalier had written bitterly of "the indifference with which my efforts to advance the cause of my country is considered by my friends." Lee felt that he had been forgotten while he was burning out his life in the swamps of South Carolina. Others with shorter service and less meritorious records, but who were nearer Washington's headquarters, were being promoted. While at Yorktown, he had seen that other favorites, such as Alexander Hamilton and John Laurens, were in the ascendancy. Few seemed to remember "the fidelity with which I have served."

Greene was sympathetic. "I believe, few officers, either in America or Europe, are held in higher estimation," he wrote. Knowing that the Virginian felt that he had not been given full credit for his accomplishments in the official reports, he continued: "Everybody knows that I have the highest opinion of you as an officer; I love you as a friend." And then he gave Light Horse Harry Lee permission to go home from the war, declaring: "My attachment to you will end only with my life."

Peter Horry was also worn out from campaigning. Quarrels, humiliations, and frustrations made him sick. During his row with Maham he became acutely ill. He could not retain his command, and the moment he relaxed his discipline the militia began deserting. Faced with a situation he could not control, he implored Marion to return from Jacksonboro and take over his Brigade.

"I fear your patience must be something longer tried with the militia," Marion replied, "as I cannot be spared without stopping the whole proceedings of the House. We have but 13 Senators, which is the least number that can do business. The other House has 74—69 can do business; but it requires 202 members of both houses to choose a Governor. As soon as they can spare me I will return."

Colonel Horry again asked Marion to return to his troops. He also wrote a violent attack upon Maham and sent it to General Greene via Marion. But the Assembly was debating a measure to fill the Continental regiments and was writing a new militia law and these, Marion replied, "oblige me to stay a little longer from relieving you." He showed Peter's letter to his brother Hugh Horry. He "thinks as I do, that it is not proper to send it, as it seems to be wrote in too much heat, and I can do the business better in person." And then, because of the shortage of forage for his horses, Marion told him: "I think you had best move to Wambaw."

"We have chosen Mr. John Mathews as Governor," Marion wrote Horry on January 29. On the following day the

Assembly would elect delegates to Congress, "after which I will return as soon as I can get orders from our new Governor."

"Col. Maham interferes with my command so much I can scarcely act," Horry complained, again urging Marion to return to his troops.

"I am surprised at Col. Maham's interfering with your command," Marion answered. "I have wrote him positive orders not to do so in any respect whatever." But confiscation and sequestration bills were coming up for debate, "and until they are passed I cannot get leave to return."

Maham was obdurate and wrote a violent letter to Greene, bitterly denouncing the Brigadier's use of his dragoons. "With regard to General Marion's having made too free use of your cavalry, you are to consider how extensive the country is he has to guard and how much he depends on your corps," Greene replied. "This will account for the hard service you have been put to. The General is a good man, and when you consider his difficulties and make just allowances perhaps you will have little to complain of but the hard necessity of the service."

Faced with an absolute necessity of settling the conflict before dissension spread among his other troops, General Greene wrote Maham orders that placed him under Colonel Horry. He also wrote Horry, urging moderation. "I have only to observe upon this subject that great delicacy on your part should be exercised on this occasion, nothing like triumph as that will wound his feelings," he said; "blinded by matters of interest and love of rank he will yield to conviction unwillingly and finding himself in this situation will feel with double force every unnecessary exercise of authority."

While Greene was settling the discord in Marion's corps, the Brigadier was trying to get away from the Legislature. He was bored by the torrent of words poured out on the confiscation bill. Simple, believing in the dignity of man, he wanted to forgive rather than chastise the Tories. A dinner guest at the table of Governor Mathews, during the heat of the debate, he was called upon for a toast. Arising, he gravely raised his glass and cried: "Damnation to the Confiscation Bill."

The Swamp Fox longed to get out into the open field again. "I asked leave of the House to return but they would not grant it," he wrote Peter Horry on February 10; "there are three laws now on the carpet which they insist I should stay until finished. If I leave the House the business will be over as many will go with me and they will not be able to make a House. Our material business is the three laws above hinted at. These reasons oblige me to stay until Wednesday next when I hope to set out. If your health is such as to require your absence from camp you will leave the command of the Brigade to Col. Maham." Then he concluded wearily: "I hope soon to get through the business here and return. I assure you I am tired of Legislating and wish myself with you."

Hezekiah Maham was as cunning as he was resourceful. Determined not to serve under Peter Horry, he turned his dragoons at Mepkin over to Captain John Caraway Smith, rode over to Jacksonboro, and took his seat in the General Assembly. Horry thereupon acted quickly. Giving in to his illness, he turned the Brigade encamped near Wambaw Creek over to Colonel Adam McDonald and retired to his plantation on the Santee.

At this critical moment of division, transfer, and confusion, the British decided to attack. On February 23 Colonel Benjamin Thompson crossed the Cooper River with five hundred infantry, two hundred horsemen, and two pieces of artillery. As a screen he sent his cavalry on a dash toward Mepkin Plantation but he sent his infantry hiking toward Wambaw Creek.

But he did not surprise the Americans. While riding through Christ Church Parish, Captain Thomas Bennett saw Thompson's advancing troops and raced back to warn Colo-

nel McDonald. Major Lemuel Benson, with Horry's dragoons, was resting at the Durant Plantation, about a mile in
front of the Brigade. Major Benson was eating dinner when
Captain Bennett raced in. Incredulous, he continued his
dinner. Bennett dashed away to warn the Brigade. Colonel
McDonald was at the home of Elias Horry, but he, too, was
at dinner and refused to be disturbed. He told the Captain
that he had ridden through Christ Church Parish on the
previous day and that there was no sign of the enemy. But
he did send Major John James, who had just reached camp
with the Williamsburg troops, to take command.

James formed Marion's brigade in the edge of the woods
on the right of the camp. He then rode toward the left to
consult Colonel Benjamin Screven. But midway in his gallop
he heard sounds of terrific firing at Durant's. Major John
Doyle had attacked with great vigor, killed Benson, and put
his dragoons to flight. Screven's six-months men, all reformed
Tories, listened and then fled, throwing the planks off Wambaw Bridge after they had crossed. By then fugitives from
Benson's scattered regiment began passing. Perceiving the
day lost, James ordered a retreat. "As he brought up the rear
on horseback, two British dragoons tried to cut him down,
and he kept them in check with his pistols, and finally leaped
a chasm in the bridge, supposed to be twenty feet in width,"
proudly wrote his son William. "He by this means gained
time to rally his men, and checked the British."

In the meantime, learning from trusted informants that
Colonel Thompson had crossed the Cooper River, General
Marion obtained leave from the General Assembly to return
to his command. On February 24 he left Jacksonboro and
with Colonel Maham dashed across country to Mepkin.
Learning that the enemy horsemen had retired, the Colonel
rode down to his plantation. Soon an express galloped up
with news of the defeat and dispersal of the Brigade.

Quickly calling out Maham's dragoons, Marion led them
galloping toward Wambaw. After covering thirty miles, he
halted at the Tydiman Plantation. Apparently he was in a

secure position. A lane flanked by rail fences led up to the Tydiman home and at its entrance lay an old field with a large pond on the right. Captain John Caraway Smith, commanding the regiment in Maham's absence, picketed his dragoons in the lane. But scarcely half an hour had passed before the enemy suddenly swung into the old field, formed their line, and prepared to attack.

After hurriedly posting a company of infantry along the fences, Marion ordered the dragoons to charge in column. In bearing down on the enemy line, Captain Smith had to veer to the left to avoid the pond. But the evolution was more than Maham's poorly trained horsemen could perform. They fell into disorder. Seeing their confusion, Colonel Thompson charged. The dragoons broke and fled. Some attempted to escape by swimming the Santee, but British riflemen swept the water. Captain Smith led his squadron to Wambaw Bridge and waited.

After heroic efforts Marion rallied the others. "We lost a fine opportunity to cut the enemy's horse to pieces, by Maham's Horse not charging as it was ordered, but I believe it was principally owing to Capt. Smith not telling his officers and men what they were going about," he wrote Peter Horry. "I rallied a part of the Horse less than half a mile, and sent them to cover the scattered men. The enemy never followed us out of the plantation."

As soon as Marion's battered and frightened troops learned that he had returned to his command, they began crawling out of brake and covert. Colonel McDonald collected those who had fled across the Santee. But they had suffered a humiliating defeat. They had lost most of their arms and many of their horses. Maham's regiment had only sixty dragoons left. Horry's dragoons were decimated. So the Swamp Fox retired to his old camp at Cantey's Plantation. His heart was heavy. At a time when all should have been working for the final liberation of their country, jealousies, frictions, and self-interest had led to the defeat of his Brigade.

Trade had again begun to flow into Georgetown, with

brigs and barkentines from the North and from the West
Indies regularly arriving in Winyah Bay. The Governor
wished to protect the seaport. "I therefore desire you would
have a party under an active and vigilant officer stationed at
or about George Town," he wrote Marion. This was an opportunity to favor Peter Horry and at the same time separate
him from Maham. On March 7 Marion wrote Horry: "You
are to act as Commandant of George Town and its vicinity."
He then laid down procedures for stimulating trade, giving
him power to set the prices of articles "necessary for the support of life, such as salt, coffee, tea, and medicines." Luxury
items could be sold at any price, but "salt must not be more
than four dollars per bushel." Public stores should be placed
under guard and hauled to Black Mingo. And then with
sympathy he wrote the senior colonel under his command:
"I hope that your disorder is not so great as to prevent you
from presiding over the above mentioned business."

With Horry commandant of Georgetown, Marion began considering the problem of the troops under Horry and
Maham. Finally he suggested that the Governor combine the
two regiments in one legion. "I have consulted General
Greene on the plan you propose of incorporating Maham's
and Horry's corps into one, and forming them into one Legion," Mathews answered on March 12. "The General and
myself both approve of the plan, and you are therefore authorized to carry it into execution and to make such arrange-
ments as you shall think best for the service."

Cleverly the Governor and the General had saddled the
unsuspecting Brigadier with a delicate task. Peter Horry was
a senior officer, with seven years of meritorious service, the
last year and a half as Marion's right hand. But he was not
a horseman. Hezekiah Maham was younger, more active, and
rode as if to the saddle born. But he was overbearing, can-
tankerous, and hard to discipline. "Governor Mathews has
informed me that you recommend incorporating Horry's
and Maham's Regiments into a Legionary corps," Greene

wrote with evident pleasure on March 19, "and that you recommend Maham for the commanding officer."

In his surprise, anger, and disappointment, Horry wrote
Marion for an explanation. The Colonel was heated and
vehement, and the Brigadier answered plaintively: "you re-
flect on me very much." He readily admitted that he had
recommended the incorporation of the two regiments, "but
I did not say which of the two officers was to be preferred."
Francis Marion, deeply hurt at being involved in a row with
one of his oldest comrades, begged Horry to withhold judgment until they could meet, sit down together, and talk over
the situation. He then truthfully summarized his proposal:
"I think it was nearly this: That Col. Maham was the best
cavalry officer and you the best Infantry, and proposed that
your corps be dismounted and serve as Infantry in George
Town, as that post was to be kept, and the horses, saddles,
and swords given to Maham."

General Greene wrote a perfunctory order for the incorporation and sent it through channels for Marion to deliver
to Horry. After its delivery came the explosion. "As you saw
the contents it is needless for me to relate any part thereof,"
Horry wrote Marion, in breaking their long friendship, "further than that I am sensible to whom I am indebted for being
turned out of service and Maham continued." With great
dignity the Colonel wrote Greene that he was satisfied, as
"you say General Marion thinks it for the good of the service." Then Peter Horry, who had fought gallantly from Fort
Moultrie to Quinby Bridge, turned the command of the
troops in Georgetown over to Captain William Allston, saddled old Janus, and sorrowfully rode home from the war.

But Hezekiah Maham did not long enjoy his triumph. Becoming ill, he retired to his home in St. Stephen's. Learning
that he was poorly guarded, Lieutenant Robins and a party
of Cunningham's Tories rode sixty miles to surprise him.
Bursting through the militia around the Colonel's house,
they found him, his doctor, and another officer sitting at the
supper table. "We shall do you no injury," said Robins while

Maham was signing his parole; "treat my men with humanity when you meet them in the field." But in his haste to
depart, the Lieutenant, who could neither read nor write,
left the signed parole lying on the table. Recovering it, Maham thought himself absolved from its terms. He began preparing to return to his Legion and again take the field. But
Marion forbade him. The Swamp Fox believed in honoring
every obligation. Since Colonel Maham had signed the document, he was bound in all honor to obey its stipulations.

CHAPTER XVIII

Master of Pond Bluff

A s the Revolution drew slowly toward its close, Francis Marion became more generous and forgiving. He was incapable of hating an individual; he could hate only the evil actions of the individual. His magnanimity was most strikingly exemplified by his attitude toward the defeated Loyalists. He had scourged Micajah Ganey, Jesse Barefield, John Harrison, and Henry Richbourg, but when they repented he was ready to welcome them back into the commonwealth.

The Carolina Loyalists had suffered greatly and, as the British power steadily crumbled, they realized that they were facing a day of reckoning. The best they could hope for was transportation. In desperation, Colonels Hector McNeil and David Fanning called out their regiments of North Carolina Loyalists and began operations. The boldness of their stroke insured its success. In the middle of September, 1781, they surprised the state capital of Hillsboro. Moving swiftly, they surrounded the church in which two hundred Continentals had taken refuge and forced them to surrender. They then captured Governor Thomas Burke, his Council, and many other leading Whigs. They released sixty Tories from jail and then started toward Wilmington, spreading fear and destruction along their route.

Repercussions from this movement were felt along the

Waccamaw and the Peedee. While the Swamp Fox was exerting his utmost energies to help Greene drive the British into Charleston, Fanning aroused some of Ganey's Tories and they began disturbing the peace. "The Tories aforesaid came only down Waccamaw where they have done a deal of mischief," Major James wrote Marion on September 20. "A small party came down Britton's Neck and carried off some horses." During the winter they continued infrequent marauding, and in early March Governor Mathews requested Marion to send an investigator to find out whether or not Ganey was harboring any Tories from North Carolina. "I apprehend this fellow will bring us and himself too into trouble very soon," said the Governor.

Governors Mathews and Martin decided on a joint expedition from the Carolinas. They gave the command to Marion, and at the head of Maham's dragoons he marched through Williamsburg and headed up the Peedee. He called out the Britton's Neck company under Captain John Dozier and sent them to man the redoubts at Dunham's Bluff and Port's Ferry. Widow Jenkins saw James, her sixteen-year-old son, march off to the war which had already cost three members of her family.

After a brief skirmish Ganey sued for an armistice. Marion invited him to cross the Peedee and come to a conference at Burch's Mill. But many of the Whig officers declared that such a meeting with a leader of banditti was beneath the dignity of the Swamp Fox.

Francis Marion was unperturbed. Guided by humane principles, he knew that there would have to be forgiveness of enemies if the country were to be united and happy after the war. To his critics he replied modestly: "I aim at no higher dignity than that of serving my Country."

Marion and Ganey met at Burch's Mill on June 8, 1782. They sat down together, negotiated, and signed an equitable treaty. They agreed that the Tories should restore all plundered property wherever possible, demean themselves as peaceable citizens and submit to the laws of the State, and sign a declaration of allegiance to South Carolina and to the United States. After submitting to these terms, more than five hundred of Ganey's followers laid down their arms at Bowling Green, midway between the Peedee and the Little Peedee.

"Honor, sir, requires that I should yield my commission to Colonel Balfour, from whom I received it," Major Ganey told Marion, in asking permission to go to Charleston. "But this done, I shall immediately return to the country and seek your protection."

Seldom has the generosity of a noble spirit been better rewarded. Micajah Ganey surrendered his commission to Colonel Balfour and resigned from the Loyalist militia. True to his promise, he returned by way of Marion's headquarters and with many of his followers enlisted for the six months required by law to obtain full pardon. All served loyally until the end of the war.

While General Marion was at Burch's Mill, a Tory named Jeff Butler came to seek amnesty. He had been cruel in his treatment of the Whigs along the Peedee and feeling against him ran very high. When the General began treating with the man, some of his militiamen sent in a message that no matter what was promised they intended to kill the scoundrel. Immediately taking Butler into his own tent, Marion told his men: "Relying on the pardon offered, the man whom you would destroy has submitted. Both law and honor sanction my resolution to protect him with my life."

"Butler shall be dragged to death from your tent. To defend such a wretch is an insult to humanity," the men replied.

Marion gave no answer. Quietly, he called in his officers and asked them to send for their most trusted followers. "Prepare to give me your assistance," he told the soldiers, "for though I consider the villainy of Butler unparalleled, yet acting under orders as I am, I am bound to defend him. I will do so or perish." That night a strong guard spirited Butler away to safety.

About the middle of July Marion marched from the Santee. Soon afterward Greene asked him to take post at Wadboo. Thereafter he kept constantly in motion, shifting his camp and roving about east of the Cooper River. Whenever possible, he camped at Fair Lawn, formerly the seat of Sir John Colleton. He chose the plantation because of its large house and wings of slave quarters on each side. He used the house for his headquarters and billeted his men in the cabins. As the buildings were strong, they were safe from rifle and musket fire. And the long lane flanked by cedars, with branches sweeping the ground, offered a perfect ambush against attackers.

The attack came on the morning of August 29. Major Fraser, with a hundred dragoons, crossed the Cooper and set out to surprise the guards at Biggin Bridge and Strawberry Ferry. Learning of the raid, Marion called in his pickets, posted his marksmen among the cedars, and sent out a reconnaissance party under Captain Gavin Witherspoon.

Meeting Witherspoon in the woods, Fraser charged. The Williamsburgers turned back toward Fair Lawn. As they were approaching the lane at full gallop, Witherspoon bore to the left and then fell back as if to cover the retreat. A dragoon darted forward to cut him down but, as he rose in his stirrups for the stroke, the Captain toppled him with his carbine. At that the concealed Americans gave a roaring shout. The surprised British wheeled and charged toward the cedars. The marksmen fired. Twenty men and five horses fell. At the sound of the volley, the horses drawing Marion's ammunition wagon bolted. Five Americans ran out and recovered the wagon, but they fled when Fraser's dragoons gave chase. Without powder, as he had so often been, Marion gave an order for his men to retreat again to the Santee. At that moment, among the cedars of Fair Lawn, Francis Marion ended his fighting days. He commanded his Brigade until the end of the war, but he never again gave a command to fire.

During the long months of autumn, as General Alexander

Leslie prepared his regiments for embarkation, Marion forbade his men to shed more blood. He was willing to spare
the enemy; he was determined to save his own men. As the
British began loading their ships, they sent men to Lam-
priere's Point to fill the butts with fresh water. Greene suggested that Marion ambush them. He refused. "My Brigade
is composed of citizens, enough of whose blood has already
been shed," he replied firmly. "If ordered to attack the enemy, I shall obey; but with my consent, not another life shall
be lost, though the event should procure me the highest
honors of the soldier. Knowing, as we do, that the enemy are
on the eve of departure, so far from offering to molest, I
would rather send a party to protect them."

On December 14, 1782, six years and six months after the
arrogant British attack on Fort Moultrie, General Leslie
evacuated Charleston. He had agreed not to destroy the city
if the Americans would allow his troops to depart in safety.
Upon the firing of a cannon in the early morning they moved
out of the forward works, and the Continentals of General
Anthony Wayne moved in. At eleven o'clock the Americans
took possession of the State House.

The South Carolina militia were disbanded here and there
in swamp or on muster field, without pity or praise, ragged,
hungry, and unpaid, to find their way home. Under the ven-
erable cedars at Fair Lawn, General Marion held his final
muster. In a short speech he thanked the men who had followed him to victory, praising their gallantry, courage, and
patriotism and wishing them happiness and prosperity. He
then mounted Ball and reined his head toward Pond Bluff.

The returning hero found his plantation in ruins. Sit-
uated only a mile from the main highway leading to the Up
Country, Pond Bluff had been ravaged by friend and foe.
The British had considered it an object of plunder and the
Americans had used it as a source of supply. They had pil-
fered Marion's goods, burned his furniture, and fired his

house. They had driven off his cattle and confiscated his horses. They had kidnaped his slaves.

Like John James, Nathan Savage, and the other veterans of his Brigade, Marion courageously began the task of rehabilitating his plantation. He was destitute, but he was unconquerable. He rose above every obstacle, every impediment. The ingenuity, daring, and faith which had brought him victory in war crowned his efforts in peace. He bought horses and cattle on credit. Unpaid for his services in the militia, he yet bought feed, seed, and tools. Never reimbursed for his losses, he somehow managed to furnish food and clothes for his loyal Negroes.

As he turned to the duties of peace, his old comrades remembered his heroism. The Senate of South Carolina on February 26, 1783, voted the resolution: "That the thanks of this House be given to Brigadier General Marion, in his place as a member of this House, for his eminent and conspicuous services to his country."

In their enthusiasm they also voted: "That a gold medal be given to Brigadier General Marion, as a mark of public approbation for his great, glorious, and meritorious conduct."

Two days later the President of the Senate presented the resolution, prefacing it with a long eulogy. "Your conduct merits the applause of your countrymen," he said in conclusion. "Your courage, your vigilance, and your abilities have exceeded their most sanguine expectations, and have answered all their hopes. Whilst the virtue of gratitude shall form a part of our national character, your important services to this country can never be forgotten."

As the Senate chamber echoed with applause, General Marion rose from his seat. "Mr. President, the approbation which this House has given to my conduct, in the execution of my duty, gives me very pleasing and heartfelt satisfaction," he replied modestly. "The honor which they have conferred on me this day, by their thanks, will be remembered with gratitude. I shall always be ready to exert my abilities for the good of the state and the liberties of her inhabitants."

Francis Marion never used his prestige, popularity, or position for his own advantage. A bill was introduced in the Legislature to exempt from suit certain officers like Sumter who had plundered the public to pay their troops. When Marion heard the clerk read his name, he rose from his seat and demanded that his name be deleted from those exempted. "If I have given any occasion for complaint, I am ready to answer in property and person," he said proudly. "If I have wronged any man I am willing to make him restitution. If, in a single instance, in the course of my command, I have done that which I cannot fully justify, justice requires that I should suffer for it."

No man had scourged the Tories with greater fury than he. Yet none more readily forgave their loyalty to their King. He defended them in public. In the Legislature he sponsored laws providing them justice and equity. In the early days of peace, an old Loyalist appeared before a meeting of the people with a petition begging for pardon. To the surprise of the Tory and the vexation of the Whigs, the venerated General spoke in spirited advocacy of the petition. "It is peace now," he cried. "God has given us the victory; let us show our gratitude to heaven, which we shall not do by cruelty to man."

Honor followed honor. On September 30, 1783, Congress promoted him to Colonel in the Continental Line. In 1784, when the General Assembly of South Carolina voted to repair and garrison Fort Johnson, Governor Guerard appointed the popular hero its commandant. The handsome annual salary of £500 was regarded as token compensation for fatigue, scars, and broken health incurred in behalf of independence. But public memory is short. Economy-frightened politicians soon forgot the rain, cold, and misery of Snow's Island and reduced his pay to $500.

When not at Fort Johnson, General Marion lived among the Huguenot relatives he so warmly cherished. He loved the children of his sister and brothers as if they were his own. His nephew Theodore, the son of Job, began wooing Charlotte, the daughter of Gabriel and the widow of Anthony Ashby, once a captain in the old Second Regiment. As his own courtship prospered, Theodore hinted to his uncle that he, too, should try matrimony. His friends and relatives also whispered that Mary Esther Videau, a very eligible spinster of St. John's Parish, always listened with glowing cheeks and sparkling eyes when anyone began reciting the exploits of the Swamp Fox.

Francis took the hint. Mary Esther was his first cousin, the daughter of his Aunt Anne Cordes and Henry Videau. She was about his age, and he had known her since girlhood. Though normally shy, now bolstered by well-wishing kin, he began paying court. She received his attentions modestly but warmly. Finally he proposed and she accepted. On April 20, 1786, surrounded by the women and children for whose safety he had fought and by the men whom he had led to victory, Francis met Mary Esther at the altar. Theodore also led Charlotte. Perhaps this was a double wedding. If so it was doubly happy, for it solemnized the union of the families of his beloved brothers.

Francis and Mary Esther had the same tastes, the same religion, and the same Huguenot kinfolk. Although their romance had none of the fire of youth, they were extremely happy. "She was in countenance the exact counterpart of the General," said William James. "She partook in all his amusements, accompanied him in his journeys, and in his absence could not be better pleased than by hearing his praises. In short, nothing could have made this matrimonial connexion more happy, but its being more fruitful. They never had an heir."

Mary Esther possessed a handsome fortune and she placed it at the disposal of her husband. He resigned as Commandant of Fort Johnson and built a simple one-story frame house at Pond Bluff, leaving it unadorned and unpainted. Here they settled for life. He cultivated his lands well, and soon the plantation was flourishing. Gradually the scars of war disappeared.

During these years when the General became tired, or the heat was oppressive, or times slack, he would heed the lure of campaign memories. Calling faithful Oscar, he would pack his tent, camp bedding, old army cooking and eating utensils, and load his two old sumpter mules. Then, with Mary Esther always his companion in his rambles, he would set out for the High Hills of Santee. Along the route, in swamp and clearing and demesne, he and Mary Esther would stop to visit his old comrades.

Sometimes his veterans called upon him in their desperate hours. Hezekiah Maham ran afoul of the law. He fell into debt, lost a lawsuit, and was served with an execution. Bad-tempered as ever, he grabbed his sword and made the deputy sheriff eat the document. High Sheriff Daniel Stevens went to arrest him, but Maham hid in the swamp. Then, like a penitent schoolboy, he sent for Marion, told him of his distress, and acknowledged that he had done wrong.

"Go, submit yourself to the laws of your country," said Marion, talking as earnestly as he had done in the tempestuous days of their campaigns, "and I then will be your friend to the best of my ability. Resist——refuse——and we are separated forever." Maham surrendered.

The aging General lived honored and beloved by all. He gave his time to the small details of rural community life, serving on committees, witnessing signatures on documents, and settling estates. As long as he would allow them, the voters of St. John's elected him to the State Senate. Never a fluent speaker nor a skilled politician, he busied himself with local bills and matters pertaining to the militia. A mild Federalist, always a follower of Washington, in 1790 he was a delegate to the convention that wrote the Constitution of South Carolina. After seeing South Carolina become a member of the Union of which he had dreamed, he refused further political honors.

Like Peter Horry, whose bitterness had turned into adula-

tion, Marion devoted his attention to the militia. He retained
command of a brigade, attending its musters, advising the officers, and training them, until the reorganization of the
militia in 1794. He then retired. Upon his retirement, the
citizens of Georgetown appointed a committee to draw up
resolutions of gratitude for his services. William James, once
a boy militiaman but now an influential young lawyer, prepared the address.

At the present juncture when the necessity of public affairs
requires the military of this state to be organized anew, to
repel the attacks of an enemy from whatever quarter they
may be forced upon us, we, citizens of the district of Georgetown, finding you no longer at our head, have agreed to con-
vey to you our grateful sentiments for your former numerous
services. In the decline of life when the merits of the veteran
are too often forgotten, we wish to remind you that yours are
still fresh in the remembrance of your fellow citizens. Could
it be possible for men who have served and fought under you,
to be now forgetful of that general, by whose prudent conduct their lives have been saved and their families preserved
from being plundered by a rapacious enemy? We mean not
to flatter you. At this time it is impossible for you to suspect it.
Our present language is the language of free men expressing
only sentiments of gratitude. Your achievements may not have
sufficiently swelled the historic page. They were performed by
those who could better wield the sword than the pen. By men
whose constant dangers precluded them from the leisure, and
whose necessities deprived them of the common implements of
writing. But this is of little moment: they remain recorded in
such indelible characters upon our minds, that neither change
of circumstances nor length of time can efface them. Taught
by us, our children shall hereafter point out the places and
say to their children, here Gen. Marion, posted to advantage,
made a glorious stand in defence of the liberties of his country;
there, on disadvantageous ground, retreated to save the lives
of his fellow citizens. What could be more glorious for the
general commanding free men than thus to fight, and thus to
save the lives of his fellow soldiers? Continue general in peace
to till those acres which you once wrested from the hands of

an enemy. Continue to enjoy dignity, accompanied with ease, and to lengthen out your days blessed with the consciousness of conduct unaccused of rapine or oppression, and of actions ever directed by the purest patriotism.

Nothing could have pleased Marion more than this tribute. His health, affected by years of warfare, days in the field and nights in the swamp, had now begun to fail. Comrades came to visit and left in anxiety. Peter Horry came for what was his last visit. As the grizzled old heroes sat and talked over their campaigns, observing that the clock was striking ten, Horry suggested that they go to bed.

"Oh, no," replied Marion, "we must not talk of bed yet. It is but seldom, you know, that we meet, and as this may be our last, let us take all we can of it in chat. What do you think of the times?"

Soon after Horry's visit, Marion was stricken. As he began sinking, he saw Mary Esther weeping beside his bed. With great tenderness he said: "My dear, do not weep for me. I am not afraid to die, for thank God, I can lay my hand upon my heart and say that since I came to man's estate, I have never intentionally done wrong to any man."

Francis Marion died at Pond Bluff on February 27, 1795. Mary Esther, other members of his family, and friends buried him in the family cemetery on Gabriel's Plantation at Belle Isle. Above his grave they laid a slab of gray marble inscribed in love and devotion:

Sacred to the Memory
of
BRIG. GEN. FRANCIS MARION
Who departed this life, on the 27th of February, 1795,
IN THE SIXTY-THIRD YEAR OF HIS AGE;
Deeply regretted by all his fellow citizens.
HISTORY
will record his worth, and rising generations embalm
his memory, as one of the most distinguished
Patriots and Heroes of the American Revolution:
which elevated his native Country
TO HONOUR AND INDEPENDENCE,
AND
Secured to her the blessings of
LIBERTY AND PEACE.
This tribute of veneration and gratitude is erected
in commemoration of
the noble and disinterested virtues of the
CITIZEN;
and the gallant exploits of the
SOLDIER;
Who lived without fear, and died without reproach.

SOURCES AND NOTES

I. *Apprentice to Mars*

The sources of *Swamp Fox* are many and varied. The incidents in the life and campaigns of Francis Marion have been derived from specific accounts, but the background for developing these incidents is the result of a lifetime of observation and study. Reared within a mile of Snow's Island, the author as a boy heard the legends about Marion. In 1929 he filled his first notebook with items from the files of the Historical Commission of South Carolina, but it was not until he was searching the unpublished correspondence of Lord Cornwallis for material used in *The Green Dragoon* (Henry Holt & Co., 1957) that he found information enough to complete his study.

The primary source for *Swamp Fox* is the correspondence, both published and unpublished, of Lord Cornwallis and of General Marion. The most important secondary sources are the biographies of Marion by General Peter Horry and Judge William Dobein James. General Horry entrusted his manuscript to the Reverend Mason Locke Weems for publication, and, to the disgust of Horry, Parson Weems turned it into a biographical romance. Many historians, therefore, have felt that James' narrative is more trustworthy. The author has found that when examined beside the correspondence of Marion and Cornwallis, the two biographies have about equal validity.

Among the sources used for background are Christopher Ward, *The War of the Revolution,* edited by John Richard Alden, 2 vols., New York, 1952; William Gordon, *The History of the Rise, Progress, and Establishment of the Independence of the United States of America . . .,* 4 vols., London, 1788; John Drayton, *Memoirs of the American Revolution . . .,* 2 vols., Charleston, 1821; and David Duncan Wallace, *The History of South Carolina,* 4 vols., New York, 1934.

Biographical information has been derived from *The Dictionary of National Biography,* London, 1921; *The Dictionary of American Biography,* New York, 1937; Lorenzo Sabine, *Biographical Sketches of the Loyalists of the American Revolution . . .,* 2 vols., New York, 1864; Francis B. Heitman, *Historical Register and Dictionary of the United States Army . . .,* 2 vols., Washington, 1903; *Year Book: City of Charleston, South Carolina,* Charleston, 1893; and the unpublished muster rolls of British regiments.

Maps used in the campaigns are Henry Mouzon, *An Accurate Map of North and South Carolina with their Indian Frontiers* . . . , London, 1775; Robert Mills, *Atlas of the State of South Carolina* . . . , Baltimore, 1825; *South Carolina State Highway Primary System,* prepared by the South Carolina Highway Department; and maps of the various counties prepared by the South Carolina Highway Department.

The story of the Huguenots is from Arthur Henry Hirsch, *The Huguenots of South Carolina,* Durham, 1928. Stories about young Marion are from Peter Horry and Mason Locke Weems, *The Life of Francis Marion* . . . , Philadelphia, 1857. Details about the Marion family are from Emma B. Richardson, "Dr. Anthony Cordes and some of his descendants," *The South Carolina Historical and Genealogical Magazine,* January, 1943.

The background of the Cherokee War is from Wallace, *South Carolina.* For Marion as a young soldier, see William Moultrie, *Memoirs of the American Revolution* . . . , 2 vols., New York, 1802. And for Marion as a farmer, see William Gilmore Simms, *The Life of Francis Marion,* New York, 1844.

The account of Marion in the early years of the Revolution is from *Yearbook: City of Charleston, South Carolina,* 1893; Robert Wilson Gibbes, *Documentary History of the American Revolution* . . . , 3 vols., Columbia, 1853; New York, 1855; and New York, 1857; Edward McCrady, *The History of South Carolina in the Revolution, 1775-1780,* New York, 1901; and Wallace, *South Carolina.*

The account of the Battle of Fort Moultrie is from Robert Bass, *The Green Dragoon: The Lives of Banastre Tarleton and Mary Robinson,* New York, 1957; and Horry, *Francis Marion.*

The names of many towns, streams, and places have been changed since Marion's time. In *Swamp Fox* the original name has been used: for instance, Cross Creek instead of Fayetteville; Drowning Creek instead of Lumber River; and St. John's Parish instead of Berkeley County. Modern spelling, however, has been used: Charleston instead of Charlestown and Winnsboro instead of Winnsborough. In the main, these spellings have come from the maps of counties prepared by the South Carolina Highway Department. The author has followed Wallace, *South Carolina,* in spelling Peedee.

The pronunciation of the names of the Huguenots is difficult. Gaillard, for example, is Gil-yard, with equal stress on the syllables; H o r r y is O - ree; and H u g e r is U - gee.

The Santee, formed by the confluence of the Congaree and the Wateree Rivers, is the largest river in South Carolina. Because of its size and location, it was of great strategic importance during the Revolution.

The birthplace of Francis Marion is a matter of conjecture. See A. S. Salley, Jr., "Introduction," offset printing of James, *Marion.*

Echoe (three syllables) was near Franklin, North Carolina.

Fort Prince George was near the Indian village of Keowee in Pickens County.

Sir Henry Clinton was the son of George Clinton, Governor of New York. After serving in the New York Militia, on November 1, 1751, he became a lieutenant in the Coldstream Guards. After distinguished service in the Army, he became a member of Parliament. In company with Generals Howe and Burgoyne, General Clinton came to Boston in 1775 and further distinguished himself in the Battle of Bunker Hill. In 1778 he became Commander in Chief of the British forces in North America. After the Revolution he engaged in a heated controversy with Lord Cornwallis. In 1790 he again entered Parliament and in 1795 died while serving as Governor of Gibraltar.

Charles, first Marquis Cornwallis, was educated at Eton and in 1756 became an ensign in the Grenadier Guards. In 1762, he entered Parliament; here he opposed the oppressive measures against the American colonies. In 1776 Lord Cornwallis came to America with British reinforcements. He advocated a strategy of capturing American seaports and then rallying the Loyalists. After his surrender at Yorktown, he was received sympathetically by the King and by the English people. In 1786 he became Governor General of India. His success in India was as great as his failure in America. He reformed the military and civil service and defeated Tippoo Sahib, Sultan of Mysore. Recalled to England upon the outbreak of war with France, in 1795 Cornwallis became Master General of Ordnance with a seat in the cabinet. In 1798 he was sent to Ireland as Viceroy and Commander in Chief. In 1802 as plenipotentiary for Great Britain, he met Joseph Bonaparte and negotiated the peace treaty of Amiens. Sent out a second time as Governor of India, Lord Cornwallis died at Ghazipur in 1805. He had been one of the most distinguished men of his generation.

II. *Commandant of the Second Regiment*

The history of the Second Regiment is from McCrady, *Revolution, 1775-1780;* Gibbes, *Documentary History;* and *Yearbook, 1889.* The behavior of the Continental troops is from John Bennett, "A list of Noncommissioned Officers and Private Men of the Second South Carolina Continental Regiment of Foot," SCHGM, January, 1915.

The story of the campaigns against Prévost is from Wallace, *South Carolina;* McCrady, *Revolution, 1775-1780; Yearbook, 1893;* and William Dobein James, *A Sketch of the Life of Brig. Gen. Francis Marion . . . ,* Charleston, 1821.

The account of Marion at Savannah is from Horry, *Francis Marion.*

The history of the British campaign against Charleston is from Sir Henry Clinton, *The American Rebellion,* edited by William B. Willcox, New Haven, 1954; and Bass, *The Green Dragoon.*

Robert Howe was leader of the Whigs along the Cape Fear River. Appointed Brigadier General of Continentals in 1776, he was sent to command in Charleston, but he was so unpopular that he was transferred to the North. After the Revolution he returned to his plantation.

Benjamin Lincoln had a long record of service in the militia, Legislature, and Provincial Congress of Massachusetts. Appointed Brigadier General in 1776, he gained the good opinion of Washington. Because of his reputation for helping defeat Burgoyne, he was put in command of the Southern Department. His surrender of five thousand troops at Charleston was the worst American disaster during the Revolution.

Richard Winn, of Winnsboro, became one of the most distinguished of the militia colonels under General Sumter. In 1793 he defeated Sumter for a seat in Congress.

Marion's orderly books and records of the Second Regiment are in the Henry E. Huntington Library, San Marino, California.

Dorchester is on the Ashley River about thirty miles above Charleston.

Tybee Island lies in the mouth of the Savannah River some fifteen miles southeast of Savannah.

John Harris Cruger was the son-in-law of Brigadier General Oliver De Lancey and was Commandant of the First Battalion of De Lancey's Division of Loyalists. He was an active and able officer. After his estate in New York had been confiscated, he settled in London.

John James was born in Ireland and brought to Williamsburg by his parents. He became a wealthy planter, horse breeder, Elder in the Indiantown Presbyterian Church, and Major in the militia. After the Revolution he represented Williamsburg in the Legislature.

John Laurens, son of Henry Laurens, was one of the bravest and most distinguished of South Carolinians. "Poor Laurens has fallen in a paltry little skirmish." Greene wrote after Lauren's death near Chehaw Creek in 1782. "You know his temper and I predicted his fate. The love of military glory made him seek it upon occasions unworthy of his rank."

Sheldon is sixteen miles north of Beaufort.

Peter Horry, passed over in the reduction of the Continental regiments, retired on half pay and remained on his plantation until he joined Marion.

III. *Release of the Prisoners*

The account of Lord Cornwallis in South Carolina is from Banastre Tarleton, *History of the Campaigns of 1780 and 1781, in the Southern Provinces of North America,* London, 1787; and Bass, *Green Dragoon.*

Banastre Tarleton, son of Mayor John Tarleton of Liverpool, was educated at Oxford and the Middle Temple. Giving up law for the army, he came to America with Lord Cornwallis and won distinction in the early years of the war. Appointed Commandant of the British Legion, he made that Tory regiment one of the best in the British Army. After the surrender at Yorktown, he became a close adherent of the Prince of Wales and the Duke of York. Although a notorious rake and gambler, he represented Liverpool in Parliament for twenty-two years. He became a full General and was made a Baronet by George IV. Tarleton wrote his *Campaigns* to remove the stigma of the loss of the Battle of Cowpens.

The story of the revolt in Williamsburg is from James, *Marion,* and William Willis Boddie, *History of Williamsburg,* Columbia, 1923. Both Clinton, *Rebellion;* and Charles Cornwallis, *Correspondence of Charles, First Marquis Cornwallis,* edited by Charles Ross, 3 vols., London, 1859, contain valuable information.

The account of Marion's going to Williamsburg is drawn from Anne King Gregorie, *Thomas Sumter,* Columbia, 1931; James, *Marion;* and Horry, *Francis Marion.* Supplementary details are from Samuel White Patterson, *Horatio Gates,* New York, 1941; William Johnson, *Sketches of the Life and Correspondence of Nathanael Greene* . . . , 2 vols., Charleston 1822; Alexander Gregg, *History of the Old Cheraws* . . . , New York, 1876; and Gibbes, *Documentary History.*

Britton's Neck is the section of lower Marion County lying between the Peedee and Little Peedee Rivers.

John Ervin (also spelled Irvin or Erwin), like his brother Hugh Ervin, lived in the Aimwell section of Florence County. Both were Elders in the Aimwell Presbyterian Church and Colonels in the militia.

Mars Bluff, where U. S. Highway 1 crosses the Peedee River, was the site of a ferry from about 1750 until 1920.

Horatio Gates, an English officer who had served under Braddock, in 1772 settled in western Virginia. Joining the Whigs, in 1775 he was appointed Brigadier General. After defeating Burgoyne at Saratoga, he became involved in the Conway Cabal and retired. In 1780, Congress sent him to command the army in the South. After his defeat at Camden, he remained at home for a year and then joined the army under Washington. He served faithfully until the end of the Revolution.

Salem is five miles southeast of Mayesville on South Carolina Highway 527.

Megert's (McGirth's) Swamp, lying north of the High Hills of Santee, is one of the branches in the headwaters of the Black River.

Baron de Kalb, a German who had served with the French, came to America with the Marquis de Lafayette. They landed at Georgetown, visited Major Benjamin Huger, and then went to Philadelphia. After serving as Major General under Lafayette, De Kalb was ordered to relieve Lincoln in Charleston. Before the Baron could reach South Carolina, General Gates overtook him and succeeded to the command of the army. After Gates had fled from the battlefield at Camden, De Kalb fought until mortally wounded.

George Turnbull was Lieutenant Colonel, Commandant of the 3rd American Regiment of Loyalists, known as the New York Volunteers. He distinguished himself during the siege of Savannah.

Francis Rawdon, of Moira, Ireland, was educated at Harrow and Oxford. Proud, haughty, and able, he was a favorite of Howe, Clinton, and Cornwallis, and served with distinction from Bunker Hill until his return to England in 1781. He was a close friend of the Prince of Wales, whom he served in the House of Lords, but he dissipated his large fortune by extravagant living. After distinguished service in the early stages of the war with France, in 1813 he went out as Governor General of India. Here he enlarged the British territory by conquest and purchased the island of Singapore. He encouraged education and allowed freedom of the press. Successively Lord Rawdon, Earl of Moira, and Marquis of Hastings, he died while Governor of Malta.

Lenud's Ferry lay near the site where U. S. Highway 17 crosses the Santee River. Lenud, a Huguenot name, was pronounced Le-noo and often spelled Lenew or Laneau.

The dragoons of Tarleton's British Legion and Simcoe's Queen's Rangers wore green coats.

Hugh Horry was a brother of Peter Horry.

Port's Ferry was about five miles below the site where U. S. Highway 378 crosses the Peedee River. Traces of the landing, road, and Marion's fort still exist.

IV. *Retreat to White Marsh*

The narrative of the release of the prisoners is from James, *Marion,* and Horry, *Francis Marion.* The report to Gates is from Marion's unpublished correspondence in Harvard Library. The published letters of Marion have been edited and the poor spelling and bad grammar corrected.

Gregg, *Old Cheraws,* is the source of information about the Loyalists in the country along the Peedee River.

The account of the expedition under Major Wemyss is from James, *Marion;* Boddie, *Williamsburg;* David Ramsay, *The History of the Revolution of South-Carolina . . . ,* 2 vols., Trenton, 1785; and Cornwallis, unpublished correspondence.

Micajah Ganey (frequently spelled Gainey) was the son of an Englishman who settled about six miles below the present town of Marion.

Jesse Barefield lived near the present village of Nichols.

The Blue Savannah lies about two miles southwest of Gallivant's Ferry, the site where U. S. Highway 501 crosses the Little Peedee River.

James Moncrief was the chief engineer for the British Army in the South. He planned the fortifications at Savannah and Charleston, winning the praise of Prévost and Clinton. He won the contempt of the Whigs by seizing and shipping nearly eight hundred slaves from Charleston as his personal property.

Abraham, Frederick, and James DePeyster were brothers from New York. Abraham was the Captain and James the Lieutenant of a company in Fanning's King's American Regiment. Frederick was an officer in the New York Volunteers. James DePeyster was with Campbell at Georgetown, and from many circumstances it is the author's reasoned belief that he was the British officer whom Marion entertained at a dinner of sweet potatoes on Snow's Island.

Britton's Ferry crossed the Peedee River at a place now called Smith's Mills some eight miles east of Hemingway.

Indiantown Presbyterian Church is on South Carolina Highway 261 about fifteen miles east of Kingstree.

Long Bluff is now Society Hill.

V. *Victory at Black Mingo*

The story of Marion's camp in the Great White Marsh is from James, *Marion;* Marion, unpublished correspondence; and Cornwallis, unpublished correspondence.

The account of the Battle of Black Mingo is from James, *Marion;* Horry, *Francis Marion;* and Boddie, *Williamsburg.*

The incident between Murphy and Blackmon is from Gregg, *Old Cheraws.* Murphy eventually died in jail. Other details are from Gates, unpublished correspondence, in the library of the New York Historical Society, and Marion, unpublished correspondence.

Kingston is now Conway.

One family spelled its name Alston; another, Allston.

The victory at Black Mingo was exaggerated by the Whigs. Boddie, *Williamsburg,* said that Ball lost seventy-four men and Marion lost seventy-one. The erroneous date of September 14 derives from James, *Marion.* The British never mentioned the skirmish in their correspondence. After his defeat Colonel Ball remained inactive until near the close of the war. Colonel Wigfall disappeared from the records.

Patrick Dollard was a man of substance. After the Revolution he represented Williamsburg in the Legislature.

Major Christian Richmond was secretary to General Gates.

Black Mingo battlefield lies near the spot where South Carolina Highway 41 crosses Black Mingo Creek.

Captain Henry Mouzon prepared the map of South Carolina used by both the British and the American armies.

VI. *Escape of the Fox*

The account of the Battle of King's Mountain is from Lyman C. Draper, *King's Mountain and Its Heroes,* Cincinnati, 1881. That of Tearcoat Swamp is from James, *Marion;* Horry, *Francis Marion;* and the unpublished correspondence of Gates, Harrington, and Marion.

The story of Tarleton's chase of Marion derives largely from the unpublished correspondence of Lord Cornwallis. See also James, *Marion;* Tarleton, *Campaigns;* and Bass, *The Green Dragoon.* For the fight between Wemyss and Sumter, see Gregorie, *Sumter;* and Bass, *The Green Dragoon.*

Logtown was the British camp on the outskirts of Camden.

Patrick Ferguson, Captain in the 71st Highlander Regiment, was one of the most humane British officers in America. Inventor of a breech loading gun and leader of a company of expert riflemen, he continued to serve after his right arm was shattered at Brandywine. Clinton promoted Ferguson to Major and sent him to organize and drill the

Loyalists around Ninety-Six. Promoted to Lieutenant Colonel, he was killed before his commission reached him.

James Conyers, liaison officer between Gates and Greene and the officers of the South Carolina militia, was a vigorous Continental officer. Promoted to Major, he was killed in 1782.

Tearcoat Swamp, called Tarcoat by the English settlers, lies between the Pocotaligo and Black Rivers. It runs into the Black River about a mile above the point where U. S. Highway 301 crosses the river.

The High Hills of Santee are a range of sand hills about a hundred feet high which begin near the confluence of the Congaree and Wateree Rivers, and extend for some twenty miles up the east side of Wateree River.

Brierly's Ferry crossed the Broad River near Strother.

Friday's Ferry crossed the Congaree River at Columbia.

Jack's Creek lies about a mile west of Summerton.

Tarleton chased Marion from near St. Paul on U. S. Highway 301, up Jack's Creek, and down Pocotaligo River to about the site of the town of Manning.

After holding Major Wemyss prisoner for several days, General Sumter paroled and sent him back to Winnsboro. Wemyss was so badly wounded that he was never again active in South Carolina.

Singleton's Mills lay on Shank's Creek, about ten miles above the confluence of the Congaree and Wateree Rivers, in the present Poinsett State Park.

Nisbet Balfour, son of an Edinburgh bookseller, was older and less educated than the other British Lieutenant Colonels. He achieved his rank by hard work and strict attention to regulations. He finally became a Major General and ended his career as a Member of Parliament.

VII. *Murder of Gabriel*

The account of the attack on Georgetown is from James, *Marion;* Horry, *Francis Marion;* and Gregg, *Old Cheraws.* The details of the murder of Gabriel are from James Jenkins, *Experience, Labours and Sufferings . . .* , 1842.

The account of the Battle of Blackstock's is from Tarleton, *Campaigns;* Gregorie, *Sumter;* and Bass, *The Green Dragoon.*

From the unpublished correspondence of Cornwallis, Gates, and Marion comes the story of Major McLeroth in Kingstree.

The New Acquisition was in general the present York County.

Major John Money was one of the bravest and most generous officers in the British Army.

Benbow's Ferry crossed the Black River thirteen miles above Kingstree.

Gapway Bay lies about eight miles east of Andrews.

Captain John Milton of Georgia and Captain John Melton of the South Carolina militia served under Marion. It is impossible to untangle the confusion in the use of their names.

The Enoree, the Tyger, and the Pacolet rise in the hills between Greenville and Spartanburg and flow into the Broad River.

VIII. *Defeat of McLeroth*

The material about Tynes and about McLeroth is from Tarleton, *Campaigns;* Bass, *The Green Dragoon;* Cornwallis, unpublished correspondence; and Marion, unpublished correspondence.

The details of Marion's camp on Snow's Island is from James, *Marion;* Jenkins, *Experience;* Horry, *Francis Marion;* Boddie, *Williamsburg;* and the author's personal observations.

The narrative of Horry and his drunken troopers is from Horry, *Francis Marion;* and Cornwallis, unpublished correspondence.

The chase of McLeroth is based on James, *Marion;* Horry, *Francis Marion;* and Cornwallis, unpublished correspondence.

John Coffin was active from Bunker Hill until the evacuation of Charleston. A Captain in the New York Volunteers, he was promoted to Major for gallantry at Eutaw Springs. Settling in New Brunswick, he was prominent in Canadian politics and rose to General in the British Army. He married Anne Mathews of South Carolina.

William Goddard became a wealthy and influential planter. The description of Goddard's house is based on the narrative by Cornet Merritt. The fields on Snow's Island were still farmed within the memory of men now living in Marion County.

Dunham's Bluff lies on the eastern side of the Peedee River, about ten miles below the point where U. S. Highway 378 crosses the river. About a hundred yards from the top of the bluff are the remains of a redoubt. Jenkins indicates that this redoubt was thrown up by troops under Colonel John Ervin.

Halfway Swamp lies north of Pinewood on South Carolina Highway 120.

Swift Creek lies east of the Wateree River. U. S. Highway 521 crosses it near Boykin, about seven miles below Camden.

IX. *Lair on Snow's Island*

The account of Greene's taking command of the American Army at Charlotte is from Douglas Southall Freeman, *George Washington: A Biography*, 6 vols., New York, 1948-1954; Greene, *Nathanael Greene;* Johnson, *Greene;* Gregorie, *Sumter;* and Gibbes, *Documentary History*. Much additional material is in the unpublished correspondence of Marion and Greene in the William L. Clements Library, Ann Arbor, Michigan.

The information about Morgan is from James Graham, *Life of General Daniel Morgan . . .* , New York, 1856. Greene's move to Camp Hicks is from Johnson, *Greene*. See also Tarleton, *Campaigns;* Bass, *The Green Dragoon;* and Cornwallis, unpublished correspondence.

Information about Watson, Campbell, and Saunders is from James, *Marion;* Cornwallis, unpublished correspondence; and Marion, unpublished correspondence.

The account of the raid on Georgetown is from Horry, *Francis Marion.* The raid by Cornet Merritt is derived from the unpublished correspondence of Marion. See also James, *Marion.*

Daniel Morgan, with a regiment of Virginia riflemen, became one of the most distinguished soldiers in the early years of the Revolution. Promoted to Brigadier General by Congress and sent to the Southern Department, he began suffering so badly from sciatica that he retired soon after the Battle of Cowpens.

Thadeus Kosciusko, a volunteer from Poland, was the chief engineer in the Southern Department. He later became very distinguished in fighting for the freedom of Poland.

Isaac Huger, cousin of Francis Marion, was an ardent Whig and member of the Provincial Congress. From a Captain he rose to Lieutenant Colonel of the Fifth Regiment. Promoted to Brigadier General of Continentals and attached to Greene's Army, he commanded a brigade at Guilford Courthouse, and the right wing of the Army at Hobkirks Hill. After the Revolution he was a member of the General Assembly.

From the color of their uniforms the 3rd Regiment of Guards was called the Buffs.

Brigadier General William L. Davidson of the North Carolina Militia was killed trying to prevent the British from crossing the Catawba River at Cowan's Ford.

John Graves Simcoe, educated at Eton and Oxford, came to America soon after the outbreak of the Revolution. Although severely wounded at Brandywine, he was made Commandant of the Queen's Rangers. After returning from Yorktown he was elected to Parliament. He served as Lieutenant Governor of Upper Canada. After being appointed to succeed Lord Cornwallis as Commander in Chief in India, he died before going out. See John Graves Simcoe, *Military Journal: history of the operations of a partisan corps called the Queen's Rangers, during the war of the American Revolution . . . ,* New York, 1844.

The Queen's Rangers (Hussars), one of the best of the Loyalist regiments, was recruited by Major Robert Rogers, whom Kenneth Roberts glorified in *Northwest Passage.* Rogers was cashiered for conduct unbecoming an officer and a gentleman.

Edmund Fanning, born on Long Island and graduated from Yale, raised and commanded the King's American Regiment. Because of illness he left his regiment at Georgetown and returned home.

Major George Benson was the Adjutant General of the British corps in Charleston.

"Small post" is the first reference to the camp on Snow's Island in Marion's correspondence.

X. *Repulse at Georgetown*

The account of Marion's appointment as Brigadier General is from Joseph W. Barnwell (editor), "Letters of John Rutledge," *SCHGM*, October, 1916–October, 1917; Horry, *Francis Marion;* and James, *Marion.*

Colonel Horry's raid down Waccamaw Neck is from Horry, *Francis Marion;* and Marion, unpublished correspondence.

Information about old Captain John Postell is from Gibbes, *Documentary History.*

The history of Tarleton's campaign against Morgan is from Tarleton, *Campaigns;* Bass, *Green Dragoon;* Graham, *Daniel Morgan;* and Cornwallis, unpublished correspondence.

Henry Lee, a Virginia graduate of Princeton, was appointed Captain of a troop of Virginia horse at the beginning of the Revolution. He early distinguished himself, earning the nickname of Light Horse Harry. At Spread Eagle Tavern near Philadelphia, he defeated British dragoons under Tarleton. A favorite of Washington, Lee was appointed Commandant of a Legion of mixed infantry and cavalry and ordered to join Greene. After the Revolution he served as Governor of Virginia and as Congressman. He was the father of General Robert E. Lee.

Light Horse Harry Lee's coming to South Carolina is from Freeman, *Washington;* and Henry Lee, *Memoirs of the War in the Southern Department of the United States,* 2 vols., Philadelphia, 1812. For the letters quoted see Johnson, *Greene;* Gibbes, *Documentary History;* Rutledge, *SCHGM;* and the unpublished correspondence of Greene and Marion.

The story of the attempt to capture Georgetown and the raids of the Postells is from Johnson, *Greene;* Lee, *Memoirs;* Gibbes, *Documentary History;* Horry, *Francis Marion;* James, *Marion;* and Marion, unpublished correspondence.

Marion's Brigade was an anomalous corps. Its composition changed frequently, as the different militia colonels brought in their regiments. Boddie, *Williamsburg,* says that at one time or another twenty-five hundred men served under Marion.

Socastee Swamp lies east of the Waccamaw River into which it runs about fifteen miles below Conway.

Bull Island lies between the Waccamaw and Peedee Rivers.

Maidendown Creek and Maidendown Bay lie just north of Mullins.

Bass' Mill was on Catfish Creek near the present town of Latta.

The Cherokee Road crossed upper South Carolina. Very roughly, it followed the route of U. S. Highway 29.

Turkey Creek is in Union County.

For a full account of the Battle of Cowpens, see Bass, *Green Dragoon.* Kenneth Roberts, *The Battle of the Cowpens,* New York, 1958, is more expansive but not completely accurate. Tarleton lost three regiments of British regulars and the infantry of his British

Legion. Cowpens was the worst British defeat between Saratoga and Yorktown, and contemporary British commentators said that Tarleton lost the battle that lost the campaign that lost the war that lost the American colonies.

Andrew Pickens, a Colonel of militia, took British protection after the fall of Charleston and returned quietly to his plantation. About the first of January 1781, he again collected his riflemen and joined Morgan the night before the Battle of Cowpens. For his part in that action he was promoted to Brigadier General.

Wadboo Creek lies east of the Cooper River and empties into it about fifteen miles below Moncks Corner. Wadboo Bridge is about a mile from the Cooper River.

XI. *Blood on the Sampit*

The story of Sumter's raid is from Gregorie, *Sumter;* and Gibbes, *Documentary History.*

The account of the Battle of Wiboo is from James, *Marion.* The letters of Ervin, Saunders, Watson, and Marion are from Gibbes, *Documentary History;* and Marion, unpublished correspondence.

The narrative of Cornet Merritt is from Jenkins, *Experience;* and from Merritt's account in the British newspapers. Marion's chase of Watson is from Horry, *Francis Marion;* and Gibbes, *Documentary History.*

Fort Granby was built around a house which is still standing and known as the Cayce House, just across the Congaree River from Columbia.

Belleville, the plantation of Colonel William Thomson, was below Fort Motte.

Colonel Henry Richburg, a staunch Whig, turned Loyalist, and took protection on November 13, 1781. Cornwallis thought that at last he had found a leader as capable as Marion.

South Carolina historians disagree as to whether Colonel Ervin sent old Captain John Postell or his son, Captain John Postell, to Georgetown. The author believes that it was young Captain Postell whom Saunders imprisoned. Young Postell was the Captain and William Futhey was the Lieutenant of a company of militia. Ervin sent Postell and Futhey to Georgetown, but Futhey escaped by outrunning the British. Postell was held until Leslie evacuated Charleston.

John Saunders of Virginia raised a troop of horsemen at his own expense and was attached to the Queen's Rangers. After the war, Saunders studied at the Middle Temple and practiced law at Fredericton, New Brunswick. He became Chief Justice of the Supreme Court of the Province.

Lower Bridge is four miles below Kingstree on South Carolina Highway 377.

Lieutenant Torriano recovered and was active around Charleston.

The Cantey Plantation lay about five miles northwest of Greeleyville.

Mount Hope Swamp lies just west of Greeleyville.

Ox Swamp, not to be confused with Ox Swamp in Clarendon County, runs ino Black River about twelve miles below Kingstree.

XII. *Raid of Colonel Doyle*

The account of Doyle's raid is reconstructed from James, *Marion;* Horry, *Francis Marion;* Cornwallis, unpublished correspondence; Cornet Merritt's narrative; and *The South Carolina Gazette.*

The dispute between Sumter and Marion is from Gregorie, *Sumter;* and Gibbes, *Documentary History.*

The narrative of Colonel Watson's visit to Widow Jenkins is from *The Experience, Labours and Sufferings* of her son James Jenkins. The story of Watson and Marion in Wahee Neck is from James, *Marion.* See also Lee, *Memoirs.*

John Doyle, who helped Lord Rawdon recruit the Volunteers of Ireland, was Brigade Major at the Battle of Hobkirks Hill. He was later Adjutant General to Gould, Stewart, and Leslie. A member of the Irish House of Commons, he became Secretary of War for Ireland. He was then secretary to the Prince of Wales. After a very distinguished career during the wars with Napoleon, Doyle was promoted to General and created a Baronet.

Welbore Ellis Doyle, younger, but senior to his brother John, commanded the New York Volunteers in the absence of Colonel Turnbull. He brought his wife with him to America. After a distinguished career in the British Army, General Doyle died while Governor of Ceylon.

While Marion undoubtedly spoke to his troops, the speech in Horry, *Francis Marion,* was probably fabricated by Parson Weems.

Burch (or Birch) owned mills and ran a ferry near the mouth of Jeffries Creek, some twelve miles below Mars Bluff.

The author's boyhood home was on the traditional site of the house of Widow Jenkins.

XIII. *Capture of Fort Watson*

Material for an account of the capture of Fort Watson comes from James, *Marion;* Lee, *Memoirs;* Johnson, *Greene;* Jenkins, *Experience;* and Gibbes, *Documentary History.*

The story of Colonel Kolb is from Gregg, *Old Cheraws;* that of Colonel Hayne from McCrady, *The History of South Carolina in the Revolution, 1780-1783,* New York, 1902.

The account of the Battle of Hobkirks Hill is from Johnson, *Greene;* Tarleton, *Campaigns;* McCrady, *Revolution, 1780-1783;* and Gibbes, *Documentary History.*

Bloom Hill is in Poinsett State Park.

William R. Davie, Commissary-General for Greene, was a distinguished soldier, lawyer, and educator. Born in the Waxhaws, he was a first honor man at Princeton, Governor of North Carolina, and founder of the University of North Carolina.

Hobkirks Hill is in the present town limits of Camden.

Saunders Creek lies about four miles northwest of Camden.

XIV. *Ruckus at Motte's*

The account of Marion's movements is from Lee, *Memoirs;* Gibbes, *Documentary History;* Greene, *Nathanael Greene;* Johnson, *Greene;* and from the unpublished correspondence of Marion and Greene.

The history of Greene's maneuvers is from Johnson, *Greene;* and that of Cornwallis, from Bass, *The Green Dragoon.* See also *Yearbook, 1898.*

The quarrel about horses is from Gibbes, *Documentary History;* Greene, *Nathanael Greene;* and Lee, *Memoirs.*

The story of the capture of Fort Motte is from James, *Marion;* Horry, *Francis Marion;* Lee, *Memoirs;* McCrady, *Revolution, 1780-1783;* Tarleton, *Campaigns;* and Gregorie, *Sumter.*

Colonel Lee carried on a secret correspondence with General Greene in which he expressed himself freely about his friends, as well as his enemies.

Buckenham's Ferry was Buchanan's Ferry on the Santee about ten miles below the confluence of the Congaree and the Wateree Rivers.

Levi Smith's account of the hanging was published in *The Royal Gazette,* April 13-17, 1782.

XV. *Partisan Generals*

The account of Greene's campaign against the British posts and against Ninety-Six is from Lee, *Memoirs;* Johnson, *Greene;* McCrady, *Revolution, 1780-1783* and Gregorie, *Sumter.*

Peyre's Plantation is described in James, *Marion.*

The material for the story of Marion's capture of Georgetown is from Gibbes, *Documentary History; Yearbook, 1898;* and Marion, unpublished correspondence.

On May 31, 1781, while General Marion was in Georgetown, his brother, Isaac, died and was buried there.

The story of the Battle of Quinby is from Gregorie, *Sumter;* Gibbes, *Documentary History;* Joseph Johnson, *Traditions and Reminiscences chiefly of the American Revolution in the South . . . ,* Charleston, 1851; Jenkins, *Experience;* Lee, *Memoirs;* James, *Marion; Yearbook, 1898;* and Marion, unpublished correspondence.

Quinby Plantation is south of the East Cooper River, about a mile from Huger on South Carolina Highway 41.

Colonel Baxter survived and commanded his regiment until the end of the Revolution.

Colonel Ball was presumably John Coming Ball.

Bonneau's Ferry crossed the Cooper River near the village of Bonneau.

Bush River is in Newberry County.

After the war Thomas Sumter became one of the most popular and distinguished men in South Carolina. He amassed an estate of some hundred thousand acres in the vicinity of Sumter. After serving in the South Carolina Legislature, he was elected to the House of Representatives and then to the United States Senate. At the time of his death at the age of ninety-eight, he was the last surviving General of the American Revolution.

XVI. *Battle of Eutaw Springs*

For the Battle of Eutaw Springs see Greene, *Nathanael Greene;* Johnson, *Greene;* James, *Marion;* Jenkins, *Experience;* and McCrady, *Revolution, 1780-1783.* The correspondence of Greene, Rutledge, Marion, and Horry is in Gibbes, *Documentary History.*

Patrick Roche (also spelled Roach) married Martha Marion, daughter of Benjamin and niece of Francis Marion.

Lord Rawdon, with Colonel Welbore Ellis Doyle and his wife, sailed from Charleston on August 21, 1781.

Some accounts date the action at Parker's Ferry as August 31.

XVII. *Breaking of Friendships*

The account of the latter phases of the Revolutionary War is from McCrady, *Revolution 1780-1783;* Johnson, *Greene;* James, *Marion;* Lee, *Memoirs;* Johnson, *Traditions;* and Gibbes, *Documentary History.*

Wambaw Creek, the eastern boundary between Berkeley and Charleston Counties, is in the Francis Marion National Forest.

When the other Tories were being transported, John Brockington refused to leave Williamsburg.

Mcpkin lies east of Cooper River about seven miles below Moncks Corner.

Benjamin Thompson, of Rumford (now Concord), New Hampshire, commanded the King's American Dragoons. After the Revolution, he was knighted by King George and created Count Rumford by the Duke of Bavaria.

XVIII. *Master of Pond Bluff*

The account of the close of the Revolution is from James, *Marion;* Simms, *Life of Francis Marion;* Gregg, *Old Cheraws;* McCrady, *Revolution, 1780-1783;* and Gibbes, *Documentary History.*

The story of Marion's return to Pond Bluff is from James, *Marion;* Horry, *Francis Marion;* and Simms, *Life of Francis Marion.*

The eulogy and the epitaph are from James, *Marion.*

Index

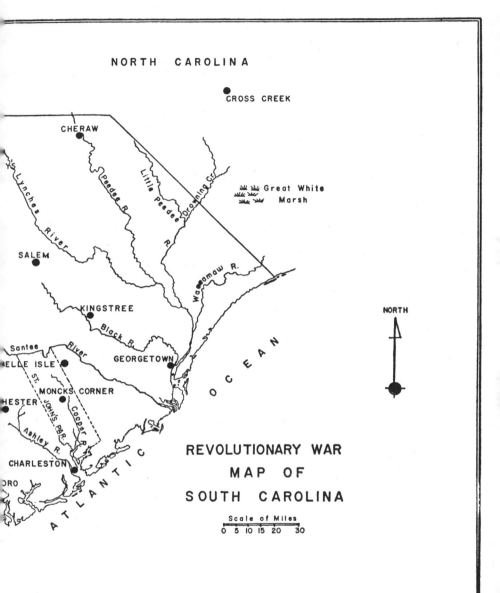

NORTH CAROLINA

CROSS CREEK

CHERAW

Lynches River

Little Peedee R.

Peedee R.

Drowning Cr.

Great White
Marsh

SALEM

Waccamaw R.

KINGSTREE

Black R.

Santee

River

BELLE ISLE

GEORGETOWN

ST. JOHN'S PAR.

MONCKS CORNER

HESTER

Cooper R.

Ashley R.

CHARLESTON

ORO

O C E A N

A T L A N T I C

NORTH

REVOLUTIONARY WAR
MAP OF
SOUTH CAROLINA

Scale of Miles

0   5 10 15 20   30

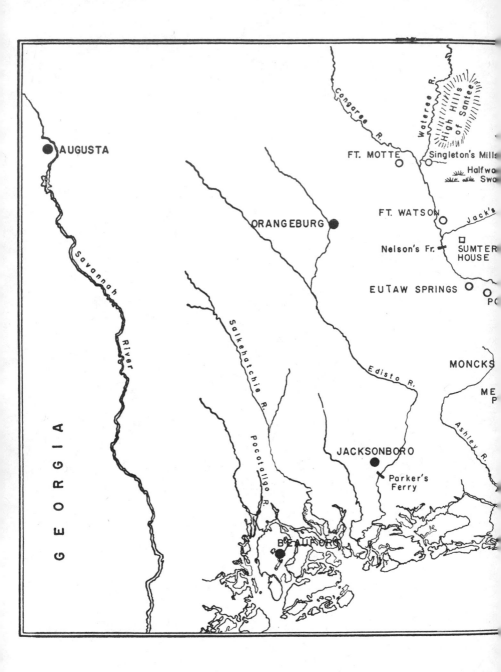

NORTH CAROLINA

Lynches R.

Mars Bluff
Ferry

Peedee R.

Catfish Cr.

WAHEE NECK

Little Peedee R.

Drowning Cr.

AMIS' MILLS

BLUE SAVANNAH

Port's Fr.

Witherspoon's Fr.

SNOW'S IS.

Britton's
Ferry

KINGSTREE

INDIANTOWN

Lower
Br.

BRITTON'S NECK

KINGSTON

Waccamaw River

CANTEY'S
PLAN.

Murry's Fr.

Black R.

Bl. Mingo Cr.

Shepherd's
Ferry

Socastee
Swamp

Santee R.

RE'S
ION

Sampit R.

Lenud's
Fr.

Br.

GEORGETOWN

NORTH

odCr.

Quinby Cr.

Wambow Cr.

Br.

OCEAN

ATLANTIC

TON

LTRIE

AREA OF
MARION'S CAMPAIGNS

SCALE OF MILES

10 5   0   5   10 15 20

About the Author

The lure of Francis Marion country remained strong throughout the life of Robert D. Bass. Born in Scranton, South Carolina, the author grew up in an area where "people talked about Marion and Lord Cornwallis as if they lived down the road." Revolutionary battle sites were the playgrounds of his boyhood days. From such beginnings Bass went on to extensive studies and a teaching career in the field of English literature. He held degrees through the Ph.D. level from the University of South Carolina, and he studied at Cambridge, Johns Hopkins, and the University of London. Yet in the midst of his professional duties Bass found time to write, and his reputation as a leading biographer of American Revolutionary figures is unquestioned today.

After retiring as a professor of English at Erskine College in Due West, South Carolina, Dr. Bass relocated to Marion, South Carolina—once again in his beloved Swamp Fox territory. In retirement he divided his time between his favorite pastimes: writing, gardening, and amateur radio.

In 1980 Dr. Robert D. Bass was inducted into the South Carolina Hall of Fame. He died May 11, 1983.